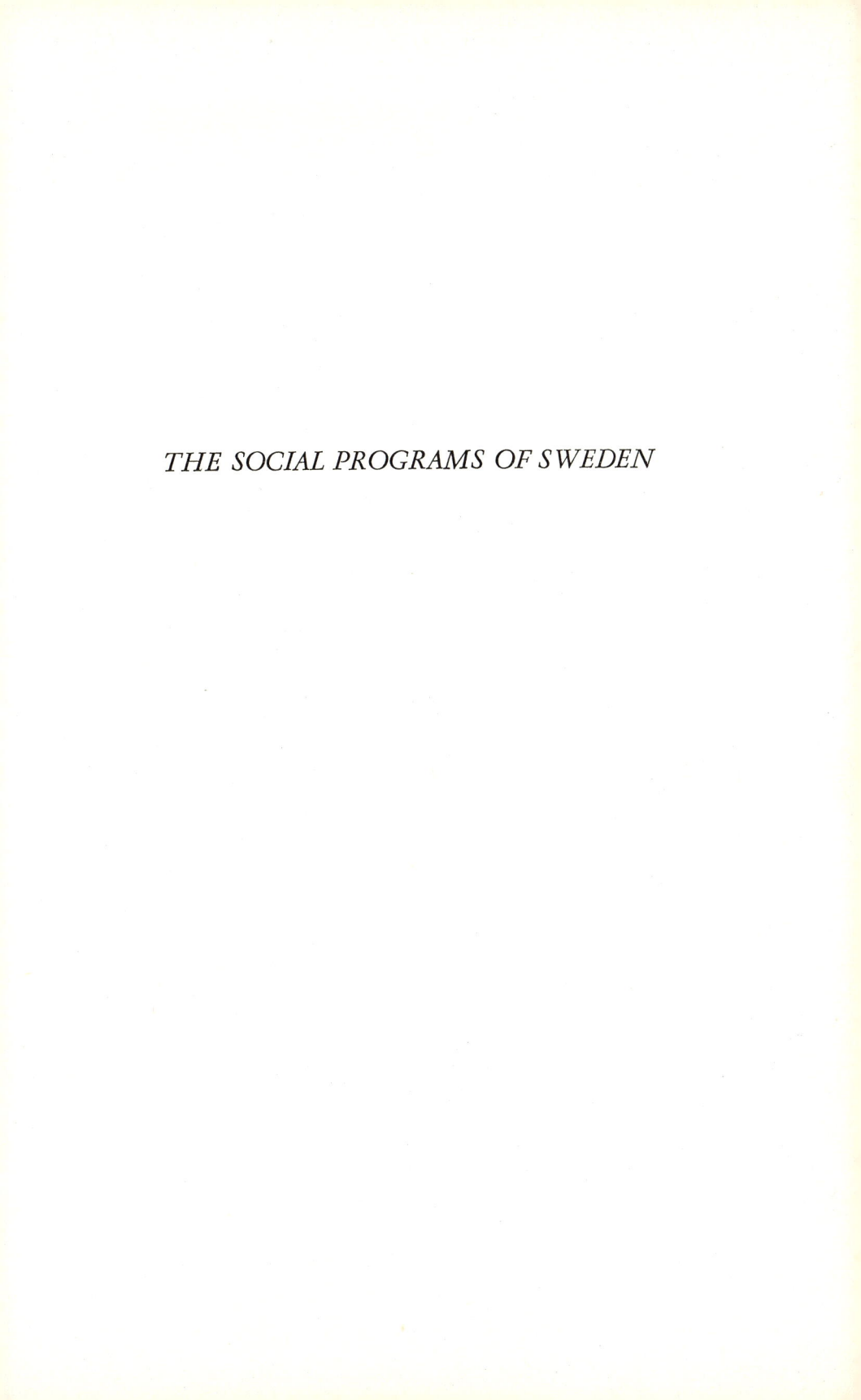

THE SOCIAL PROGRAMS OF SWEDEN

"Freedom is the finest thing
We seek in all the world's wide ring,
Who well can bear his freedom.
Wouldst thou be both wise and bold,
Then love thy freedom more than gold,
For glory follows freedom."

      Bishop Thomas of Strangnas (1443)
          TRANSLATED BY MARTIN A. ALLWOOD

*THE SOCIAL PROGRAMS
OF SWEDEN ⚹ A SEARCH
FOR SECURITY IN A FREE
SOCIETY by Albert H. Rosenthal*

THE UNIVERSITY OF MINNESOTA PRESS, MINNEAPOLIS

© Copyright 1967 by the University of Minnesota. All rights reserved. Printed in the United States of America at the North Central Publishing Company, St. Paul

Library of Congress Catalog Card Number: 67-27098

Published in Great Britain, India, and Pakistan by the Oxford University Press, London, Bombay, and Karachi, and in Canada by the Copp Clark Publishing Co. Limited, Toronto

The lines from "At the Salvation Army" by Pär Lagerkvist, on page 36, are taken from *Seven Swedish Poets* (Staffanstorp, Sweden: Bo Cavefors Bökforlag) and appear by permission of the editor and translator, Frederic Fleisher.

TO THE MEMORY OF THE MANY HAPPY, TREASURED
YEARS WITH MY FATHER

Max L. Rosenthal

"And remember that the companionship of Time is but of short duration. It flies more quickly than the shades of evening. We are like a child that grasps in his hand a sunbeam. He opens his hand soon again, but, to his amazement, finds it empty and the brightness gone."

Yedaya Penini 14th Century

Foreword

CANTATA

"Thy noble thoughts, thy acts of love,
Thy dreams of beauty — these Time can never devour.
Eternity like some great storehouse teems
With sheaves safe-garnered from destruction's power.
Go forth, Mankind! Be glad, thy cares at rest,
Thou bear'st Eternity within thy breast."

      Victor Rydberg (1828–1895)

THIS book fills a long felt need. Ever since the publication of *Sweden: The Middle Way*, now nearly thirty years ago, the Swedish social system has been a subject of controversy. There has been a great deal of emotional writing about the effort of the labor government in Stockholm to regulate capitalism and provide a decent standard of living for every citizen.

Much of this emotional writing has come from those who for one reason or another have sought to discredit the Swedish experiment. Reporters have been sent to Sweden with a preconceived view of how harmful the social security system has been to the morals and the stamina of the Swedish people. And they have duly written their preconceptions after taking a quick look at the middle way. Other writers have given an exaggerated idea of the degree of state intervention in a system that is 95 percent free enterprise and, at most, 5 percent socialism or public ownership.

The net result of much of this highly colored writing has been to ignore the real contribution that Sweden has made in a half dozen fields and particularly in the fields of social security and public health. But now comes an author ideally equipped to appraise this contribution by reason of his background. This is the great virtue of the book. It is a careful and thorough examination of Sweden's achievement by a specialist familiar with our own social security, public health, and welfare systems. In this respect it is a unique contribution to a way of life that has much to offer the rest of the world. It should do a great deal to obviate the emotional pros and cons of which we have heard so much. No subsequent appraisal of what Sweden has done can be made henceforth without this basic work.

MARQUIS CHILDS

Washington, D.C.

Preface

THE PORCELAIN FACTORY
"The simple form which all men understand,
The form which offers hearty bread to all,
To still their hunger, not luxury recall."
Carl Snoilsky (1841–1903)

MOST American citizens are quite satisfied by the fact that extensive public health and social security programs have been established in the United States. No one seriously proposes the elimination of, or an extensive reduction in, these programs. Social security has become an institution in the American way of life.

At the same time, the history of the development of the social programs in the United States, particularly the extensive compromises reflected in the passage of the Medicare program, make it clear that most Americans have not developed a consistently affirmative attitude toward the extension of government responsibilities to meet social needs. Politicians are applauded when they object to increased government activity — especially at the federal level. Most Americans rarely think of the over-all question of the role of government or consider it in philosophical terms. When the question is raised it is usually presented in the context of political debate or used by a group or organization with some special interest in the particular issue being considered at that time.

Stripped of political or partisan overtones, the question is a genuine one. It is essentially that of the appropriate role for government — the

THE SOCIAL PROGRAMS OF SWEDEN

part that the public agencies at federal, state, and local levels should play in the provision of health, social insurance, and welfare services. The need for these services is not questioned as much as who should perform them. Many Americans feel that it is quite appropriate to support large national private organizations working to establish health and welfare facilities. They are not as sure whether their government, which actually spends much more money in these fields, belongs at all in this area. This reluctance to accept government responsibility for health and welfare has many roots. The American citizen, particularly at election time, hears charges of paternalism and socialism applied to government activities in social areas. He has been repeatedly warned about the development of a welfare state; he sees his taxes rise as large expenditures are made for health, welfare, and social security programs; and he is presently being asked to support increased programs in these areas.

Sweden is used as an example by both those who favor the extension of social programs through government action and those who feel that such extension of the role of government will result in greatly increased taxes and the loss of personal freedom and incentive. Some have used the example of Sweden as a country which, because of the expansion of government welfare programs, has become socialistic and presumably decadent; others have enthusiastically described Sweden as a country that has solved all or most of its social problems in the context of a free society. Here are two opposite evaluations of the social programs of the same country. What are the health and welfare programs of Sweden? How extensively do the public programs protect the Swedish citizen against the hazards of illness, poverty, and old age? Has the establishment of these programs made Sweden a socialist country? Have incentive and initiative been reduced because of government administration of public programs? Has the taxation, necessary to finance these programs, become so great as to be confiscatory? Is the high suicide rate in Sweden a result of the expansion of the social programs?

How did it happen that Sweden, with a democratic tradition older than that of the United States, with the second oldest democratic constitution in the world, should be leading in the provision of government services in health and welfare programs for its citizens? Has freedom become less in this secure society?

PREFACE

Some years ago, a book by Marquis Childs, descriptively entitled *Sweden: The Middle Way*, called the attention of the world to Sweden's extensive development of a privately owned system of cooperatives as an effective adjustment of capitalism in a rapidly developing industrial society. Could it be said that Sweden has developed a parallel "middle way" in the provision of social security for its citizens if it is found that this country has constructed a means of protecting its people against the major social hazards and of meeting their health and basic economic needs and, at the same time, maintaining a society characterized by individual freedom, free enterprise, and high personal incentives?

This book was undertaken on the premise that a description of the major Swedish social programs would be of value to Americans and others seeking to improve the social programs in their own countries. Perhaps a study of the social laboratory of Sweden will be of assistance in answering two significant questions discussed by planners of social policy all over the world. The first is the broad philosophical question, "Are security and freedom compatible?" The second is more specific and more easily answered. "Can a desirable balance of meeting social needs and preserving individual freedom and incentives be achieved if great care is taken not only in the design of broad social policies, but also in the nature of the administrative practices through which these policies are carried out?" It is this area, the forms of administrative organization and the built-in methods of ensuring the responsiveness of the bureaucracy to the needs and desires of the citizenry, and other unique characteristics of Swedish government, that may offer some useful ideas for Americans seeking expanded social programs but fearful of an authoritarian government.

The usefulness of a review of a national system of social programs depends largely on the extent to which an author has achieved the desirable goals of accurate description and balanced evaluation. Recognizing the difficulty of this task, the writer has sought to distinguish description from evaluation both in the methodology of this study and in the organization of the presentation.

The procedure for research has included an analysis of the full reports of parliamentary commissions, debates in the Riksdag, laws enacted by the Riksdag, regulations established by departments and boards, and reports of the agencies concerned. Three visits were made to Sweden to gather data and observe the operation of the programs. The first of these was for an extended period in 1956 when several of the current programs in health and welfare were being considered. For the ensuing seven years the development of these programs was closely observed. A return visit to Sweden was made in July through September 1963. This period was selected because it was possible to examine the newly established Supplementary Pension program which had been in operation for six months. Finally, the writer visited Sweden in May 1965 for a brief review of the programs and to obtain the most recent data. These visits have made it possible to conduct a series of interviews with the officials administering the social programs and to obtain statements about objectives, evaluations, and problems from many of the people who participated in the development of the programs and are responsible for their operation today. In addition, discussions were held with members of opposing political parties, businessmen, labor leaders, representatives of interest groups, and the general public to obtain as wide a spectrum of views as possible.

However, laws, reports, and official documents, as well as interviews with officials, may provide statements of objectives rather than actual accomplishments. Thus, the writer has checked the statements in the light of actual practices in the day-to-day operation of each program by an examination of cases in the files of each agency administering the social programs. From a relatively large number of cases reviewed, the author has selected representative cases which are presented in summary form to illustrate each of the major programs. As a significant exception to the Swedish Freedom of the Press Act, the social insurance and welfare records are kept confidential as are such records in the United States. Consequently, special permission was required for access to and use of actual case files, on the condition that the names of the persons concerned would be changed.

The chapter arrangement reflects the author's effort to present each of the social programs by a description that is predominantly free from evaluation. Conclusions have been confined, in the main, to the last chapter. The opening chapter, "Growth of the Social Programs," traces the background of the current programs and offers an over-all view of the complex of programs organized to meet the total needs of the Swedish people. The second chapter, "The Social Security Programs," describes the Basic and Supplementary Pension programs designed to

PREFACE

meet the catastrophic effect of loss of income because of retirement, death, or disability of the family breadwinner. Chapter III, "Health Insurance," presents a description of the organization and operation of the extensive insurance program designed to ameliorate the economic consequences of illness. The fourth chapter, "Public Health," reviews the administration of the public health programs, the hospital system, and government activities in the fields of mental health, sex education, birth control, abortion, and dental health.

Chapter V, "Welfare and Related Programs," describes the system of social administration designed to provide assistance on the basis of need for those who for one reason or another are ineligible for social insurance protections. Attention is also given to the special programs for children, the aged, and the disabled. Chapter VI, "The Government and the Individual," points up the salient and unique features of Swedish government. This review and analysis is significant not only for an understanding of program administration but also for an examination of some of the built-in devices in Swedish government which protect the rights of the individual citizen. This discussion may help to explain the lack of concern over expanded government activity in social fields which is typical in Sweden today. The seventh chapter, "Program Comparisons: Sweden and the United States," provides an evaluation and comparison of the social programs in the two countries. The eighth and concluding chapter, "Freedom in the Secure Society," offers an analysis of the impact of the Swedish social programs on individual freedom and other significant social values which are frequently discussed by those concerned with possible negative side effects of the Swedish programs.

In brief, this book has been written in the belief that people living outside of Sweden are interested in knowing about the social programs of that country, and with the hope that an examination of the Swedish experience may provide some guidelines and new ideas in the world-wide search for ways of meeting human needs in a free society. The search continues for the way to achieve the ultimate goal—providing maximum security while, at the same time, preserving the greatest possible degree of personal freedom.

ALBERT H. ROSENTHAL

University of New Mexico
October, 1967

Acknowledgments

THE excerpts of Swedish poetry, opening each chapter, have been selected from many traditional and widely known poems and serve to exemplify the cultural expression of Swedish social philosophy underlying the development of the current health and welfare programs.

Appreciation is expressed to:

The Rockefeller Public Service Award Program and Princeton University which administers the program, whose award in 1956 afforded the opportunity for travel and research in Sweden in 1956 and 1963.

The leaders in government, universities, business, and labor in Sweden who cooperated wholeheartedly and frankly in the review of the Swedish social programs and their impact on Swedish life, including: Dr. Per-Axel Hildeman, Director, the Swedish Institute, and John W. Walldén, Assistant Director, for their helpful guidance and encouragement, and excellent resource material; Mr. Ernst Michanek, Chairman of Sweden's International Assistance Board and formerly Undersecretary of the Department of Social Affairs, for his generous expenditure of time, excellent publications, and thoughtful counsel in the development of this study; Mr. Sten Wengström of the National Insurance Board; Mr. Ingemar Lindberg of the Ministry of Social Affairs; Dr. Arthur Engel, formerly Director General of the National Medical Board; Mr. Helge Dahlström, Director of the Social Welfare Office of the Stockholm Department of Public Welfare; and Professor Nils Andrén, Department of Political Science, University of Stockholm.

The Swedish Embassy in the United States, particularly Ambassadors Gunnar Jarring and Hubert de Besche, Mr. Thorbjörn Carlsson, Labor

Attaché, and Mr. Nils-Gustav Hildeman, Cultural Attaché; and Ambassador Graham Parsons and officials of the United States Embassy in Stockholm, particularly Mr. Earl Dennis, formerly Public Affairs Officer; Mr. Lawrence Carlson, formerly Cultural Officer; and Mr. Jorma L. Kaukonen, Labor Attaché.

Mr. and Mrs. Sten Klosterborg for their friendship and encouragement and for the translations by Mrs. Gunila Klosterborg of the Swedish poetry used at the opening of most chapters.

Professors Reuben Gustavson, Ben M. Cherrington, William Anderson, Lloyd M. Short, and the late Peter Odegard for their long friendship and guidance in the completion of this study.

The late Mr. Chester B. Lund, the former Director, Office of Field Administration, Office of the Secretary, Department of Health, Education, and Welfare; Mr. Bradshaw Mintener, formerly Assistant Secretary; and Mr. Marion Folsom, formerly Secretary of the Department of Health, Education, and Welfare, for their encouragement and counsel. Mr. John Ervin, Jr., Director of the University of Minnesota Press, for his patience and thoughtful advice, and Mrs. Eleanor Earle Rolf, Editorial Assistant, the University of Minnesota Press, for her editorial ability and interest in the final preparation of the manuscript.

The responsibility for the accuracy, reporting, and the soundness of conclusions reached in this study is, of course, the author's alone.

ALBERT H. ROSENTHAL

Table of Contents

I Growth of the Social Programs   3

Old-Age Pensions (Social Security), 4. Health Insurance, 6. Welfare, 8. Program Development, 10.

II The Social Security Programs   12

THE BASIC PENSION, 12: Coverage and Eligibility, 13. Retirement Benefits, 14. Other Benefits: DISABILITY PENSION, 15; WIDOWS' AND CHILDREN'S PENSIONS, 16; SUPPLEMENTS, 16. Financing, 17. Administration, 18. Basic Pension Number, 19. Case Example, 20. THE SUPPLEMENTARY PENSION, 22: Coverage and Eligibility, 22. Retirement Pension, 23. Disability Pension, 24. Survivor's Pensions, 25. Benefits and Cost-of-Living Adjustments, 26. ADMINISTRATION, 29. THE INSURANCE FUNDS, 32. APPEALS, 34. CASE EXAMPLE, 34.

III Health Insurance   36

Characteristics of the Program, 37. Coverage and Eligibility, 38. Benefits: PHYSICIANS' SERVICES, 38; HOSPITAL CARE, 41; MEDICINES, 42; TRAVEL COSTS, 42; DENTAL CARE, 43; CASH ALLOWANCES, 43; MATERNITY BENEFITS, 45. Financing, 46. Health Insurance Statistics, 48. Administration, 49.

IV Public Health   52

Administration, 53. Hospitals, 56. Mental Health, 58. Sex Education, 60. Birth Control, 62. Abortion, 63. Dental Health, 67.

V Welfare and Related Programs   69

Administration, 72. Statistics, 74. Child Welfare, 80. Care of the Aged, 83. Rehabilitation, 86.

VI The Government and the Individual 92

A Parliamentary Democracy, 94. Public Interest and Participation, 98. Decentralized Government, 99: THE DEPARTMENTS, 100; THE SEMI-INDEPENDENT BOARDS, 103. Local, County, and Province Government: THE STAD AND KOMMUN, 104; THE LANDSTING, 106; THE LANSSTYRELSE, 108. Civil Service, 111. Citizen Controls of Government, 117: THE OMBUDSMAN, 120. The Tax System, 129.

VII Program Comparisons: Sweden and the United States 135

The Social Security Programs, 138. The Health Programs, 144: COVERAGE, 145; BENEFITS, 147. The Welfare Programs, 150.

VIII Freedom in the Secure Society 154

Individual Liberty, 155. The Role of Government, 157. Free Enterprise, 159. Loss of Incentive, 161. Costs of the Social Programs, 163. Moral Standards, 164. A Public Philosophy for the United States, 168.

Bibliography 175

Index 183

List of Tables

1. Amounts Received and Expended under the National Pension (in Millions of Dollars and Kronor)   18

2. Supplementary Pension Annual Benefit, According to Year of Birth and Average Earned Income   28

3. Total Annual Benefit for a Married Pensioner, According to Year of Birth   29

4. Total Daily Sickness Allowances, According to Earned Annual Income   44

5. Premiums for Supplemental Daily Allowances, According to Earned Annual Income   47

6. Expenditures under the Health Insurance Funds for 1961 (in Millions of Dollars and Kronor)   49

TABLE OF CONTENTS

7. Distribution of Seats in the 1967 Riksdag	97
8. Civil Service Employee Status in 1963, by Department	114
9. State Business Enterprise Employee Status in 1963, by Enterprise	114
10. Examples of Total Taxes for a Married Couple	131
11. Examples of U.S. Social Security Monthly Payments, According to Average Earned Income after 1950	142
12. Comparative Examples of Monthly Benefit Payments by the Swedish Supplementary and Basic Pension Programs and by U.S. Social Security, According to Average Annual Income after 1950	143
13. Percentage of Private, Public, and Cooperative Enterprise in Swedish Industry	159
14. Expenditure and Investment in the Public and Private Sectors of Swedish Economy	160

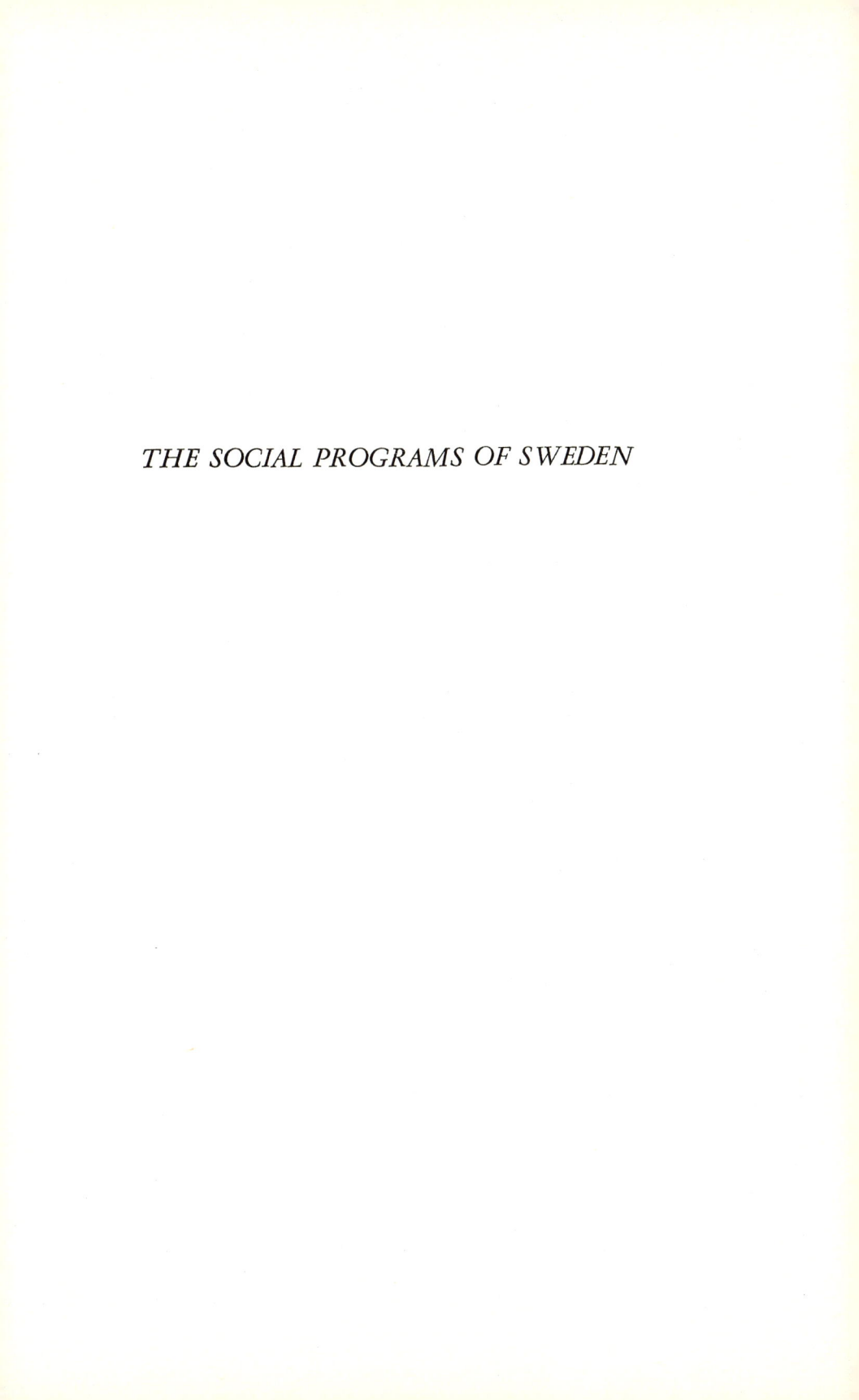

THE SOCIAL PROGRAMS OF SWEDEN

I

Growth of the Social Programs

SAYINGS AFORISMER
"What is a book?
No man can see or gain from a book
More than just as much as he has a
Real true need to see and gain from it.

Only the need can make the syllable alive.
The truth is an empty word, but the need for
Truth is everything."
Wilhelm Ekelund (1880–1949)

IN SWEDEN, the individual is protected from almost every social hazard by some form of legislation. The emphasis in Swedish social policy today is on the prevention of dependency, by means of full employment and extensive insurance plans, but public assistance is also available for those who are unable to provide adequately for their own needs or who are ineligible for insurance. Governmental programs have been developed to meet the problems an individual may encounter because of serious illness, disability, death of the family breadwinner, old age, substandard income, or unemployment. Public agencies have assumed responsibility for a wide range of services that in many societies are left to private initiative — for instance, provision of vacations for low-income families.

The complexity of the social programs is perhaps the first thing that strikes an observer. There appears to be an overlapping or a lack of coordination among some governmental activities. As in the United

States, agencies administering closely related programs often operate independently of each other, hence sometimes at cross-purposes. This has resulted from the historical fact that, in both countries, social legislation was enacted piecemeal in response to particular social problems. There is a bewildering array of supplements and allowances for those considered to be dependent. Certain consistent philosophical premises, however, do underlie the Swedish system, and a long step toward consolidation of administrative machinery for insurance plans was taken in 1962 with the passage of the National Insurance Act. But several of the welfare, health, and education programs are still administered under separate legislative acts and by different agencies.

It is difficult to determine the number of social programs operating in Sweden today. Depending upon the definitions used, authorities may list from eighteen to more than one hundred. Similarly, classification of programs into broad categories for purposes of analysis varies from writer to writer. Some simply classify programs by administrative agency, others by type of client — the aged, the disabled, children. One elementary but graphic classification uses these divisions: "In the Normal Course of Life," "In Case of Need," and "Pension Reform."[1] For our purposes here, a simple breakdown under three headings seems logical and useful: old-age pensions (or social security), health insurance, and welfare.

Old-Age Pensions (Social Security)

The present old-age, disability, and retirement pension system has its roots in the National Pension Act of 1913, which was the first national effort to provide social insurance for the entire population. This program was dual in nature. One part was financed by individual contributions and utilized the premium reserve system of private insurance companies. The other part was financed by taxation. The first part of the plan guaranteed every citizen upon retirement or disability a pension related to his previous earnings. However, it was found that most of these payments were inadequate and consequently the retired or disabled had to rely to a large extent on benefits provided under the second part of the plan: a small "block" pension and a house or rental allowance, eligibility for which was determined by an income or needs test administered at the municipal level. Even so, many of the aged found it necessary to

[1] *Social Benefits in Sweden*, p. 1.

apply for welfare benefits to supplement the small payments they received. As late as 1930, the average monthly benefit under the National Pension Act was only $7. The depression of the thirties, combined with inflation, resulted in great pressure for increased payments and an improved pension plan.

The next milestone was the National Pension Act of 1946, which went into effect on January 1, 1948. This law provided that, at age 67, all citizens would receive the same pension regardless of previous income or taxes paid. The pension was fixed at $200 (1,000 kr.) per year. In addition the law continued the practice of providing municipal rental allowances and other supplements on a needs basis, to permit a standard of living befitting citizens of "modest means." Disability payments and survivor's benefits for the husband, wife, or young children were provided on the basis of need — an income test, in the more pleasant term of the Swedish law, administered at the municipal level. This law also established the concept of periodic adjustments to the cost of living. Under this principle, a cost-of-living index was developed and applied to all payment benefits to protect beneficiaries from the effects of inflation. Adjustment to the cost of living has remained an important feature of Swedish retirement insurance.

Even before the National Pension Act of 1946 went into effect, many people, including government leaders, objected to the application of a means test in determining eligibility for the housing and other allowances. They also criticized the Basic Pension as insufficient to meet the needs of many in the retired, disabled, or survivor's categories without special allowances. As a result of these protests three high-level committees were appointed by the government in 1946 to study different possibilities for the establishment of an income-related, compulsory, and contributory social insurance program which would provide more substantial benefits than the recent act.

The three committees worked over a period of ten years. Each developed a different approach to a system of supplementary pensions. The three proposals were presented to the voters under a rarely used referendum procedure. None of them gained a majority. However, since 46 percent of the votes cast in the referendum were in favor of some form of legislation,[2] the Social Democratic party in 1958 introduced in the Parliament a bill providing for supplementary pensions; but it failed to

[2] Ernst Michanek, *Sweden's New National Pension Insurance*, p. 4.

pass. In 1959 another bill was proposed and this time the measure was approved. The new act has been in effect since January 1, 1960, and provides for all employees and self-employed persons an inflation-safe Supplementary Pension. Payments of Supplementary Pensions did not begin until 1963, however. Each person covered will eventually receive a total pension — Basic Pension plus Supplementary Pension — equal to about two-thirds of the income from work during "the best years." [3]

The 1959 Pension Law has since been modified. On the basis of recommendations by a Royal Commission of Inquiry, legislation was introduced and passed in the 1962 Riksdag that codified and consolidated the provisions of the 1959 Pension Law with all other insurance programs, provided for coordinated administration, and liberalized the amounts paid for Basic Pensions and the daily allowances in health and maternity insurance. The Introduction to the published copy of the act states the purposes of the new law: "With the National Insurance Act, which was passed by the Swedish Parliament in 1962 and which went into effect on January 1, 1963, the most important branches of Swedish social insurance — health and maternity insurance and basic and supplementary pensions — have been welded together into one whole. Thus Sweden has obtained a unified, materially and administratively coordinated social insurance scheme which provides for payments in case of childbearing, illness, disability, old age and death of the family breadwinner. It is characteristic of the Swedish social insurance scheme, as the Act shows, that it covers the whole people and gives benefits to all, regardless of their occupations." [4]

Under the 1962 law, only two special allowances based on a determination of need remain: the municipal housing allowances and the wives' supplement. Anyone eligible for the Basic Pension and with an income under a certain fixed limit is automatically eligible for these allowances. Since the legal right to these allowances is clearly defined the sense of dignity of the individual receiving them is not threatened.

Health Insurance

The establishment of compulsory health insurance in Sweden was greatly facilitated by two factors: First, most of the hospitals in Sweden have been traditionally owned and operated by the government; second,

[3] *Ibid.*
[4] *The National Insurance Act,* May 25, 1962, p. 1.

GROWTH OF THE SOCIAL PROGRAMS

"providence societies" or "sickness funds" have existed in Sweden since the time of the medieval guilds. A number of these guilds administered sickness insurance benefit programs, which continued to exist even after the abolition of the guild system. Many of these programs eventually grew into the voluntary benevolent societies that began to flourish in Sweden in the 1870's. In addition, trade unions and other societies included sickness benefits at an early date as part of the programs of their organizations.

This pattern of development existed throughout the Nordic countries. In Denmark and Finland the majority of the population is still covered by "voluntary" health insurance plans with a government subsidy of 25 percent, despite the fact that health insurance became compulsory in Denmark in 1961 and in Finland in 1964. The *Scandinavian Times* describes the emphasis as maintaining the historical pattern of the program: "This system is more than non-governmental. It is a 25 per cent subsidized co-op chain forged by mutual consent from voluntary local cooperative clubs founded more than a century ago." ("Health Care for All," May 1965, p. 3.) In 1892, a statute in Denmark provided that government subsidies would be granted to sickness benefit societies that met government standards. The voluntary health insurance plan in Denmark was limited to lower income employees until 1960. Even today low-income workers receive a more favorable premium rate. Norway established the first compulsory health insurance plan in the Nordic countries in 1909. It covered only workers with a low income. Other employees were covered by voluntary insurance until 1956 when the compulsory program was extended to everyone regardless of income. Today, health insurance is compulsory in all of the Scandinavian countries: Sweden since 1955, Norway since 1956, Denmark since 1961, Finland since 1964.

In Sweden the first government legislation concerning the operation of voluntary sickness insurance societies was passed in 1809. In 1891, formal regulations were approved concerning the cash benefits of the voluntary funds. This legislation was superseded by new laws in 1910 which were subsequently replaced by the Act of 1931. This act provided subsidy to and supervision of approved sickness benefit societies, and resulted in the development of a great number of central and branch sickness funds to which a relatively large proportion of Swedish citizens belonged. By the end of 1950, there were 37 regional and 1,116 local sickness benefit societies in Sweden. The number of voluntarily insured persons at that time was about 3,088,000, or 58 percent of the population over 15 years of age. In addition, approximately 1,289,000 children were covered by the insurance of their parents.[5]

It is estimated that by 1954 almost 70 percent of the population was covered by the sickness funds. However, only 25 percent of the old-age pensioners held membership in a voluntary health insurance plan. In addition, it had been found that many people felt that they could not afford the premium rates of the programs and others were disqualified from membership because they were in poor health by the time they applied. Consequently, the Riksdag had passed the Act of January 3, 1947, providing for compulsory sickness insurance. This act did not take effect for a number of years because it was believed that Sweden did not have sufficient hospitals and physicians to meet the demands for service that would arise under the compulsory health insurance program.

The national health insurance program finally went into effect on January 1, 1955. It has since been amended twice. In 1959 the voluntary sickness funds were transferred into the administrative structure of the compulsory national health insurance program. In 1962 the National Insurance Act made the following changes: (1) The administration of the program was coordinated with that of the other national public insurance plans — old age, survivor's, and disability; (2) the statutes and amendments were codified into one coherent system; (3) the scale of daily allowances was raised; (4) the self-employed were made eligible for supplementary allowances (previously they were eligible for only the basic daily allowances); (5) a substantial increase was provided in maternity benefits; and (6) the time limit on hospital and daily allowances for any one disease, previously restricted to a two-year period (except in the case of pensioners) was eliminated.

Welfare

The earliest social legislation in Sweden, as in most countries, was in the field of welfare. The first formal actions were taken in the 1760's. Laws were passed which established that each county and municipality was responsible for providing public assistance to those who could not

[5] *Social Sweden*, pp. 158–167, and Göran Tegner, *Social Security in Sweden*, pp. 72–75.

GROWTH OF THE SOCIAL PROGRAMS

care for themselves or their families. Even though the laws provided only minimum assistance for the poor, they were significant because they represented a shift in responsibility from religious orders or individual philanthropy to the local government unit.

The first law which can be considered primarily a public welfare act was passed in Sweden in 1847. This listed the needy classes such as the ill, widows, orphans, and the disabled, including the blind, and called on local governments to provide food, shelter, and medical care for them. However, as a result of a serious economic depression the progressive nature of the law was sharply restricted in 1871 by a limitation of the classes of eligible recipients.

The laws of 1847 and 1871 were replaced by the Poor Relief Act of 1918. It too was based on the concept that the provision of aid to the needy is a local responsibility. Under this act each local government, known as a *kommun*, was charged with the duty of providing adequate care and relief to any person in need. Each kommun was required to establish a public assistance committee selected by the kommunal council. The public assistance committee consisted of at least five members in cities and towns and three members in rural kommuns. The law also called for the appointment of deputy members and staff. Even then the role of women in welfare administration was recognized in that the law required that at least one of the regular members and one of the deputies be a woman.

Two classes of assistance were established: "compulsory assistance" and "permissive assistance." Compulsory assistance, the care local governments were required to provide, was given to ". . . any destitute minor, aged, infirm, disabled or feeble-minded person incapable of maintaining himself by gainful employment and not receiving adequate support from some other source such as a relative, employers, charity organization, insurance or aid society." [6] There was no residence requirement: The law provided that compulsory assistance be given to people in need wherever they happened to be, even if under the Swedish registration system they were domiciled in another kommun. Even foreigners in need received assistance under the same conditions as Swedish citizens. The central government reimbursed the local government in full for the costs of compulsory assistance to non-residents. The public assistance committee was authorized to recover costs of com-

[6] *Social Sweden*, p. 242.

pulsory public assistance to residents from the recipient when his financial status improved or from relatives legally liable for his maintenance, including the husband, wife, parents, or adult children. If the recipient had no relatives and could not pay, the central and local governments were not reimbursed.

The local committees were also empowered to provide "permissive assistance" — aid beyond what was statutorily required or to cases not eligible for compulsory assistance. For example, partially disabled persons who were destitute and ineligible for pension disability payments or persons for whom the compulsory assistance payments were insufficient could be granted permissive assistance. The costs were not automatically reimbursed by the central government, but recovered, where possible, from the recipient when he was able to meet such obligations.

In 1937, on the premise that the Poor Relief Act of 1918 should be modernized, a Social Welfare Commission was established to study the operation of the program and recommend legislation to the Riksdag. After thirteen years of study, the commission finally published a report in 1950; it eventually led to the passage of a new Law on Social Help by the Riksdag on January 4, 1956, which became effective on January 1, 1957. The Law on Social Help superseded the Poor Relief Act of 1918 and provided the basic legal structure for the administration of public welfare in Sweden today.

In 1924, the passage of the Child Welfare Act had called for the establishment of local child welfare committees and transferred responsibility for the care of children from the local public assistance committees to the new child welfare committees. The local public assistance committees, however, were still held responsible for the provision of public relief to children living with their parents and until 1956, when the health insurance program came into effect, they were responsible also for the payment of hospital and medical expenses for needy children.

Program Development

A review of the growth of the social programs in Sweden indicates their evolutionary development. Statutes in 1847, 1871, and 1918 represented steps in the development of a social philosophy completely different from the poor laws of the 1700's. Half a century elapsed between the establishment of the first Basic Pension program in 1913 and the

GROWTH OF THE SOCIAL PROGRAMS

authorization of Supplementary Pension payments in 1963. Sixty-four years separated the first legal regulation of voluntary health insurance funds in 1891 and effectuation of the current plan in 1955. The present humanitarian Law on Social Help passed in 1956 was adopted only after years of study. This pattern is continuing at present, for there are several royal commissions and committees currently examining refinements in the Supplementary Pension, further possibilities for rehabilitating welfare recipients, and extension of the health insurance program to include dental care for adults.

II

The Social Security Programs

> A POOR MONK FROM SKARA
> "But ahead through long lasting struggle
> Better times will dawn
> When no one is evil
> And no one is good
> But brothers who fight
> In the stream of evil
> And extend each other the hand
> To help reach the shore."
> Gustaf Froding (1860–1911)

THE TERM "social security," although not commonly used in Sweden to designate the retirement, disability, and survivor's insurance program, is descriptive of its broad coverage and objectives. Use of this term here will facilitate comparison with the similar program in the United States.

To provide means of meeting the financial hazards of loss of regular income because of age, disability, or death of the breadwinner Sweden has developed — as noted in Chapter I — an insurance system consisting of two closely related programs: the Basic Pension of flat-rate benefits, with a complex of supplements and allowances, and the income-related Supplementary Pension.

THE BASIC PENSION

The Basic or National Pension in Sweden may be described as having (1) evolutionary development; (2) universal coverage; (3) comprehensive and complex benefit provisions; (4) no relation to income, except

THE SOCIAL SECURITY PROGRAMS

for certain supplements; and (5) limited benefits so that, without supplements and allowances, it is insufficient to meet the needs of most families.

As indicated in the preceding chapter, the concept of the block pension was initially formulated in law by the National Pension Act of 1913. The social philosophy of equal treatment for citizens became a cornerstone of the Social Democratic party, which supported retention of the block pension throughout many changes of the program. Constant review and change have marked the development of the Swedish pension programs through legislation of 1946, 1959, and 1962. The efforts of the Riksdag in this field have been typical of Swedish lawmaking. The Riksdag has considered alternate viewpoints before passing the bills and then has provided a period of delay before their enforcement.

The accompanying tabulation shows the number of persons receiving Basic Pension benefits in January of 1958, 1962, 1967, and 1970 (figures for 1967 and 1970 are estimated); this information is from *The Swedish Budget, 1967/68*, p. 51.

	1958	1962	1967	1970
Old-age pensioners (67 or older)	707,000	771,000	872,000	950,000
Disability pensioners	139,000	146,000	157,000	165,000
Others	80,000	138,000	176,000	185,000
Total	926,000	1,055,000	1,205,000	1,300,000

Coverage and Eligibility

Coverage under the present Basic Pension is practically universal for all Swedish citizens and is extended, by mutual agreement, to nationals of other Scandinavian countries and of Switzerland, Italy, Great Britain, and other nations covered by European conventions on social security. Swedish nationals who reside abroad are eligible if they have lived in Sweden and been registered for tax purposes during a specified period. All employees and self-employed persons are covered by the Basic Pension. No group is excluded.

The law states that "Swedish nationals as well as such aliens and nonnationals who are registered as residents of the country for census purposes shall be insured under this Act" (Chapter 1, Article 3). However, Part 3 of the law, which outlines the regulations for the Basic Pension, restricts this broad eligibility: "Every Swedish national who is census-registered in Sweden or who was census-registered here for the year during which he attained sixty-two years of age, as well as for the five preceding years, is entitled to a Basic Pension subject to the following provisions" (Chapter 5, Article 1). Residence in Sweden immediately before eligibility is thus required. The law on this point is clear. In addition to being a citizen, the applicant must have been legally domiciled in Sweden for the year immediately preceding eligibility — 63 for the reduced pension or 67 for the full pension — and the five preceding years. In practice, five and one-half years has been considered sufficient. The question is frequently asked whether a Swedish citizen who has been living abroad may return to Sweden and be eligible for the Basic Pension. As indicated, he would be required to return to Sweden at least six months before his 58th or 62nd birthday and maintain residence there for the succeeding five and one-half years. At the age of eligibility he may then live abroad and receive a Basic Pension.

The residence requirement is comparable to that of the state-administered old-age pension programs in the United States which differ somewhat from state to state but almost universally require citizenship and a minimum residence period of five of the nine years preceding application for pension, including the immediately preceding year. The amount paid in these programs varies widely among the several states and is, in accordance with the Social Security Act of 1935, determined on the basis of need of the recipient. However, in certain periods in states such as California and Colorado the payments were almost identical for all beneficiaries (as in a block pension).

Both the previous and the present Swedish Basic Pension laws provide for full benefits to be paid at the age of 67. The new provisions in the amendments of 1962 permit receipt of the old-age pension at age 63 with a reduction of six-tenths of 1 percent for each month between the present age and the month the recipient becomes 67. Conversely, the eligible recipient may elect to postpone receipt of the pension and gain six-tenths of 1 percent for each month until he attains the age of 70. In accordance with this formula the recipient at age 63 will receive 71.2 percent of a full pension while one who waits for seven years will receive 121.6 percent of the Basic Pension.

Retirement Benefits

Increased benefits for retirement because of age became effective on July 1, 1962. (This is in contrast with other changes in the law, including

THE SOCIAL SECURITY PROGRAMS

the actual payment of benefits under the Supplementary Pension, which became effective on January 1, 1963.) For 1963, the Basic Pension was established at $680 (3,400 kr.) per year for a single person, an increase from $570 (2,850 kr.) under the previous law. A husband and wife who are both eligible under the old-age or disability provision will receive a combined pension benefit payment of $1,066 (5,330 kr.) per year, an increase from $902 (4,510 kr.) under the old law.

Other Benefits

The Basic Pension program may be described as comprehensive because of the complex of family pensions that are included. While the structure of special allowances and supplements appears exceedingly confusing to an American observer and almost as confusing to the Swedes, there is a definite rationale underlying it. The 1962 National Insurance Act provided needed coordination. The special allowances and supplements include disability pensions, widows' pensions, children's pensions, wives' supplements, children's supplements, disability supplements, and municipal housing supplements. The four supplements were formerly "means-tested," but under the 1962 amendments only the wives' supplement (a widows' pension payable to women widowed before July 1, 1960) and the housing supplement are now dependent upon proof of need.

Disability Pension.[1] Any Swedish citizen or resident alien between the ages of 16 and 67 whose working capacity is reduced by at least one-half is entitled to a disability pension under the Basic Pension plan, provided that the cause of the disability, as medically determined, is illness, mental retardation, or a permanent physical or mental handicap. These ages were chosen because at 16 the general children's allowances cease, and at 67 the full Basic Pension payments begin. Household work is equated with other work, giving disabled housewives the same benefits as wage earners.

Benefits are in direct ratio to the degree of disability: full payment for total disability, two-thirds if disability is more than two-thirds of working capacity, and one-third in all other cases. The standards for determination of disability as set by law require consideration of what ". . . can reasonably be expected of [the applicant] in view of his edu-

---

[1] The Swedish name was changed by the Act of 1962 from *invalidpension* to *förtidspension* or "advance pension."

cation and previous work, as well as age, living conditions and comparable circumstances" (Chapter 7, Article 3). The 1962 law eliminates the income test which was previously required for the approval of a National Disability Pension.

A temporary disability allowance is paid if the disability does not appear to be permanent but if it can be assumed that it will last for at least one year. For 1963 the full disability pension was $680 (3,400 kr.). From July 1, 1968, the full disability pension will be the same amount as the old-age pension with a reduction in percentage when other pension benefits are received in the same family.

Widows' and Children's Pensions. All widows are entitled to a pension if they were 36 years of age or older at the time of their husband's death or have a child under 16 years of age living in the home. These eligibility requirements also apply to common-law wives or divorced women who are on an equal footing with widows in being entitled to a widows' pension. The benefit payments cease, however, if the widow remarries. This parallels the provision for widows' benefits under social security in the United States. Since July 1, 1963, a full widow's pension has been established at 90 percent of the base amount of the Basic Pension, with proportionate reduction provided if the widow is not 50 years of age at the time of the husband's death. At present it amounts to $680 (3,400 kr.).

Every child in Sweden under 16 years of age receives a general children's allowance which amounts to $110 (550 kr.) per year. In addition, since 1960 the Basic Pension has provided for an extension of the children's pension in the form of a survivor's benefit which is payable to children under 16 years of age who have lost one or both parents and are Swedish citizens permanently residing in Sweden. This benefit is not means-tested and at present amounts to $280 (1,400 kr.) a year for a child who has lost both parents and $200 (1,000 kr.) a year for a child who has lost one parent. No cost-of-living increments are added for the children's pension.

Supplements. The most significant parts of the pension received by many recipients are the benefit supplements.

The wives' supplement is a means-tested benefit payable to the wife of a pensioner who is 60 years of age or older and has been married to her husband for five years or longer. If granted, the couple receives a maximum pension, at present $1,066 (5,330 kr.) per year.

THE SOCIAL SECURITY PROGRAMS

The children's supplement provides, without the means test formerly required for a supplementary payment, a pension of $200 (1,000 kr.) per year for each child under 16 years of age. This supplement is coordinated with other pensions and is reduced or eliminated as disability or supplementary payments exceed the established maximum (see pp. 23–25).

Disability supplements add $240 (1,200 kr.) to the disability pension of blind persons, disabled persons who need another's help, and disabled persons who work and have extra expense because of their employment. The disability supplement is not payable to persons in hospitals or institutions (Chapter 9, Article 2).

Municipal housing supplements are unchanged by the 1962 law with respect to the requirement that each municipality provide municipal housing supplements, to all persons eligible for the Basic Pension, on the basis of a means test. Every municipality is expected to add a supplement necessary to pay the rent or other housing expenditures of national pensioners either entirely or in part depending upon the income of the pensioner. Each municipality has established rules governing the housing supplement for its residents. The municipality initially pays the total costs but subsidies are provided by the central government under a cost-sharing formula. Every municipality is required to conform to the regulations and provisions of the National Insurance Board to be eligible for the central government grants. The means test is based on deduction of any income received by a pensioner from the amount of the full supplement. No supplement is paid if the income exceeds established limits. Adult children or other relatives of pensioners are not required to provide any part of the expenses of the parent or relative in the calculation of need by the means test.

Financing

The cost of the National Basic Pension is paid by the central government with a large part of the supplements and allowances, especially the municipal housing allowance, paid by the local governments.

While each taxpayer pays an amount noted on his tax bill as a pension fee, the central government adds almost an equal amount to meet costs of the National Pension program. In 1960–61, the total amount expended in the program was $515,200,000 (2,576,000,000 kr.). Of this, $206,800,000 (1,034,000,000 kr.) was received from pension fees, and

$80,200,000 (401,000,000 kr.) was expended by local governments.[2] The total cost of the program for fiscal year 1963, that is 1962–63, was $692,000,000 (3,460,000,000 kr.) including $78,800,000 (394,000,000 kr.) for improvements and increases authorized by the Act of 1962 and effective July 1, 1962. Table 1 shows the trend of expenditures by fiscal years: the total expended, the amounts collected for pension fees, and the contribution by local governments.

Table 1. Amounts Received and Expended under the National Pension
(in Millions of Dollars and Kronor)

	Amount Received		Amount Expended
Year	Pension Fees	Local Government	
1939.....	$ 9 (45 kr.)	$ 6.2 (31 kr.)	$ 30.6 (153 kr.)
1949.....	25.8 (129 kr.)	15.2 (76 kr.)	162 (811 kr.)
1959.....	125 (625 kr.)	65.2 (326 kr.)	436 (2,179 kr.)
1961.....	206.8 (1,034 kr.)	. . .	515 (2,576 kr.)
1962.....	. . .	96 (480 kr.)	590 (2,950 kr.)

Administration

The administration of the Basic Pension, along with that of the Supplementary Pension and the National Health Insurance program, is under the supervision of the National Social Insurance Board (the *Riksförsäkringsverket*), a series of 28 regional insurance funds or agencies (called *Allmänna Försäkringskassorna*), and approximately 600 local insurance offices called *Lokalkontor*. (The National Insurance Act of 1962 consolidated the administration of the Basic Pension, the Supplementary Pension, and health insurance and took over the field structure of the previous local sickness insurance offices and regional funds.) Because the applicant for a Basic Pension is generally not required to deal personally with any of these offices, the description of the administrative organization and structure is presented in more detail in the discussion of the Supplementary Pension program (see pp. 29–32).

The procedure for obtaining the Basic Pension is very simple and almost automatic. The regional social insurance office sends out an application form to each person three months before he reaches 67 years of age. If the person wants to retire at the age of 63 or at any time between 63 and 67, or becomes disabled, he or his representative must take the

[2] *The Development of Sweden in Figures*, p. 8.

THE SOCIAL SECURITY PROGRAMS

initiative and visit the nearest local social insurance office, the Lokalkontor. Proof of age must be submitted with the application; a birth certificate is sufficient and most frequently used. However, a letter from the pastor of the parish in which the person resides confirming his age is considered proof enough. Since excellent records and vital statistics have been maintained in Sweden for many years most applicants find little difficulty in obtaining a birth certificate as proof of age.

Those who do not automatically receive the pension application form, i.e., if they have recently moved and their names are not on the local registration list, are required to visit the local social insurance office, complete a form, and present evidence of residence for the required period of time. The local social insurance office reviews all the forms for eligibility and submits them to a representative of the local pension committee, *pensions delegation*, established in every municipality by the law (Chapter 18, Article 24). The local pension committee reviews applications closely to sift out those requesting allowances or supplements which require the application of the means test. The major function of the local committee is the determination of the amount of the municipal housing allowance. The pension committee, composed of residents of the same municipality as the applicant, ascertains his actual income level and standard of living, and makes a recommendation to the local office. The local office certifies the pension supplements and allowances for which the applicant is eligible and forwards the application, together with the report of the pension committee, to the appropriate regional social insurance office with a recommendation on the amount to be paid. In cases of disability application the reports of the medical examiner are attached. The regional social insurance office acts upon the application, determines the amount to be paid, and places the account on an individual punch card for record and control purposes. The certification is sent to the National Social Insurance Board in Stockholm, where members of the staff review the regional determination. An automatic punch card system is used to print the checks, which are mailed from the National Social Insurance Board directly to the recipient (see pp. 20–21).

Basic Pension Number

Sweden has one of the best developed and most extensive statistical systems of any country in the world. Records are opened at birth for every Swedish national and maintained at the local or parish level. To be eligible for any of the social programs each individual must be census-registered in the locality in which he lives. (The term in Swedish is *Mantalsskrilven*, and means registered with the tax-collecting authorities.)

A Basic Pension number is assigned to every citizen. It consists of four sets of digits providing a numerical statement of the year, month, and day of birth and the number of people registered up to that time with the identical birthdate. For example, a person born on November 26, 1914, who was the tenth to be registered as having that birthdate would have the Basic Pension number of 14-11-26-10.

This system not only has the value of simplicity but also authenticates the date of birth at the time the number is assigned (although current procedure still calls for submission of proof of birthdate or age at the time of application for a Basic Pension). In addition, this method greatly helps a person remember his Basic Pension number.

CASE EXAMPLE

Mrs. Andersson Applies for a Basic Pension. Mrs. Brigit Andersson had lived in Sweden all of her long and industrious life. Her husband had operated a small shoe repair shop in the older section of Stockholm until his death, and Mrs. Andersson not only maintained their home but also assisted her husband in the shop. When he died, Mrs. Andersson found it impossible to operate the business and sold it for the value of the materials and equipment. They had no children.

As she approached 67 years of age, Mrs. Andersson visited the Stockholm office of the National Social Insurance Board and indicated that she would be eligible for a pension on August 4, 1963. (She could have received a widow's pension right after her husband's death but did not.) Although an application form is sent automatically to those who are eligible for a pension, the National Social Insurance Board encourages all who are able to come to a local office and discuss their pension. Mrs. Andersson brought with her a document indicating that she was a Swedish citizen and census-registered in Stockholm.

After reviewing the document and talking briefly with Mrs. Andersson, the interviewer stated that she was apparently eligible for the Basic Pension and suggested that she also apply for a municipal housing supplement since she had no source of regular income and very meager savings. Mrs. Andersson concurred with the suggestion. With the help of the interviewer she completed the form *Ansokan om Allman Pension*, "Application for Public Pension," which asked for her full name, her address, the place at which she had been census-registered, her occupational status, her marital status, the names of members of her family living with her, and the sources of her income. She signed the form under the statement "I hereby certify on my honor that the information today in this application is truthful," and was told that she would be notified of the action taken.

Her application was sent to one of the four Insurance Committees of the Stockholm Regional Fund for Stockholm, which determined her other annual income as "none" and recommended the payment of a municipal housing allowance of $228 a year (1,140 kr.). Her papers were then sent to the office of the regional insurance fund. A staff member of this office reviewed the application and determined that Mrs. Andersson was not qualified for a Supplementary Pension since she did not have a qualifying number of pension points (see next section). It was also concluded that the amount recommended for the housing supplement was too low, according to the standards established for the city of Stockholm, and this amount was raised to $333 a year (1,665 kr.). The amount of the Basic Pension itself was established at $680 (3,400 kr.), which includes the cost-of-living index addition.

A notice of the approved pension was sent by the central insurance office to Mrs. Andersson on July 31, 1963. A simultaneous notification of the decision was sent to the finance bureau of the regional insurance board authorizing issuance of a pension check to Mrs. Andersson beginning in August 1963. The notice Mrs. Andersson received was in the nature of a completed form letter. It opened with this statement: "The Insurance Fund grants you a public pension to be paid as from August 1963, with the following annual amounts. The amount is calculated according to the pension price index and the base amount valid from July 1963." Following this opening, the letter detailed for Mrs. Andersson the amounts she would receive annually as Basic Pension and municipal housing supplement and indicated she would receive the total of $1,013 (5,065 kr.) in monthly installments of approximately $84 (422 kr.). Since her home and furniture had long since been paid for and her wants were very simple, Mrs. Andersson was able to manage on this income.

THE SOCIAL PROGRAMS OF SWEDEN

THE SUPPLEMENTARY PENSION

The General Supplementary Pension is known throughout Sweden as "ATP," an abbreviation taken from its full Swedish name, *allmän tilläggspension,* which means "general supplementary pension." The Supplementary Pension is very similar to the social security program in the United States. Both programs are compulsory and contributory, and include survivor's and disability benefits as well as retirement payments.

The major characteristics of the newly established General Supplementary Pension program may be stated as follows: (1) there is practically universal coverage, with all employees and most self-employed included; (2) it is comprehensive in benefits, in that it includes retirement, disability, and survivor's insurance; (3) it is compulsory, in that the taxes are paid by all employers for all employees (with certain relatively minor exceptions); (4) the full tax is contributed by the employers (in contrast to the Basic Pension fees which are paid entirely by the employees); (5) it is income-related in contrast to the Basic Pension; (6) it is adequate to meet the needs of most retirement beneficiaries, the disabled, and survivors; and (7) it is related to cost of living in the calculation of both pension credits and benefit payments.

Coverage and Eligibility

The three significant dates in the immediate development of the General Supplementary Pension program are 1959, when the Riksdag passed the Supplementary Pension Act; January 1, 1960, when payroll tax contributions on income earned from any gainful occupation began; and January 1, 1963, when the first Supplementary Pension benefits became payable.

No special groups are exempted from the Supplementary Pension, such as the initial exclusion of medical doctors in the United States program. However, while coverage is compulsory for all classified as employees, a self-employed person may, on application to the regional social insurance office, be exempted from the Supplementary Pension insurance program, both in contributions and in benefits, with respect to income earned from his self-employment. Approximately 10 percent of the employees covered by the Supplementary Pension have taken advantage of this option and have contracted out of it; most of these are farmers. It should be noted that the exemption of a self-employed person

THE SOCIAL SECURITY PROGRAMS

from coverage under the Supplementary Pension also causes him to forfeit insurance for supplemental daily allowances under the health insurance program, since the daily allowances are related to income earned through gainful work. However, a self-employed person remains covered if he earns any income simultaneously or at a future date because of work done as an employee.

A second type of exemption was permitted early in the program through the mechanism of collective agreements made before July 1, 1961, which gave employees the right to contract out of the Supplementary Pension plan collectively through their trade unions or professional organizations and adopt an alternative pension plan. The employers had to submit a proposal to the National Social Insurance Board specifying all of the factors in the alternative proposed pension plan. No groups of employees took advantage of this option, which was only available for two years.

The law states the minimum period for the accumulation of credits in order to be eligible for benefit payments at the age of 67. This period is at least three years for a Swedish citizen (two years if he was born in 1896 or earlier) and ten years for an alien residing in Sweden. It should be noted that the requirement of citizenship established for the Basic Pension is not included as a requirement for the Supplementary Pension.

The Supplementary Pension may be described as comprehensive in benefits because it includes (1) a retirement pension, normally from age 67; (2) a disability pension, known as the "advance pension"; and (3) a survivor's pension, payable to the widow or widower and surviving children. These pensions are paid in addition to the Basic Pension.

The total payment of benefits, including the retirement, disability, and family benefit programs amounted to $7,100,000 (35,500,000 kr.) in 1963.

Retirement Pension

The retirement pension under the Supplementary Pension program becomes payable at 67 years of age, as in the Basic Pension plan. At the beneficiary's request, the payment of Supplementary Pensions can begin at 63 years with a reduction in the amount or be postponed until the age of 70 years with an increase in the amount of the pension, as in the Basic Pension (see p. 14). The total retirement benefit for those eligible for the Supplementary Pension usually includes the retirement pension for the Basic Pension. This total amount will ultimately constitute two-thirds of the average annual earnings during the beneficiary's 15 best income years of employment. In the initial period during the installation of the Supplementary Pension, 20 years with a pension-earning income have been required to earn a full Supplementary Pension, and one-twentieth of the full amount is deducted for each missing year. The 20-year requirement will ultimately be increased to 30 and consequently one-thirtieth will be deducted for each missing year. The minimum amount included in the calculations for total retirement benefit is $800 (4,000 kr.) per year of earnings and the maximum is $7,050 (35,250 kr.) per year.

Supplementary Pensions are paid whether or not the beneficiary continues work or has other sources of income. This is in contrast with the work clause provision in the social security program in the United States, which, until age 72, provides for a deduction of earnings from employment which exceed a stated amount. This concept was rejected in the consideration of the Swedish program. The report of the committee of the Riksdag pointed out that a provision that stimulated older people to quit their jobs represented unsound social policy. It is preferable, the committee concluded, to permit older people to continue in their jobs and maintain their sense of usefulness and contribution to society. No consideration was given to the concept which won organized labor support for the work clause provision in the American social security program. In Sweden there was no fear that a subsidized, older working force might tend to reduce wage levels, and the pensioner may continue at full salary, taper off and use the pension as a supplement, or quit work and depend entirely on his pension. The choice is up to him. This system of continuing employment for the older segment of the working force is indeed working very satisfactorily. Retirement benefits under the Supplementary Pension plan were paid to 24,600 persons in 1963.

Disability Pension

The National Insurance Act of 1962 coordinates the provisions for disability benefits of the Basic Pension with the disability provisions in the Supplementary Pension program. The same standards are used in determining eligibility in both programs. The applicant must be a Swedish citizen or a resident alien covered by an international convention. Disability must be medically ascertained.

Three levels of payment, identical to those of the Basic Pension, have been established. They are based upon the degree of reduction in working capacity. Those who have lost all or almost all of their working capacity receive the full Supplementary Disability Pension (the same as the full Supplementary Retirement Pension normally received at age 67). Two-thirds of a full pension is given to those with a loss of considerably more than one-half of their working capacity, and those who have lost one-half of their working capacity, the minimum required for eligibility, receive one-third of a full pension. But the full Supplementary Pension is paid to those who become disabled, to whatever degree, in the year preceding the birthday on which they would become eligible for the full pension.

To qualify for the advance or disability pension under the Supplementary Pension program the applicant must have earned pension points for at least one year and is required, at the time when he became disabled, to have been earning an income in excess of $960 (4,800 kr.) a year, or must have earned pension points during at least three of the four years immediately preceding the disability. This is in contrast with the Basic Pension program under which all persons, irrespective of previous incomes, are eligible for the disability pension. In 1963, 7,650 people received disability pensions under the Supplementary Pension program.

Survivor's Pensions

In addition to the pensions provided under the Basic Pension plan for all children under age 16 who have lost one or both parents there are survivor's benefits under the Supplementary Pension for widows and children under 19 years of age. In cases in which there is one survivor 40 percent of the Supplementary Pension which the deceased received or would have received is paid. If there are two survivors 50 percent is paid. This percentage increases by 10 percent with each additional survivor.

In 1963, a total of 16,550 surviving dependents — 9,340 widows and 7,210 children — received survivor's benefits under the Supplementary Pension program.

Benefits and Cost-of-Living Adjustments

There has been a long-standing tradition in Sweden that pensions should be adjusted to a cost-of-living index and thus have a constant purchasing power. This concept has been used for many years in the administration of the Basic Pension by the addition of cost-of-living supplements. This concept is also maintained in the new Supplementary Pension in two ways: (1) by the method in which pension credits are calculated with respect to the base amount, and (2) in the adjustment of benefits to a cost-of-living index related to the dates when contributions were paid.

While many pension systems, including several state pension programs in the United States, utilize a cost-of-living index to adjust benefits to actual purchasing power, the Swedish plan of adjusting pension credits as well as benefits is somewhat unusual and deserves special attention. There is almost universal agreement that pension benefits should be related to the cost of living to guarantee purchasing power, but some question has been raised about the value of also adjusting pension credits to the cost-of-living index. Perhaps the architects of the Swedish program saw some psychological value in the dual plan. However, the highly complicated method of calculating benefits is an obvious disadvantage and makes it difficult for Swedish citizens to fully understand how the figure on their benefit checks is arrived at. The following description, simplified as it is, indicates the complex and rather technical nature of the formula used in the determination of the Supplementary Pensions.

The system starts with an artificially designated amount of money called the base (or basic) amount, which fluctuates in accordance with current monetary value. This concept is specified in the law itself: "The base amount is determined for each month by the Crown and amounts to 4,000 kronor multiplied by the figure showing the relation between the general price level for the third month preceding that to which the base amount refers and the price level in September 1957" (Part 1, Chapter 1, Article 6). The law prohibits any change in the base amount unless the price levels have varied by 3 percent since the last change, and provides for rounding off the amount to the nearest 100 kronor. The national consumer price index is used as the basis for the adjustments. The amount of $800 (4,000 kr.) was used as the standard for the base money value as of September 1957. The almost constant rise in the cost of living is reflected in the subsequent adjustments made in this amount, indicated in the following list:

	Dollars	Kronor
September 1957	800	4,000
January 1960	840	4,200
January 1961	860	4,300
January 1962	900	4,500
January 1963	940	4,700

The base amount is used as the lower limit in the collection of contributions for the Supplementary Pension, as well as in calculating pension earnings. (Incomes under the base amount are not included in the calculations; the Basic Pension is considered to cover those earning under this amount.) Also, it automatically sets the upper limit since the law provides that the upper limit is ". . . income from employment and other gainful activity which exceeds a sum that is seven and a half times greater than the base amount in force at the beginning of the year" (Chapter 11, Article 5).

Pension points are arrived at by dividing the pensionable income by the base amount in force at the beginning of the year. For example, a man earning 140,000 kr. in 1963 would have a pensionable income of 130,550 kr., on which he would earn 27 pension points. Pension points for the self-employed are credited only when contributions are paid by a specified date. Premiums for the employed are paid by the employer as a percentage of wages paid to each employee within the lower and upper limits.

Benefits are computed by multiplying the annual average of pension points earned during the 15 best years of employment by 60 percent of the current base amount. Since the amounts of disability pensions and survivor's benefits have been set in relation to the amounts of old-age pensions, the same system governs all parts of the Supplementary Pension program.

An example of payment under the retirement provisions of the Supplementary Pension is as follows: "We will assume that you were born in 1900 and that during every year of the period 1960–1965 you had an earned income of Swedish kronor 10,000 [$2,000]. Your old age pension from ATP in 1967 will then be Swedish kronor 1,032 [$206.40] (assuming unchanged prices level)."[3] To this would be added auto-

[3] *A Short Guide from the National Insurance Office* (Stockholm: Kunglia Boktr., 1963), p. 5.

matically the Basic Pension of $680 (3,400 kr.) for a total of $886.40 per year or $73.86 per month, a subsistence income for a person of modest means. It would frequently be supplemented by the municipal rental allowance.

Under this system of calculating benefits, the amount received from

Table 2: Supplementary Pension Annual Benefit, According to Year of Birth and Average Earned Income*

Year of Birth	Income of $2,000 (10,000 kr.)	Income of $5,000 (25,000 kr.)	Income of $7,050 (35,250 kr.)
1896	$ 76.80 (384 kr.)	$ 275.20 (1,376 kr.)	$ 366.60 (1,833 kr.)
1897	110.80 (554)	403.60 (2,018)	550.00 (2,750)
1898	143.20 (716)	525.60 (2,628)	733.20 (3,666)
1899	174.80 (874)	647.20 (3,236)	916.60 (4,583)
1900	206.40 (1,032)	769.80 (3,849)	1,099.80 (5,499)
1901	238.80 (1,194)	890.20 (4,451)	1,283.20 (6,416)
1902	270.80 (1,354)	1,013.00 (5,065)	1,466.40 (7,332)
1903	302.00 (1,510)	1,134.40 (5,672)	1,649.80 (8,249)
1904	332.80 (1,664)	1,257.80 (6,289)	1,833.00 (9,165)
1905	366.00 (1,830)	1,377.20 (6,886)	2,016.40 (10,082)
1906	399.40 (1,997)	1,499.20 (7,496)	2,199.60 (10,998)
1907	429.00 (2,145)	1,620.40 (8,102)	2,383.00 (11,915)
1908	462.00 (2,310)	1,745.00 (8,725)	2,566.20 (12,831)
1909	495.00 (2,475)	1,865.40 (9,327)	2,749.60 (13,748)
1910	528.00 (2,640)	1,989.80 (9,949)	2,932.80 (14,664)
1911	560.80 (2,804)	2,114.20 (10,571)	3,116.20 (15,581)
1912	593.80 (2,969)	2,238.60 (11,193)	3,299.40 (16,497)
1913	626.80 (3,134)	2,362.80 (11,814)	3,482.80 (17,414)
1914 or later	659.30 (3,299)	2,487.20 (12,436)	3,666.00 (18,330)

SOURCE: *A Short Guide from the National Insurance Office* (Stockholm: Kunglia Boktr., 1963), p. 5.
*The figures are based on the price level of spring 1963.

the Supplementary Pension is based within established limits on two variables: the year of birth and the annual earned income. The amounts range from $76.80 per year for a person born in 1896 who has had an average earned income of $2,000 (10,000 kr.) per year, to the potential benefit of $3,666 (18,330 kr.) per year for a person born in 1914 or later with an average earned income of $7,050 (35,250 kr.) per year. Table 2 gives examples of the annual Supplementary Pension based upon year of birth and average earned income.

Table 3 indicates the total annual benefit — Basic Pension plus Supplementary Pension — for a married pensioner whose average annual earnings were $7,050 (35,250 kr.) or more.

THE SOCIAL SECURITY PROGRAMS

ADMINISTRATION

Regional insurance funds have been established on the basis of the counties known as *län*. There are 24 län throughout Sweden and four additional fund offices have been provided, one in each of the cities of Stockholm, Göteborg, Malmö, and Norrköping. A separate office serves the people located outside each city in the län. Each län social insurance office has jurisdiction over the programs of the county or the city in which it is located. The name of the regional public insurance funds in Swedish is *Allmänna Försäkringskassorna* which, translated literally, means "public insurance funds." While the term also refers to the agency or office from an administrative point of view, the term "fund" may have been used because the law actually places a fiscal responsibility in each local office.

Table 3. Total Annual Benefit for a Married Pensioner, According to Year of Birth

Year of Birth	Total Annual Benefit*
1896	$1,432.60 (7,163 kr.)
1897	1,616.00 (8,080)
1898	1,799.20 (8,996)
1899	1,982.60 (9,913)
1900	2,165.80 (10,829)
1901	2,349.20 (11,746)
1902	2,532.40 (12,662)
1903	2,715.80 (13,579)
1904	2,899.00 (14,495)
1905	3,082.40 (15,412)
1906	3,265.60 (16,328)
1907	3,449.00 (17,245)
1908	3,632.20 (18,161)
1909	3,815.60 (19,078)
1910	3,998.80 (19,994)
1911	4,182.20 (20,911)
1912	4,365.40 (21,827)
1913	4,548.80 (22,744)
1914	4,732.00 (23,660)

SOURCE: *A Short Guide from the National Insurance Office* (Stockholm: Kunglia Boktr., 1963), p. 5.

* The total annual benefit is equal to the sum of the Basic and Supplementary Pensions. The Basic Pension, calculated at the price level of spring, 1963, was established at 5,330 kronor (444.1 kr. per month) or approximately $1,065.84 ($88.82 per month) for a married couple. The Supplementary Pension benefits for a married pensioner are given in Table 2, column 3.

Each län fund is administered by a board and an executive director established as a semi-autonomous public corporation with assets and liabilities. The regional fund is supervised by the National Insurance Board, the Riksförsäkingsverket, which establishes and enforces regulations and policies in accordance with the law for the operation of the regional funds. This supervision is specified in the Act of 1962: "The National Insurance Board shall exercise supervision of the regional insurance funds, which are required to comply with the Board's directives" (Chapter 18, Article 2). The board of a regional fund normally consists of seven members. The chairman is appointed by the central government. One member is named by the National Board of Health, one by the provincial or regional government, and the four remaining members are appointed by the county or town council. If the fund has jurisdiction over more than one province (*länsstyrelsen*), the law provides that each of the two provinces should appoint one member, making the total eight instead of the usual seven. A deputy is appointed for each member. Each member serves for a term of four years and may be removed by "the body that appointed him" (Chapter 18, Articles 7 and 8). Standards for membership include Swedish citizenship, a good financial record, and a good reputation. The person appointed may not be a minor or a "person incapacitated for managing his own affairs" (Chapter 18, Article 9). He may not be an employee of the National Insurance Board, a regional social insurance fund, or the National Insurance Court. At meetings of the board, members are prohibited from discussing any matter in which they have either a business or a personal interest. Minutes, including a record of any dissent from decisions, are required for all meetings.

The staff of each regional fund (which varies from 800 employees in Stockholm to 50 in Göteborg) includes in addition to the executive director one or more pension and one or more medical officers. The law indicates that the regional funds should cooperate with the medical doctors in each area. "It shall be the duty of a medical officer to assist the Regional Fund in questions which require medical knowledge and to foster co-operation between the Regional Fund and the medical practitioners within its jurisdiction" (Chapter 18, Article 12).

The law is specific on the manner and authority for the appointment of key officials. The executive officer, officers for pension matters, and other officers in the higher grades are to be appointed by the National

THE SOCIAL SECURITY PROGRAMS

Social Insurance Board. The medical officers are appointed by the National Board of Health. Other staff members are appointed by the board of the regional fund. The law requires that the National Public Insurance Board and the National Board of Health consult with the board of management of each regional fund in making appointments or dismissals. Similarly, the salary scale, retirement, and conditions of employment of officers appointed by the National Social Insurance Board are determined by the National Board after consultation with the regional fund. With respect to medical officers, the regional fund is required to comply with directives issued by the National Insurance Board on the advice of the National Board of Health. In this way, the participation and coordination of the activities of the two major national public agencies involved in insurance and in health are provided for in the administration of the programs (Chapter 18, Article 13). The law goes into great detail on requirements for reports, audits, and annual balance sheets. It provides for the establishment of a board of three annually appointed auditors to review all financial activities of the board. Members of the board of a Regional Social Insurance Fund and the executive director are held personally responsible for any action which "willfully or negligently inflicts loss" on the fund or on a third party, and the official is liable for damages resulting from such action.

Two types of committees are established in the administration of the Basic Pension, Supplementary Pension, and health insurance programs. The first is the pension committee established at the regional fund level to decide matters involving disability pensions, supplements, and allowances. The pension committees are known as pension delegations and consist of five people: the chairman who is also, as a rule, the chairman of the Fund Board of Management, two medical practitioners (appointed by the National Board of Health), and two members appointed by the county council or *landsting*.

The second committee is the insurance committee, *Försäkringanamnd*, which is established in every municipality to ". . . assist the Fund Board of Management, the pension committee and local offices with advice and information pertaining to local business" (Chapter 18, Article 23), and to examine the work of each fund with respect to the administration of such allowances under the Basic Pension that are means-tested. The insurance committee consists of from five to seven members all appointed by the municipalities, and each member has a deputy. The committee selects its chairman and vice-chairman. Each regional fund is required to have an officer ". . . to present matters before the insurance committee" (Chapter 18, Article 24).

The salaries and expenses for the chairman of the regional fund boards and members of the pension committee are determined by the central government and paid by each regional public insurance fund from the income it receives. The National Social Insurance Board determines all other salaries, such as those for the members of the regional fund board, insurance committees, and auditors.

THE INSURANCE FUNDS

A National Pension Insurance Fund, *Allmänna Pensionsfonden,* was established in 1959 at the time of the creation of the Supplementary Pension system to receive the contributions payable from January 1, 1960, and to build up a reserve for payments to begin on January 1, 1963. The National Pension Insurance Fund is actually composed of three funds, each with its own board. The constituent funds are designated by number. The First Fund is responsible for the contributions paid by public agencies and organizations for their employees. The Second Fund receives and administers the contributions paid by private employers who employ at least 20 persons, and the Third receives and administers the contributions of employers employing fewer than 20 persons and contributions of the self-employed.

Each fund is composed of representatives of the groups concerned, the employers and employees (and self-employed in Third Fund). The government appoints the chairmen of the three boards.[4] Swedish business is afforded a significant investment opportunity by the provisions which permit a "loan back" of a maximum of one-half of the total of premiums paid in any calendar year to employers, public authorities, or societies which have paid contributions. These loans are administered through the National Bank, commercial banks, the Post Office Savings Bank, and other savings banks which are required to assume all risks involved. The amounts remaining that are not required for the payment of benefits in that year are invested in public and private bonds. The provisions regulating the purchase of private bonds require special guarantees to ensure the soundness of bonds purchased.

[4] The membership of the three fund boards for 1962 and the groups represented are described in *The National Pension Insurance Fund, Report for the Year 1962* (Stockholm: Tryckeri AB Fylgia, 1963), pp. 2–4.

THE SOCIAL SECURITY PROGRAMS

It is significant to note that the funds may not invest capital in real estate or in the stocks of commercial companies. The purpose of this prohibition is to prevent the funds, whose investments will be extremely large in the future, from exercising any direct control over private businesses. A somewhat unexpected result of this restriction against investing in real estate is that the funds are required to rent property since they may not even own the buildings that house their administration.

In 1962, the total amount collected by the three funds was more than $269.5 million (1,346.2 million kr.). Of this amount, the First Fund Board collected $74.1 million (370.3 million kr.), the Second, $145.5 million (726.3 million kr.), and the Third, $49.9 million (249.6 million kr.). Of the total amount collected, the First Fund received 27 percent, the Second 54 percent, and the Third 19 percent.

The system of borrowing back up to one-half of the premiums paid has been extensively used by employers. By the end of 1962, the so-called retroverse loans amounted to more than $11.1 million (55.5 million kr.). The amounts loaned back by each of the funds were as follows: the First Fund, $80,000 (400,000 kr.); the Second, $11 million (55.1 million kr.); and the Third, $20,000 (100,000 kr.).

The investments by the funds are significant in the Swedish economy. At the close of 1962, the total fund administered a security holding amounting to $569.5 million (2,846.4 million kr.) with an average rate of interest of 5.66 percent.

In January 1961, the pension funds held 480 million kronor; in January 1964, 4,800 million kronor; and in January 1967, 14,600 kronor. It is estimated that the funds will hold 32,000 million kronor by January 1970. (*The Swedish Budget, 1967/68*, p. 51.)

To meet the costs of the National Insurance Board administration of the National Pension insurance programs, the funds paid out during 1962 the following amounts: treasury expenditure for 1961–62 fiscal year, $1,950,000 (9,750,000 kr.); Stockholm Governor's Office expenditure, $81,000 (405,000 kr.); supplement for expenses of health insurance funds, $183,320 (916,600 kr.); as fund advance for 1962 (the advance funds are provided until actual costs are determined) $500,000 (2,500,000 kr.); to the city of Stockholm for the years 1960 and 1961, $27,657 (138,284 kr.); to municipalities other than the city of Stockholm, $118,198.75 (590,993.75 kr.); and an advance for 1962, $657,327 (3,286,634 kr.). The expenditures in total in 1962 amounted to $3,517,-

502.75 (17,587,511.75 kr.). The administrative expenses of the fund boards in 1962 totaled $129,835.95 (649,179.73 kr.).[5]

APPEALS

Any individual who feels that his Basic Pension or the amount established for his contributory pension is not in accordance with the law may appeal, within twenty-one days of notification by the fund of the amount he is to receive, to the regional fund in the area in which he lives. However, since the regional fund is the agency which determines the amount the pensioner may prefer to appeal directly to the National Social Insurance Board. A relatively large staff has been established in a complaints division to hear the initial appeals of dissatisfied pensioners or individuals whose application for a pension has been denied.

The decision of the National Social Insurance Board is not final. Appeals from the decision of the National Board may be made by filing a brief with the National Insurance Court. The National Insurance Court was established by the Act of 1960 (it became operational on July 1, 1961) solely for the purpose of hearing appeals on matters involving the Basic Pension, the Supplementary Pension, or health insurance payments. The decisions of the National Insurance Court are final. When there are questions involving interpretation of the law or regulation, the National Insurance Board may, on its own initiative, ask the National Insurance Court for an advisory opinion.

CASE EXAMPLE

Mr. and Mrs. Swenson Receive Their Retirement Pension. Mr. and Mrs. John S. Swenson both were born and had lived all their lives in Stockholm. Mr. Swenson was born on July 4, 1897, and his wife on July 27 of the same year. When they learned of their impending eligibility for the Basic and Supplementary Pension at age 67, they visited the office of the Stockholm Insurance Fund and obtained, completed, and submitted their application forms on May 5, 1964.

Mr. Swenson had been employed regularly as a maintenance electrician and, according to the records of the Insurance Fund, had earned credits for pension points as follows: 3.74 for 1960 (the first year of the Supplementary Pension program), 4.12 for 1961, and 5.02 for 1962 (when he was 65). Since Mrs. Swenson had been a housewife no pension

---

[5] *Ibid.*, p. 6.

THE SOCIAL SECURITY PROGRAMS

points had been registered on her card. Her Basic Pension retirement benefit was approved at $590 (2,950 kr.) annually, the Basic Pension amount for a married pensioner that year.

Mr. Swenson was entitled to the same Basic Pension and, in addition, to an annual Supplementary Pension of $370.60 (1,853 kr.), calculated as follows:

$$\left(\frac{60}{100} \times 4{,}800 \text{ kr.}\right) \times \left(4.29 \times \frac{3}{20}\right) = 1{,}853.28 \text{ kr.}$$

In the formula, 60 percent of the current base amount (4,800 kr. in 1964) is multiplied by the average of pension points which, for Mr. Swenson, was 4.29 for three years. The formula is based on a twenty-year earning period so Mr. Swenson was eligible for 3 out of 20 years.

On July 19, 1964, an official notification of approval of the pension — a total of $1,550.60 (7,753 kr.) — and the amount to be paid on monthly basis was sent to Mr. and Mrs. Swenson. On July 15, 1964, the first monthly payment of $127.55 (637.75 kr.) was made.

III

Health Insurance

AT THE SALVATION ARMY
"Little hand, that is not mine,
to whom do you belong in this world wide?
I found you in the darkness. You are not mine.
But I heard someone who cried."

Pär Lagerkvist (1891–   )
Translated by Frederic Fleisher

THERE are two reliable objective measurements that allow public health officials to assess the effectiveness of health care in any nation.[1] One, commonly called infant mortality, is the rate at which infants die immediately after birth and during the first year of life. The second is the life expectancy for males and females at the time of their birth. If we apply these measures to Sweden we find that its citizens are receiving health care superior to that provided by most countries of the world, including the United States.

According to 1962 statistics issued by the Children's Bureau of the U.S. Department of Health, Education, and Welfare, Sweden and The Netherlands were the countries with the lowest infant mortality rates in the world.[2] The statistics for these two countries showed the rate of 15.3 deaths for each 1,000 live babies. In the same year the United States dropped from tenth to eleventh place. In 1956, the United States

---

[1] Louis I. Dublin, *Factbook On Man: From Birth to Death* (New York: Macmillan, 1965), p. 395. See also "Indicators of Health," *American Journal of Public Health*, Vol. 54 (Aug., 1964), p. 1194.

[2] *Reduction of Infant Mortality, Selected Countries, 1950–1962.*

had ranked fifth among countries with the lowest infant mortality rate. While the infant mortality rate has improved in the United States, the improvement has been less than in other countries during the same period. In 1962, 25.3 of every 1,000 live babies in the United States died in their first year of life, a mortality 40 percent higher than in Sweden. A report of the studies by the Department of Preventive Medicine at the Harvard Medical School points out the importance of this measurement: "Infant mortality is regarded by the Harvard group as important because it is a reflection of what people really care about in their society."[3]

The second indicator used by the Department of Preventive Medicine at Harvard also suggests a more adequate or effective health care program in Sweden than in the United States. During a study of life expectancy at birth, the Harvard group analyzed United Nations statistics, compiled in 1960, which showed that Sweden, together with Norway and The Netherlands, ranked first in life expectancy for males while the United States ranked thirteenth. Sweden was also listed with the other two countries as ranking first in life expectancy for females, while the United States ranked seventh.

It is clear that Sweden provides significant attention to the health of its citizens. The Swedish health insurance program is the subject of this chapter, and a closely related topic, public health, will be discussed in Chapter IV.

Characteristics of the Program

The Swedish health insurance program, established in 1955 and amended in 1959, was, as we have already noted, coordinated with the other insurance programs by the National Insurance Act of 1962. In addition to codifying the separate statutes into one coherent system, the 1962 Act increased daily allowances and generally improved the benefit provisions of the program.

The current Swedish health insurance program may be described as having six major characteristics: (1) it is universal in coverage; (2) it is compulsory; (3) it provides comprehensive benefits; (4) it operates on a cash basis with a deductible feature; (5) it is contributory; and (6) it is income-related in that it has graduated premiums and benefits.

[3] Robert K. Plumb, "U.S. Health Care Is Found Lagging," *New York Times*, Nov. 6, 1963. See also "Infant Mortality: No Change," *Time*, Sept. 6, 1963, p. 48.

THE SOCIAL PROGRAMS OF SWEDEN

Coverage and Eligibility

The Swedish health insurance program has universal coverage: all Swedish citizens and those foreign nationals who have been census-registered in Sweden for a specified period of time or covered by a convention agreement between their country and Sweden are covered under the program. All children are covered under their parents' registration until the age of 16 when they are registered under their own name. By convention, foreigners from other Scandinavian countries, Great Britain, and Italy are covered just as Swedish nationals without any delay for census registration. All residents receive medical and hospital benefits and all gainfully employed persons earning more than a minimum amount, as well as housewives, are insured for sickness cash benefits. Certain groups of the population may also insure voluntarily for a supplementary cash benefit.

The Swedish program is compulsory since all individuals and employers are required to pay the premium whether or not the benefits are used. The program is paid for by the insured, the employer, and the government.

Benefits

The Swedish health insurance program provides comprehensive benefits since it includes physicians' services, hospital care, travel costs to and from the hospital and doctors' offices, medicines, sickness cash payments, and maternity benefits.

Physicians' Services. All insured persons are entitled to reimbursement for the cost of physicians' services. A nonresident of Sweden is covered for medical benefits if the need for medical care arose during his period of residence in Sweden. An insured person obtains medical care by calling the doctor of his choice, who may be in private practice, a member of the medical staff of a hospital outpatient clinic, or a government-employed district doctor. A doctor attending a patient privately may charge whatever fee he desires. However, the health insurance program, in consultation with medical and hospital organizations, has established a fee schedule and the patient is reimbursed only on the basis of this schedule. It is customary for a patient calling a doctor for the first time to ask whether or not he bases his fee on the approved schedule.

The doctor bills the patient and acknowledges receipt of payment on a form prescribed by the health insurance program. The insured person either takes or sends the receipted bill to the local office of the regional social insurance fund, where he is reimbursed three-fourths of the amount specified in the fee schedule for the actual care received or three-fourths of the amount specified in the fee schedule for the general class of care, whichever is lower. The fee schedule is based upon the fees usually charged by general practitioners and includes allowances for X-ray examinations and X-ray and radium treatment given by specially trained laboratory technicians. The fee schedule also includes allowance for the travel expenses of doctors. In larger cities there is frequently a difference between the bill received by the patient and the fee schedule, while in smaller communities most doctors charge fees in accordance with or close to the amount set in the fee schedule.

In rural areas or other locations where there is no private medical doctor in practice the insured person may consult the district doctor. The district doctor, a government employee who also supervises public health programs, charges according to the established fee schedule. The same procedure is followed as with private practitioners.

The insured person may go to the outpatient department of a county hospital to consult one of the doctors of the hospital staff. In these cases, the patient is billed according to a fee schedule established by agreement between the hospital doctors and the *landsting* (county council). In most cases the charge is the same as that in the health insurance fee schedule. The patient is again reimbursed three-fourths of the amount billed. In the major cities such as Stockholm, Göteborg, and Uppsala the patient may go to the outpatient department of a hospital where he pays one-fourth of the fee schedule to the hospital. The balance of the fee is paid by the health insurance fund directly to the hospital.

The fee schedule provides for three main kinds of service: Group I includes simple consultations with examination and treatment; Group II covers consultations involving treatment including minor surgical operations; Group III covers consultations including special treatment with fees classified by the extent of treatment required. In Group III would be cases involving internal medicine, major surgery, gynecology, and ophthalmology; ear, nose, and throat treatment; and psychiatry classified as simple, complicated, or serious. The fee schedule includes charges established for home visits, laboratory examinations, and special tests.

Many medical practitioners, while generally approving of the program, have recommended increases in the fee schedule, particularly for simple consultations. In 1963, the fee schedule provided only $1.60 (8 kr.) for a simple consultation (Group I) in Stockholm and $1.20 (6 kr.) in other parts of the country. The fee for consultation and treatment of cases in Group II is set at $3 (15 kr.) in Stockholm and $2 (10 kr.) outside of the city. For Group III, depending upon the severity of the case, the fee established is $4 (20 kr.), $5 (25 kr.), or $6 (30 kr.) in Stockholm and $3 (15 kr.), $4, or $5 for the rest of the country.

Since many doctors are charging more than the fee schedule, an increasing number of patients are seeking to obtain medical care at fee-scheduled rates from hospitals with outpatient clinics, or from the local or district medical officers. (The same tendency of doctors to charge more than the established schedule is limiting the value of the voluntary medical insurance program in the United States.) However, a well-known Swedish professor of medicine had this to say on the subject of the doctors' fees: "A special comment regarding doctors' fees may be warranted. The free choice of a doctor is completely retained in the interest of both patients and doctors. Physicians who are partly salaried, such as 'provincial physicians,' most hospital doctors, etc., have to charge their fees according to special schemes. All other doctors may charge as they find reasonable, but the patient will in no case get back more than 3/4 of the standard fee from the insurance. This does not seem to prevent many patients, regardless of their social-economic class, from seeing the doctor of their choice."[4]

The problem of obtaining medical care at the established fee schedule arises from a number of factors. First of all, as indicated in the statement above, not only patients but doctors have complete freedom of choice. The doctor in private practice has the same freedom in accepting his patients as the patient has in choosing his doctor. The doctor may limit his practice to patients who are willing to pay above the fee schedule. Second, many doctors feel that the established fee schedules are too low in comparison with earnings in other professional fields and in the light of a steadily rising cost of living. Physicians object to the lack of separate, higher fee schedules for specialists.[5] Third, the shortage of doctors in private practice in certain areas and specialties limits choice of physician in many locations. The problem, as in the United

[4] Gunnar Biörck, "Socialized Medicine in Sweden," *Trends in Swedish Health and Welfare Policy*, p. 8.
[5] *Ibid.*, p. 9.

States, is more one of the geographic distribution of doctors than of too low a ratio of physicians to the population. In 1960 Sweden had 7,130 licensed physicians. Of these, 3,144 were in private practice, 2,904 were attached to hospitals, 851 were government-employed medical officers, and 231 were members of the faculty at medical schools. In 1961 the total number of physicians in Sweden had grown to 7,380, a ratio of 98 to each 100,000 inhabitants.

Hospital Care. An insured person who is in need of hospitalization receives such care in a ward free of any expense except for a token charge by the insurance fund. Hospital care includes maintenance, medical and nursing care, medicine, and all auxiliary services. The patient is admitted to a hospital ward through referral by his attending physician or through the outpatient department of the hospital. The hospital notifies the appropriate health insurance fund of each admission. Normally, an insured person is admitted to the hospital of the city, town, or county in which he lives. If the patient should need special treatment unavailable at a rural hospital he is referred to a hospital where such treatment is obtainable.

If he prefers to be in a private or semi-private room the patient pays a daily fee, which in the public hospitals of Stockholm is $4 (20 kr.) a day for a semi-private room or $7 (35 kr.) a day for a private room. A private room is provided without charge when, in the doctor's judgment, it is required for special treatment. This would include post-operative or terminal cases.

Even with the extra charge the demand for semi-private and private rooms in hospitals exceeds the supply. As in a ward the patient receives, without additional charge, all necessary operations, medical treatment, laboratory tests, blood transfusions, X-ray examinations, and medicines. In public hospitals all treatment is given by the medical staff of the hospital. A patient who prefers to be treated by a privately practicing physician is required to go to a private hospital and pay all expenses including hospital costs. However, since most hospitals in Sweden are public hospitals, this situation arises only rarely. In 1963 only 2.7 percent of all beds in general hospitals were privately managed and 3.3 percent of all beds in mental hospitals were nonpublic.

It should be noted that while the hospital charges the health insurance fund $1 (5 kr.) per day per patient, this is only a small fraction of the actual cost for the care provided. In 1961, the cost of operating general hospitals in Sweden amounted to $15.80 (79 kr.) daily per patient. The difference between the small fees collected from the health insurance fund and the actual cost of operating the hospitals is made up by the county government for most hospitals, although the central government administers and pays the cost directly for a few hospitals.

Medicines. The Swedish health insurance program considers the purchase of drugs and medicines an important factor in the cost of medical care and provides for reimbursement in full or in part depending upon the type of medicine required. The full cost is paid by the insurance fund for medicines required for chronic diseases including insulin for diabetes, cortisones for arthritis, and tetracyclines and other antibiotics. The physician uses a special form to prescribe these medicines. This form is validated by the health insurance office for a one-year period and the patient is given a requisition form. The patient submits this form to the pharmacist, who supplies the medicine without charge to the patient periodically as needed for the one-year period. The pharmacist submits these requisitions to the appropriate health insurance fund for reimbursement. For other medicines the patient receives a prescription from the doctor and submits it to the pharmacist. The patient pays the first $.60 (3 kr.) per prescription and one-half the balance of the cost; the insurance fund pays the rest.

As in the plan for obtaining medical care the patient has complete freedom in purchasing drugs and medicines. He may go to the pharmacist of his choice and, on presentation of his doctor's prescription, purchase his medicine with the deduction described above. The pharmacies and pharmaceutical companies are privately owned and operated.

At the end of each month, the pharmacist submits his bill to the health insurance fund and is reimbursed for the medicines he has provided. The central government pays the health insurance funds $.23 (1.15 kr.) of each $1 (5 kr.) expended for costs of medicines. The remainder, almost 80 percent, is paid by the social insurance fund.

Travel Costs. The cost of going to and from the doctor's office or the hospital is reimbursed at the lowest rate for transportation available that is suitable in the light of the patient's condition. The standard for reimbursement is the cost of travel to the nearest district physician. If a patient in a rural area prefers to consult a doctor in the city he may do so but is reimbursed for transportation only to the location of the nearest district doctor. The full cost of transportation to the nearest hospital

HEALTH INSURANCE

is paid in the following cases: a severe accident, a physician's referral to the outpatient department of a hospital, or a case in which the patient is in urgent need of medical care but has been unable to consult the district physician.

As with medical care or ordinary medicines, the travel reimbursement contains a deductible feature so that the patient pays a small amount of the cost. The patient pays the first $1 (5 kr.) of the cost of travel in visiting a physician in the larger cities of Stockholm, Göteborg, Malmö, and Norrköping. In these cities the patient need not choose the nearest doctor or hospital. In other areas, the patient pays the first $.80 of the travel cost.

The transportation expense to the nearest hospital for treatment in a ward is reimbursed in full but the patient pays the first $.80 (4 kr.) of the return trip. When the doctor determines that it is necessary to have someone accompany an elderly or helpless patient the travel cost of the companion is reimbursed.

Dental Care. Dental care is not a significant part of the health insurance program. It is limited to maternal care and dental needs related to serious operations, plastic surgery, and X-ray examinations. During pregnancy and for a period of 270 days after childbirth, a woman may obtain dental care and be reimbursed. She may choose the dentist and is reimbursed three-fourths of the fee charged up to the amounts allowed in the dental fee schedule.

Dental care is provided without charge to all children in school until the age of 15; this is not directly related to the health insurance program.

A commission of the government is currently studying the feasibility of expanding dental care as part of the health insurance program for the entire population. One limiting factor is the availability of sufficient dentists and dental facilities.

Cash Allowances. To compensate, at least in part, for the loss of income due to illness, the Swedish health insurance program provides for a daily allowance of money to begin on the fourth day of each illness. When illness occurs within twenty days of a previous illness the first waiting period covers the second illness as well.

All employed persons, including the self-employed, who earn $360 (1,800 kr.) or more per year, and housewives, are insured for cash benefits of $1 (5 kr.) per day. A supplementary daily sickness allowance provides additional payments for all employees or self-employed who earn $520 (2,600 kr.) or more. The self-employed who contract out of the Supplementary Pension insurance program are automatically exempted from insurance for supplementary sickness allowances. The rate of supplementary sickness benefits varies between $.20 (1 kr.) and $4.60 (23 kr.) per day, depending upon the insured person's annual income. The total daily payments thus range from $1 (5 kr.) to $5.60 (28

Table 4. Total Daily Sickness Allowances, According to Earned Annual Income

Income	Allowance
$360–$519 (1,800–2,515 kr.)	$1.00 (5 kr.)
520–679 (2,600–3,395)	1.20 (6)
680–839 (3,400–4,195)	1.40 (7)
840–999 (4,200–4,995)	1.60 (8)
1,000–1,159 (5,000–5,795)	1.80 (9)
1,160–1,359 (5,800–6,795)	2.00 (10)
1,360–1,679 (6,800–8,395)	2.40 (12)
1,680–2,049 (8,400–10,245)	2.80 (14)
2,050–2,499 (10,250–12,495)	3.20 (16)
2,500–2,799 (12,500–13,995)	3.60 (18)
2,800–3,199 (14,000–15,995)	4.00 (20)
3,200–3,599 (16,000–17,995)	4.40 (22)
3,600–4,199 (18,000–20,995)	5.00 (25)
4,200 (21,000)	5.60 (28)

kr.). Table 4 shows the scale of daily cash sickness allowances related to income levels. Since the sickness daily allowance is tax free, it is estimated that the amounts paid approximate two-thirds of the daily net income of an employee earning up to $4,400 (22,000 kr.) per year.

The amounts shown in Table 4 are payable to those whose earning capacity has completely ceased because of illness. In cases in which working capacity is reduced by one-half, one-half the amount of the sickness cash allowance is paid. No sickness allowances are paid when earning capacity has been reduced by less than one-half.

A children's supplement is added to the amount paid when the family of the insured includes children under 16 years of age. The amount of this supplement is related to the number of children in a family: $.20 (1 kr.) per day for one or two children; $.40 (2 kr.) for three or four children; and $.60 (3 kr.) per day for more than four children. A mother, if she or her husband is ill, who has a child under ten years of age receives a children's supplement of $.40 per day.

During the time spent by the insured in a hospital the sickness cash allowance is reduced by $1 (5 kr.) per day, but the reduction is limited to one-half of the total sickness cash allowance. During hospitalization a mother with a child under ten years of age at home would receive a daily cash allowance of $.90 — the minimum sickness allowance of $1, reduced by one-half, plus the supplement for a child under ten.

There is no time limit for the receipt of hospital care and sickness daily cash allowances in the current program. Before the 1962 Act cash allowances were reduced after 180 days of illness and ended after 730 days. Now, after a period of three months, the social insurance fund is required to determine whether the insured person might be able to work in a different occupation. If rehabilitation is possible the patient must take special vocational training to fit himself for a job in which his illness would not be limiting. If it is determined that rehabilitation is impossible and that the working capacity of the patient cannot be restored by medical care or retraining, the incapacity is designated permanent or of considerable duration. If the disability is permanent and reduces earning capacity by at least one-half, the sickness cash benefit is replaced by payments under the advance pension program.

The procedure for obtaining sickness cash allowances is relatively simple. The insured person notifies the appropriate social insurance fund by telephone or letter of his illness and incapacity. This is actually done on the first day of illness since this day would then be counted toward the waiting period of three days. The social insurance fund sends the insured person a form which is a self-declaration about the illness and is returned to the social insurance fund after one week, or, if the person recovers more quickly, as soon as he resumes work. For the first week of incapacity no medical certificate is required; if the illness extends longer than one week it is required. The certificate includes the doctor's estimate of the duration of illness. The payment of cash sickness allowances is made each week and covers each calendar day. The payments are made by mail or, if the patient prefers, at the local office of the social insurance fund.

Maternity Benefits. Three types of benefits are provided for pregnant mothers: (1) medical, hospital, and dental benefits related to pregnancy and childbirth; (2) a maternity cash payment; and (3) a supplementary cash payment.

The costs of medical care, hospital treatment, and travel related to pregnancy and childbirth are reimbursed in whole or part to the mother by the health insurance program. The standards are the same as those followed for general illness. The mother is reimbursed three-fourths of the cost of the physician's services, provided hospital care in a ward without charge (or at a modest charge in a semi-private or private room), receives medicines at one-half of the regular price, is reimbursed three-fourths of the dental fees, and is reimbursed the cost of travel to and from the doctor's office and the hospital (except for the deductible sum).

A maternity cash allowance of $180 (900 kr.) is payable for the birth of each child to all women covered by the health insurance program and residing in Sweden. If more than one child is born the amount is increased by $90 (450 kr.) for each additional child. The mother may receive one-third of this amount, or $60 (300 kr.), in advance of the expected date of confinement. A supplementary maternity cash allowance is also paid to women who are gainfully employed and insured for supplementary sickness cash allowances. This payment may be made from the sixtieth day before the expected date of confinement and is payable as long as the woman is restricted from gainful employment (but not for more than 180 days).

Women who are insured for sickness cash allowances may increase their insurance voluntarily. (Students may also insure voluntarily for the sickness cash allowances.) However, in these cases, the voluntary sickness cash allowance may not exceed $2.40 (12 kr.) per day, including the basic sickness cash allowance. Although modest, the voluntary cash allowance is a significant part of the maternity benefits.

Financing

Almost all phases of the health insurance program include a small payment by the beneficiary for the services provided. As previously mentioned, the patient pays one-fourth of the cost of medical services, one-half the cost of most medicines in addition to the first $.60 (3 kr.), and the first $.80 or $1 (5 kr.) of travel costs in returning from the doctor's office. The deductible feature, in addition to reducing the costs of the program, serves as a deterrent to overuse of the program by those who do not have a genuine need for the services. Since the patient must pay part of the initial costs, even if only a token payment, there is less tendency to call for a doctor's services or medicines unless they are really needed. At the same time, after the partial cost is met, the insurance

HEALTH INSURANCE

benefits prevent the total medical cost from being catastrophic to the lower or middle income citizen.

The total cost of the health insurance services is shared by the insured, who pay premiums covering one-half of the cost, the employers, whose payments cover one-fourth, and the government, whose subsidies pay one-fourth of the cost. The insured pay amounts which vary according to their income from employment (each income group is one of the "sickness benefit classes"), and the particular social insurance fund administering the account.

Table 5. Premiums for Supplemental Daily Allowances, According to Earned Annual Income

Income	Premium Stockholm	Rest of Sweden
$520–$680 (2,600–3,400 kr.)	$ 1.60 (8 kr.)	$ 1.40 (7 kr.)
1,680–2,040 (8,400–10,200)	15.20 (76)	12.00 (60)
2,800–3,200 (14,000–16,000)	22.50 (111)	17.60 (88)
3,600–4,200 (18,000–21,000)	34.40 (172)	27.20 (136)
4,200 (21,000)	39.80 (199)	31.40 (157)

Health insurance premiums paid by the insured are of three types: for medical care including hospitalization, for basic daily allowances, and for supplemental daily allowances. The first two are compulsory and the premiums are as follows: for medical care including hospitalization,[6] $15 (75 kr.) in Stockholm and $12 (60 kr.) in the rest of Sweden; for daily allowances, $14 (70 kr.) in Stockholm and $11 (55 kr.) in the rest of Sweden. Table 5 provides examples of employee premiums payable annually as of January 1, 1963, for supplemental daily allowances. Employer contributions were established for the year 1963 at 1.5 percent of the cash wages up to the amount of $4,400 (22,000 kr.) earned by an individual in any one year.

The self-employed, who, under the amendments of 1962, are automatically covered for supplemental daily allowances unless they exempt themselves from this benefit, are required to pay premiums amounting to the entire cost of these allowances. A self-employed person earning $3,000 (15,000 kr.) per year pays a premium of $72.80 (364 kr.) per year. A self-employed person may reduce his premium substantially by

[6] Payable by those who receive $480 (2,400 kr.) or more in annual taxable income for that year. Those with a lower taxable income, those who have reached the age of 67, or who receive an advance pension receive these benefits without cost.

electing a waiting period of 33 or 93 days in place of the statutory 3 days.

The subsidies paid by the central government in 1963 amounted to 50 percent of the expenditures by the health insurance funds for the following: for medical care outside of hospitals, transportation to and from doctors' offices or hospitals, basic sickness cash benefits, the children's supplement, and maternity cash benefits. The government subsidizes 20 percent of the expenditure for voluntary sickness benefits and contributes toward the cost of prescribed drugs, although this program is covered by special legislation not included in the codification of 1962. For the fiscal year 1962 the National Social Insurance Board's total health and maternity expenditure was $246.8 million (1,234 million kr.). The amendments of 1962 increased the cost of health and maternity insurance by $70 million (350 million kr.) for that year. This includes a $10 million (50 million kr.) increase in subsidies by the central government.

Health Insurance Statistics

On December 31, 1961, there were 661 public sickness funds which insured 5.7 million people above 16 years of age for medical benefits. Children under 16, estimated at 1.8 million, received all benefits through their family insurance. During 1961, 4.6 million people were insured for daily cash allowances and of these 3 million were insured for supplementary daily cash allowances. During that year there were 2.3 million reported cases of sickness for which the public sickness funds paid daily allowances for reimbursements for the cost of hospital treatment. This represents 51 cases per 100 people insured for daily allowances. Daily allowances or hospital treatment benefits were paid by the funds for approximately 59 million days, representing 12.8 days per person and 25.3 days per case. (Each illness is considered a case.) The number of days per person was higher for women, 13.3 days, than it was for men, 12.3 days. Daily cash allowances paid for 3.7 million days of illness, and of this amount 1.3 million days were paid for illness of housewives.

Hospital treatment costs were paid for 14 million days representing slightly more than 2 days per person. Hospital treatment costs for children under 16 represented 1.5 million days. Basic maternity allowances were paid for 107,000 cases and additional maternal allowances were paid for almost one-half of these cases. Maternity assistance in 1961

HEALTH INSURANCE

was provided to 16,640 mothers involving the expenditure of $1,281,600 (6,408,000 kr.) or an average of $80 (400 kr.) per mother.

During 1961, contributions, premiums, and subsidies paid to the funds were distributed as follows: $110.9 million (554.7 million kr.) paid as premiums by the insured; $71.8 million (359.2 million kr.) paid as contributions from employers and $52.7 million (263.4 million kr.) paid as subsidies from the central government. In addition, the funds received $1.7 million (8.6 million kr.) in interest and $.6 million (3.1 million kr.) in miscellaneous receipts. Expenditures of the funds in 1961 are shown in Table 6.

Voluntary insurance for additional cash allowances as of December 1961 included 101,000 self-employed, 143,000 housewives, and 6,800 students. Payments of additional voluntary daily allowances were made for 3.3 million days during the year. The amount paid out was $3.2 million (16,000,000 kr.). The contributions for daily cash allowances exceeded the amount paid out and the balance was used to establish a reserve fund. During 1961, contributions from members amounted to $3.8 million (19 million kr.) and the central government subsidies consisted of $.6 million (3 million kr.).

Administration

The administrative structure of the social insurance programs including the health insurance program, integrated by the Act of 1962, has al-

Table 6. Expenditures under the Health Insurance Funds for 1961
(in Millions of Dollars and Kronor)

Item	Expenditure	
Daily allowance	$118.9	(594.6 kr.)
Medical attendance	34.8	(174.0)
Administration	25.6	(77.8)
Medicines	20.5	(102.4)
Hospital treatment	16.5	(82.5)
Maternity benefits (except confinement)	13.3	(66.7)
Other sickness benefits	4.3	(21.3)
Transportation to and from doctors	4.1	(20.6)
Transportation to and from hospitals	3.1	(15.5)
Children's supplement	2.9	(14.5)
Miscellaneous	.6	(3.2)
Total	$234.6	(1,173.1 kr.)

SOURCE: *Allmanna Sjukkassor 1961* (Stockholm: The National Social Insurance Board, 1963), p. 13.

ready been discussed at some length (see pp. 29–32). Reviews of two cases taken from the files of the regional health insurance fund of Stockholm will illustrate the operation of the Swedish health insurance program.

Mr. Lundgren Has a Kidney Operation. This is a general case of illness requiring hospitalization and an operation. Mr. Tage E. Lundgren is 35 years of age, married, and works as an engineer at the Phillips Tele-Industry at a salary of more than $4,200 (21,000 kr.) per year. He has one child 15 years of age in the home. Mr. Lundgren was taken ill with a kidney infection on March 6, 1963, and his doctor sent him to St. Erik's Hospital for an operation.

Mr. Lundgren stayed in a ward in the hospital and thus was covered completely by illness insurance. He was in the hospital a total of 44 days and the health insurance fund paid the hospital costs of $1 per day, amounting to $44 (220 kr.). Mr. Lundgren was in the hospital during the following periods: March 6 to 28, April 3 to 6, and April 21 to May 7. He received a daily cash allowance of $4.60 (23 kr.) for the periods he was in the hospital, excluding the three-day waiting period. He was also required to be at home during his illness for the following periods: March 29 to April 2, April 7 to 20, and May 8 to 31. He received a daily cash allowance of $5.60 (28 kr.) for the periods he was at home since the regulations provide for an additional $1 (5 kr.) in the payment of daily cash allowances at home. He also received $.20 (1 kr.) per day during both periods, the allowance for the child in his home under 16 years of age.

In summary, Mr. Lundgren had his hospital bill paid in full, including the doctor's fees while he was in the hospital, cost of the operation, examinations, medicines, and room. He received payment amounting to three-fourths of the doctor's fees for treatment outside the hospital and 50 percent of the cost of all medicines above $.60 (3 kr.) per prescription. In addition, he received a total of $446 (2,230 kr.) in cash as his daily sickness allowance, plus the children's allowance, for the time he was absent from work.

Mrs. Chilstrom Has a Baby. This case involves a maternity confinement with insurance under the Stockholm social insurance fund. The case is that of Mrs. Eva Marguerita Chilstrom, twenty-one years old, who, although married, works as a kitchen helper at the Southern Hospital, *Södersjukset,* and receives an annual income ranging from $2,000

HEALTH INSURANCE

(10,000 kr.) to $2,400 (12,000 kr.). Mrs. Chilstrom worked until the day before delivery and became a patient in the Southern Hospital maternity ward on February 11, 1963. She gave birth to a child on February 12 and was confined in a ward during the period from February 12 to 19.

The hospital received payment of $7 (35 kr.) from the Stockholm social insurance fund at the rate of $1 (5 kr.) per day. Mrs. Chilstrom received the following health insurance maternity benefits: On January 16 she was given $60 (300 kr.) in cash as an advance payment of her maternity benefit, on February 20 she received $120 (600 kr.), or the balance due to her of the maternity benefit known as the *moderskopspenningen*. She received a supplementary daily allowance, from February 12 until August 10, totaling $392 (1,960 kr.) or $2.20 (11 kr.) per day for a total of 180 days. (Under the regulations a sick person is given $3.20, 16 kr., per day, but maternity cases only $2.20, or 11 kr.) She got a total of $572 (2,860 kr.) in cash, her hospital bill was paid in full, and her medicines came without cost from the pharmacist. Mrs. Chilstrom did not claim dental benefits although she was eligible to receive three-fourths of the cost of any dental treatment she may have needed related to the birth of her child.

IV

Public Health

> THE RUSTIC
> "Each plague has its own scream.
> Only health keeps silent.
> The mighty men with scream and thunder
> Destruct villages and countries.
> Silently the peasant and his son
> Will build them up again
> Sowing in the bloodstained soil
> What right is
> I give my God and King
> And the rest
> I freely will enjoy."
> Erik Gustaf Geijer (1783–1847)

IN SWEDEN, all activities in the field of public health and care of the sick are either operated or controlled by public authorities. The sophisticated and advanced Swedish programs for public health, hospitals, and preventive health service have developed from the historically effective role of the government in the field of medicine. Governmental activities in medicine have long been widely accepted. This is probably a major factor in explaining the ease with which the health insurance funds were placed under government control in 1955.

In September 1963, Sweden celebrated the 300th anniversary of the public health program in that country. The first health department, the Kollegium Medicum, was established in 1663. The Kollegium was the government agency assigned to certify the qualifications of doctors for the practice of medicine in Stockholm, approve the qualifications of

PUBLIC HEALTH

midwives, and supervise pharmacies in the preparation of drugs and medicines. In 1813, the Royal Health Kollegium succeeded the Kollegium Medicum. The present agency, the National Board of Health, Kungliga Medicinalstyrelsen, was created in 1877 as the central government agency responsible for all health, medical care, and related services.

Administration

Initially, the responsibility for the development of legislative programs and appropriation requests in the field of public health was lodged with the Department of Interior, since this was the ministry through which the National Medical Board worked. However, in 1963 general responsibility in the field of public health was transferred to the Department of Social Affairs, in the effort to coordinate certain aspects of the public health program with the health and retirement insurance and public welfare programs. As will be indicated in Chapter 6, the Swedish departments do not administer but are responsible for legislative and appropriation matters in the fields under their jurisdiction. The semi-independent boards, responsible not to the minister but to the crown, conduct the day-to-day administrative functions in their respective fields. Consequently, as with the other independent boards, the director general of the National Health Board reports to the king-in-council rather than to the minister of social affairs. As a result, the National Board of Health is endowed with a large measure of autonomy in the administration of the public health programs throughout Sweden. Its responsibility includes supervision over health and pharmaceutical services, the operation of both general and private hospitals, and the work of medical personnel, hospitals, pharmacies, and related institutions throughout the country.

The organization of the National Board of Health consists of nine major bureaus.[1] The medical bureau works in the field of preventative and corrective treatment outside of hospitals. The bureau of hygiene administers programs in environmental sanitation and epidemiology. The bureau of hospitals is responsible for the general hospitals. The bureau of mental health deals with the problem of mental illness and establishes standards for, and inspects, institutions for the mentally deficient, epileptics, and psychiatry for children. The bureau of social and forensic psychiatry is responsible for the legal aspects of decisions

[1] Gillis Albinsson, *Public Health Services in Sweden*, pp. 10–11.

in the field of psychiatry, and handles requests for abortions and sterilizations. The bureaus of dentistry and pharmacy work in those fields. (All of the medical bureaus are headed by medical doctors, the dental bureau by a dental surgeon, and the bureau of pharmacy by a pharmacist.) The bureau of legal and administrative affairs includes a department of statistics, and the bureau of finance has as one of its responsibilities the administration of the fiscal affairs of the state mental hospitals.

The director general of the National Board of Health, known also as the National Medical Board, is a medical doctor and his deputy is a lawyer. The National Board of Health maintains standing committees of experts who are authorized to make decisions in the name of the board. In addition to licensing all medical doctors the National Board of Health establishes qualifications for, and gives licenses to, dentists, nurses, pharmacists, physiotherapists, midwives, and others working in the field of health. Complaints of mistreatment or malpractice are reviewed by a disciplinary committee on which the senior staff of the board serves as an administrative tribunal. The standing advisory committees include a Scientific Council and a Council of Responsible Authorities. The Scientific Council is made up of leaders in the several scientific fields related to health. The Council of Responsible Authorities is composed of representatives of the Federation of Swedish County Councils and the Swedish Federation of Cities. The work of this council is significant since the county councils and cities are responsible for the provision of hospital and related health services in their respective jurisdictions.

The work of the National Board of Health has been carried out by district medical officers and members of their staffs employed by the länsstyrelsen and located in each of the 28 provincial headquarters throughout the country. The district medical officers, senior physicians, and sanitarians have been responsible for the supervision of the public health services in each district or have served as consultants to local governments in matters of environmental health and hygiene. By an act of the Riksdag in 1961, the work of the district medical officers and their staffs has been transferred to the county council organization which traditionally has supervised the hospital system. An observer has written about this change: "The success of the county hospital scheme has convinced the public, and reluctantly the medical profession, of the advantage of having the county councils as responsible for all medical

PUBLIC HEALTH

care including preventive measures. The county councils will therefore according to a parliamentary act of 1961 take over the district doctors and their stations (today serving a population of about 6,000 in a rural area). A better integration between medical care inside and outside the hospital will thereby be achieved." [2]

Immediately under the supervision of the National Board of Health are the state mental hospitals, state hospitals for epilepsy, schools for midwives, state laboratories for forensic chemistry and pharmacy, and a center for mass radio-fluorography. This center reviews the results of the nationwide lung examination program which is carried out as a cooperative effort by the National Board of Health and the county councils.

The medical aspects of civil defense have been assigned to the medical defense planning committee of the National Board of Health. This committee operates almost autonomously and is composed of representatives of the National Board of Health, the Federation of County Councils, the Federation of Cities, the Department of Defense, and civil defense agencies. This committee has established a network of emergency hospitals throughout Sweden with stocks of medical supplies and has assigned all doctors and nurses registered with the committee to specific positions in case of a national emergency.

The central government directly operates several scientific and health institutions. The National Institute of Public Health is a major research agency for investigating methods of public health improvement. The institute works in the fields of hygiene, environmental research, and factory hygiene. It is responsible for a training program for inspectors in the field of environmental hygiene and general sanitation. The central government also operates the National Bacteriological Laboratory, which is responsible for epidemiological research and administration. The laboratory receives information and materials from doctors located in all parts of Sweden and assists in the diagnosis of patients suspected of suffering from an infectious disease. Specialists on the staff of the laboratory are available to make epidemiological studies in areas where infectious diseases have been located. The laboratory also manufactures vaccines and serums for the immunization program.

The National Laboratory for Forensic Chemistry and the National Forensic Medical Offices are also operated by the central government.

[2] Arthur Engel, *The Swedish Regionalized Hospital System*, p. 276.

The National Pharmaceutical Laboratory is somewhat comparable to the Food and Drug Administration in the United States in that it is responsible for investigation concerning safety and accuracy in the production and sale of medicines and drugs.

Hospitals

The significant characteristic of the Swedish hospital system is that by far the majority of the hospitals are owned and operated by public authorities. Only 3.7 percent of the hospitals in Sweden are privately owned. Most of the hospitals, 64.8 percent, are owned and operated by the counties. At present, almost all of the mental hospitals, 24.5 percent of all hospitals, are operated by the central government. The central government also has managed 7 percent of the general hospitals. Even the private hospitals frequently receive some government subsidies and may have a representative of the county or central government as a board member.

The number of hospitals in Sweden has increased dramatically in the past twenty years. In 1940 there were 51,073 hospital beds in general hospitals and in 1960 there were 67,986. By 1961, this number was 70,971, an increase of more than one-third over the number available in 1940. For the care of patients with mental diseases the number of beds had increased from 24,673 in 1940 to 34,408 in 1960, and to 34,804 in 1961.[3]

The plans for the construction of all hospitals throughout Sweden are reviewed by the Central Board of Hospital Planning, which encourages high standards, standardization of equipment, and continuous research and consultation in matters of hospital organization and administration. The board is composed of representatives of the Federation of County Councils, the Federation of Cities, the National Board of Health, and industrial associations. The board publishes results of its research and studies, and these documents are available for the guidance of county councils and city officials in the planning and operation of hospitals. A review of all hospital plans by the Central Board of Hospital Planning is mandatory, even though the hospitals are built, operated, and financed by the county councils.

Traditionally, mental hospitals have been constructed and operated by the central government while general hospitals have been constructed

[3] Gillis Albinsson, *Public Health Services in Sweden*, p. 33.

PUBLIC HEALTH

and operated by county councils. Several royal commissions, established by the minister of the Interior Department, conducted studies over several years, and they recommended the transfer of the mental hospitals to the county councils. This step has been approved, and it is anticipated that mental hospitals will be under the jurisdiction of the county councils by the end of 1967.

The central government operates three major somatic disease hospitals, all of which are teaching hospitals. These are the Karolinska Hospital and the Serafimer Hospital in Stockholm, and the Akademiska Hospital in Uppsala. Since a large part of the financing of the hospitals is paid by the county councils, including most of the cost of hospital operation under the health insurance program, consideration has been given to the desirability of transferring these hospitals to the jurisdiction of the county councils. The landsting population, which averages about 250,000 inhabitants, has been able to support general hospitals — in fact has been the basis for the hospital system in Sweden. However, this population base was not considered sufficient to support the advanced specialties, as the director general of the National Board of Health has written: "Without a sufficient population basis you cannot organize hospital departments of an optimal size and effectivity and the specialist himself will not have a clientele that gives him the necessary experience and routine."[4] Continuing, he said: "Experience has shown that these self-governing territories have been capable of building up highly differentiated hospital facilities but otherwise there is full evidence that they are not large enough in respect to population to support such specialties as neurosurgery, thoracic surgery, radiotherapeutic cancer clinics, virus laboratories, etc."[5]

The advantages of a centralized hospital system, i.e., the support of specialization and staff for teaching and research, and the values of a decentralized system, reflecting the ". . . understandable wish of the public to have medical facilities within a convenient distance," have been compared for some time. A regional hospital plan has been proposed as a means of balancing the advantages of both the decentralized and centralized plans.[6]

In 1960, on the basis of more than six years of study and consultation,

[4] Arthur Engel, *The Swedish Regionalized Hospital System*, p. 273.
[5] *Ibid.*, p. 277.
[6] *Ibid.*

the director general of the National Board of Health presented proposals to the Riksdag for the establishment of a regional hospital system in Sweden. With slight modifications, his proposal was approved by the Riksdag during that year. This plan called for the establishment of six regional hospitals as soon as possible and the seventh in 1970. The regional hospital system, currently being established, utilizes the present five teaching hospitals: Karolinska Hospital, Stockholm; University Hospital, Lund-Malmö; Sahlgrenska Hospital, Göteborg; Akademiska Hospital, Uppsala; Umeå Hospital in Umeå in the northern part of the country. The sixth to be drawn into the system is Linköpings Central Hospital. In 1970, Örebro Central Hospital will become the seventh regional hospital.[7]

An adequate and developing hospital system in Sweden has been not only a significant factor in the provision of adequate health service conveniently located throughout the country, but also has provided an essential resource for the successful extension of all elements in the comprehensive health insurance program.

Mental Health

As noted previously, the organization of mental hospitals is currently undergoing a major change. A recently completed study, comparing the mental health programs in Sweden with programs of other countries, describes this change: "The organization of Swedish mental health services is in a state of transition. Traditionally, the bulk of hospital care for the mentally ill in Sweden has been given by about 25 State mental hospitals, but the system is now being changed in favor of county-wide and city-wide patterns of service, with emphasis on psychiatric units in general hospitals, day hospital programs, and smaller mental hospitals near general hospitals, as in Denmark. There are 24 counties in Sweden and each will eventually have its own system. Already, each county in Sweden has a community clinic at the general hospital, in addition to available mental hospital beds."[8] In 1962, there were approximately 30,000 adult mental patients in government mental hospitals in Sweden. This represented almost 100 percent occupancy of available hospital beds. The current trend to include mental health care in län hospitals

[7] *Ibid.*, p. 279.
[8] Sylvan S. Furman, *Community Mental Health Services in Northern Europe*, p. 134.

PUBLIC HEALTH

throughout Sweden is part of the effort to meet the shortage of hospital facilities for mentally ill patients.

Three large central government hospitals, in or near Stockholm, provide care for mentally ill patients. They are the Southern General Hospital, Beckomberga Hospital, and the Stockholm Län Hospital at Danderyd. Southern General has 84 beds in the psychiatric unit and, in addition, psychiatric service is provided for patients in the general wards which contain 1,200 beds. A special unit of the hospital provides emergency services to attempted suicides. Beckomberga Hospital has 1,400 beds including 450 for geriatric patients. Thirty-five psychiatrists are located in Beckomberga Hospital and are assisted by three psychologists and graduate students. Danderyd Län Hospital was opened in 1960 and includes facilities for 900 patients, including 100 beds for psychiatric patients.

Special care for children is provided by child welfare centers located throughout Sweden. While not directly focused on mental health problems, these centers serve as both a preventative and a discovery facility. As one observer comments: "In the course of giving the usual protective and medical services (health maintenance, immunization, dietary advice, etc.), attention is given in the course of home visits to environmental problems and to early detection of behavior difficulties."[9] Most mental health services are provided in the larger cities through school mental health programs and municipal outpatient clinics for children. In Stockholm a program initiated in 1964 provided for nine psychologists and nine social workers to work in teams throughout the school system, assisting school psychiatrists and school nurses in testing, counseling, and treatment. Special classes have been opened for children with difficulties including retarded mental development, reading and writing problems, temperament problems, immaturity, hearing and sight problems, and cerebral palsy. A special school has been opened for retarded children whose difficulty is too great for the special classes. Approximately 5 percent of the 80,000 children in the Stockholm schools receive treatment for behavior difficulties.

Stockholm and its suburbs are served by five psychiatric clinics for children. These are located at Kungsholm in the center of Stockholm, Liljeholmen, Hökaranger, Vällingby, and Högdalen. Each clinic has a nursery school staffed by a part-time psychiatrist. In addition, Stock-

[9] *Ibid.*, p. 143.

holm has a child guidance clinic at Kungsholm which includes a therapeutic nursery school, a special day school for children with behavior problems, and outpatient psychiatric and psychological services.

Sex Education

The laws, tradition, and attitudes relating to sex in Sweden are widely misunderstood. One contemporary Swedish writer opens a treatment of this subject by saying: "In many parts of the world, Sweden is known as a country with free erotic practices. The picture circulated to a news hungry public is made up of facts taken out of context and of misconceptions. It is colored by wishful thinking or indignation. The power of these misconceptions is tragically illustrated by the stream of women who have come to Sweden during recent years in the hope of receiving a legal abortion. All too many of them have found that the regulations governing this controversial question are restrictive and that their trip was in vain."[10] It is true, however, that certain subjects related to sex are approached somewhat differently in Sweden than in many other countries. These include sex education, birth control, and abortion.

Since 1940, education in the anatomical, physiological, and psychological aspects of sex has been included in the curriculum of the Swedish schools. The first manuals for teachers on sex education were published by the Swedish National Board of Education in that year. Sex education has been a compulsory feature of the Swedish schools since 1956.

The purpose of the courses in sex instruction is stated in the Preface of a teacher's manual entitled *Sex Instruction in Swedish Schools*, first published by the National Board of Education in 1957. "The purpose of sex instruction in Swedish schools is to present biological information and to impart knowledge in a manner that will help not only in molding ideals but also in building character. Instruction on these lines is intended to have a pronounced ethical basis." The content of the manual is described in the Preface as follows: "It contains, among other things, general views on sex education and instruction in what should be presented to pupils in different age groups. Suitable ways in which this can be done are outlined in suggested lessons on the subject."

The manual is divided into sections based on the age and school year of the child. Instruction begins during the first school year and even the problems of the preschool child are considered. During the first year

[10] Birgitta Linner, *Society and Sex in Sweden*, p. 3.

PUBLIC HEALTH

particularly instruction is based on the interests, curiosity, and comprehension of the child. The curriculum includes a presentation of how the sexes differ, where children come from, how they develop before birth, the process of birth, the dependence of the child on his parents, and the importance of home life.

From the age of eleven to thirteen years the curriculum covers such subjects as the sexual organs, puberty, menstruation, wet dreams, masturbation, conception, pregnancy, development of the fetus, delivery of babies, and determination of sex. Segregated classes were used for discussions of menstruation and menstrual hygiene until 1956 when it was decided that it was more desirable to discuss these and related subjects in mixed classes.

During the eighth and ninth school years, when the students are fourteen to sixteen years old, intensive sex instruction is conducted. The ninth school year is the final year of the compulsory program, but an intensive voluntary program is offered beyond the ninth year. The curriculum includes such subjects as the structure and function of the sexual organs; development of the fetus and pregnancy; labor; sex and youth, including moral considerations and the values of abstention from sexual relations during adolescence; illegitimacy; spontaneous and induced abortions; venereal diseases; contraception; sterilization; the menopause; sexual abnormalities; moral and social aspects of sex; the family; public welfare programs for advice about setting up a family, pregnancy, confinement, and nursing; and public welfare programs available for the care and training of children and adolescents.

While the biology courses are used as the academic location of courses in sex instruction, the manual recommends that courses in religion, sociology, and other subjects discuss sex education. Since 1954 the Swedish Broadcasting Corporation has conducted sex education programs in the schools and several continuous educational television programs are presented.

As indicated earlier, there is far from a consensus on the desirability or appropriateness of the sex education courses presently conducted in Sweden. As an authoritative writer states: "The teacher's guide for sex education has been criticized by conservative groups as well as by radical groups. The former want strict and clear ethical norms to be taught and the information about contraceptives to be reduced, if not excluded altogether. In the latter group, some people feel that factual

THE SOCIAL PROGRAMS OF SWEDEN

information alone should be supplied, leaving the question of norms to the individual."[11] Because of these widely divergent views a royal commission was appointed in 1964, with membership representing the different ideas and organizations, to develop recommendations concerning the entire sex program.

Birth Control

The liberal attitude toward birth control in Sweden dates from 1938. Before that year, the dissemination of birth control information was prohibited by law. Since 1950, all maternal health clinics have been required to provide information concerning birth control and family planning. These clinics provide information about contraceptives and, irrespective of the marital status of the patient, provide diaphragms or other contraceptive devices to women who request them following the birth of a child.

At the present time booklets and pamphlets about birth control, as well as contraceptive devices, are readily available throughout Sweden. One of the most widely known pamphlets in Sweden is the brochure entitled *The Sexual Relationship* (*Den sexuella samlevnaden*), which strongly recommends family planning and offers a detailed description of various contraceptive methods. The booklet lists the places where both married and unmarried persons may obtain counsel and contraceptive devices for birth control.[12]

A widely read book in Sweden entitled *The Ideal Marriage* by Van der Velde gives further endorsement of contraceptive practices: "Too frequent childbirth is unsuitable both for the mother and for the children. A rule which an experienced professor of pediatrics used to teach is both wise and easy to remember. He said that every mother ought to enjoy the sun of two summers between each childbirth. If better reasons need to be put forth in justification of the use of contraceptives by married couples, one may point out the sharp reduction of infant mortality that has occurred during the past century."[13] The availability of information concerning contraception in modern Sweden is pointed out by another writer: "Nowadays, planned parenthood is fully accepted and facilities for obtaining knowledge about contraceptives are available to the general public. In public places, one can see posters bearing

[11] *Ibid.*, p. 6.
[12] Gunnar af Geijerstam, *Den sexuella samlevnaden*, p. 6.
[13] Linner, p. 27.

messages directed to young people. Such posters, sponsored by the National Association for Sex Education, say: 'Both of you are responsible. Can she depend upon you? Can you depend upon yourself? — to be safe is the most important thing to both of you.'"[14]

One of the most active organizations in Sweden is the National Association for Sex Education, known as RFSU, an independent, nonpolitical organization composed of individuals and those persons representing organizations. The RFSU conducts an active informational program; operates clinics for planned parenthood employing gynecologists, psychiatrists, social workers, and nurses; operates a laboratory for determining pregnancy; and maintains an organization of more than forty small RFSU stores located throughout Sweden where prophylactics are sold, mail orders for contraceptives are filled, and automatic coin-operated machines are supplied and serviced.

Abortion

The present relatively liberal law on abortion in Sweden is of recent origin, as are the laws and practices concerning information on contraception and sex education.[15] Before 1939, therapeutic abortions were illegal in Sweden. During the seventeenth century abortions were punishable by death and the legal code of 1734 retained this penalty. In 1864, the law was amended to provide for a jail sentence with a maximum of six years. The law was liberalized by amendments in 1890 and 1921. Although the law of 1921 did not sanction abortions for any reason, abortions for certified medical reasons were generally permitted.

The number of illegal abortions began to increase and it is estimated that by 1930 seventy women a year died of complications resulting from illegal abortions. In 1934, a royal commission was established to develop new legislation on abortion and the commission submitted its recommendations in 1935. The current law on abortions was approved by the Riksdag in 1938 and became effective on January 1, 1939.

The law of 1939 permitted therapeutic abortion under certain medical, humanitarian, and eugenic conditions listed in the law as follows: "When, because of disease, deformity or weakness in the woman, the birth of the child would endanger her life or health; or when the wom-

[14] *Ibid.*, p. 21.
[15] An excellent treatment of this subject is provided in Birgitta Linner's *Society and Sex in Sweden.*

an was impregnated under certain conditions set forth in the penal code, particularly if she was made to submit to intercourse against her will, as in rape, or if she was impregnated before she was 15 years of age; or when there is reason to believe that the expected child will inherit a mental disease, mental deficiency and/or a severe disease or deformity of other nature, either from its mother or its father."

In 1946, the law was amended adding social reasons to the medical justifications for an abortion. The amendment provided that "Abortion is also permissible when, in view of the woman's living conditions and other circumstances, it can be assumed that the birth and care of the expected child will seriously undermine her mental or physical health." In 1963, another amendment permitted additional medical reasons for legal abortion: "When there is reason to assume that the child will suffer from severe disease or deformity because of injury during fetal life . . ." The purpose of this amendment was to protect against the effects or injury caused by diseases such as German measles, drugs like thalidomide, by Rh blood sensitization, and by the adverse effects of radiation.

The regulations of the National Medical Board provide that abortion may be authorized (1) by the National Medical Board on any of the grounds stipulated in the law (the authorization of the board is required if the abortion is sought on eugenic grounds or in cases in which the woman is legally incompetent, except in an emergency); (2) by two doctors, one of them a government official, except in cases where the authorization of the National Medical Board is required; and (3) by the licensed practitioner performing the operation in a case of emergency, for example, if pregnancy has to be interrupted owing to a disease or physical defect in the woman and if the procedures under (1) or (2) above cannot be followed without harmful consequences owing to delay or other attendant circumstances. An abortion usually may not be performed after the twentieth week of pregnancy except for reasons of disease or a physical defect in the woman. However, the National Medical Board may make exceptions and authorize performance of the operation up to the twenty-fourth week of pregnancy.

While the law on abortions in Sweden today is liberal and provides social or psychological as well as medical reasons for legal abortions, the procedure established for obtaining approval is a thorough one. Applications to the National Medical Board must include a birth certificate, a detailed history of the applicant, and a certificate and recommendation from a Swedish licensed physician. The history must cover all circumstances in the woman's life pertaining to the application and show that she is a person of moral character and good reputation.

Usually, a woman seeking an abortion is advised by her doctor to visit one of the mental health clinics located throughout Sweden. Since 1945, central government grants have been given to the län or cities to provide the mental health clinics with qualified counselors for women seeking interrupted pregnancies. In 1964 twenty clinics operated programs in this field. "The task of these social-medical agencies is to establish, after investigation, whether or not a legal abortion is indicated."[16] The staffs of the clinics include psychiatrists, gynecologists, and social workers who work as a team on each case. The application, together with the recommendations of the team of the clinic, is forwarded to the National Medical Board. The board has established a special committee to deal with these applications. The committee consists of both medical and lay members with a gynecologist as chairman.

In 1962, 4,257 applications for abortions were received by the National Medical Board. During that year there were 108,179 live births in Sweden, indicating that less than 4 percent of the pregnant women sought legal abortions. Of the applications received, only 69 percent, or 2,957, were approved in one of three ways: 2,772 were approved by the National Medical Board, 183 were authorized by two doctors, and 2 were performed as emergencies. The distribution, according to grounds, of legal abortions approved by the National Medical Board in 1962 is shown in the following list.[17]

Justification	Number
Weakness	1,581
Disease	948
Anticipated weakness	151
Humanitarian	80
Eugenic	12
Total	2,772

The liberalization of abortion laws has resulted in a reduction of illegal abortions and the resulting deaths. As a 1964 report states: "Analysis of the statistics from 1930 through 1946 revealed a rapid decline in the

[16] Linner, p. 24.
[17] For greater detail, see *Therapeutic Abortion and the Law in Sweden.*

frequency of criminal abortions. In the first half of the 1940's there were 35 deaths a year from the sequels of criminal abortion, as opposed to 70 during the first half of the 1930's before the new law on abortion in 1939." [18]

The relative liberality of the laws cited above and the humanitarian philosophy underlying the Swedish medical administration have caused many pregnant women to come to Sweden in the mistaken hope of obtaining an abortion. As far back as 1958, the influx of women seeking abortions brought a memorandum from the National Medical Board stressing the fact that few abortions are authorized for women from abroad primarily because the necessary investigations cannot be promptly conducted and the background of such women is not known in Sweden.

The only exception is in the case of a severe disease, the use of a medicine dangerous to the unborn child, such as thalidomide, or a physical defect which indicates that the continuation of pregnancy or the birth of the child might endanger the mother's life or health.

The liberal provisions concerning social or psychological grounds for abortion will not be used to authorize operations for women from abroad. As one writer states, "When social reasons are the primary grounds for a desired abortion (medical-social reasons such as 'weakness' as well as social-medical reasons such as 'expected weakness'), the application, in most cases, must be rejected since the necessary social investigation of the case cannot be performed satisfactorily. Such an investigation must be made in conformity with Sweden's legal regulations and must follow the procedures outlined on official forms. The Swedish National Board of Health cannot cooperate in arranging the necessary contacts with Swedish doctors, hospitals and abortion authorities to carry out these investigations." [19] The Swedish Foreign Office has sent memoranda to all its embassies abroad giving the reason stated above and concluding, "This would consequently rule out cases where foreign women travel to Sweden with the sole purpose of applying for a legal abortion."

Foreign women living in Sweden are eligible to apply under the same conditions as Swedish women. As one booklet states: "Aliens registered at the annual census and liable to taxes in Sweden come under the

[18] *Ibid.*, p. 7.
[19] Linner, p. 26.

abortion law and may seek permission for abortion through the counseling centers."[20]

Dental Health

A national dental health program is planned and supervised by the Dental Division of the National Board of Health.[21] The program is conducted by the public health committees of the county councils.

Under each county public health committee a principal dental officer, known as a dental inspector, serves as head of the dental program in the county. The county or län operates a central clinic as part of the general county hospital. Each county is divided into districts, and each district operates a permanent dental clinic with branch and mobile units. The hospital dental clinic treats complicated cases referred by the district clinics and serves hospital patients. The number of dentists varies with the number of children in each district. A work load of 500 to 600 children has been established as the norm for each district.

The National Board of Health and the chief medical and dental officers of each län supervise conformity to standards relating to the construction and operation of the clinics. For example, a surgery and dental laboratory is required in each clinic housing two or more dentists.

The Dental Division employs all dentists, dental nurses, and technicians working in the clinics. All dentists must be accredited and licensed. In 1961, 1,812 dentists were employed in the Dental Health Service. Of these 1,670 worked in 751 district dental clinics, 55 in 30 orthodontic clinics, and 87 in 22 central hospital clinics. The dentists in the public program represented almost 35 percent of the total of 5,100 dentists practicing in Sweden in 1961.

While more than 60 percent of the working time of the clinic dentists is devoted to the dental care of children (the regulations require a minimum of 55 percent), some dental care is provided to adults. Children's dental treatment is provided without charge but adults (defined as those over 15 years of age), pay according to a modest fee schedule. However, treatment of adults is provided without charge to patients in the general hospitals that contain a dental clinic. The dental care provided includes care of both deciduous and permanent teeth of children,

[20] *Therapeutic Abortion and the Law in Sweden*, p. 8.
[21] Olof Osvald, *The Swedish Public Dental Health Service*, p. 3.

periodontics, orthodontics, and oral, maxillofacial, and preprosthetic surgery.

The central government provides subsidies for the construction and operation of the dental clinics. The county councils receive grants for buying equipment for new dental clinics and annual subsidies of $3.20 (16 kr.) for each child provided with dental care. The municipalities also share the cost, being charged $1 (5 kr.) for each child treated living in the municipality.

An educational, or preventative, dental health program is conducted both by the Public Dental Health Service and the Tandvärnet, the association of dentists in private practice.

As noted earlier, one of the major reasons, in addition to costs, given for the delay in extending the health insurance program to include dental care has been the shortage of dentists, auxiliary staff, and facilities. A commission of the Riksdag is currently studying this subject. The opening of two new dental schools (a third is planned) may provide sufficient dentists to permit the extension of the health insurance program to include dental insurance in the near future.

V

Welfare and Related Programs

> CITIZEN SONG
>
> "As sure as we have a fatherland
> We are heirs to it one with another,
> By common right and in equal bond
> The rich and his needy brother."
>
> Werner von Heidenstam
> (1859–1940)

As IN most other countries, including the United States, the development of public welfare programs in Sweden has been characterized by frequent controversies reflecting at least two distinct philosophies.[1]

One philosophy emphasizes that poverty is a result of an unwillingness to work and to save and can be controlled by the individual. It implies that poverty results from immorality and a lack of incentives and proper conduct. In earlier times, this philosophy incorporated religious concepts and asserted that people in need or suffering from the death of the family breadwinner, disease, or disability were paying for their sins. The old English poor laws reflected this philosophy and provided for the most severe treatment of the poor. The minimum provisions for the poor authorized by these laws were as degrading as possible so that no one would want to be poor and the poor would have the incentive to better their lot. The laws and regulations concerning the early poor-

---

[1] For a consideration of differing welfare philosophies see Wayne Vasey, *Government and Social Welfare*.

houses in England, and still in effect in parts of Ireland, prohibited heat, painted walls, comfortable beds, or desirable food.

As indicated in the opening chapter, the early poor laws of the 1760's in Sweden were not much more generous than those of England.[2] In Sweden in 1847, the first public welfare act that provided more than a minimum subsistence for the poor became law. However, as the result of a depression, this act was sharply restricted by legislation in 1871. The next poor laws, passed in 1918, stated humanitarian concepts and, while continuing the practice of placing primary responsibility for welfare administration on the local governments, provided central government assistance, mainly through the assignment of welfare and children's counselors to assist the local governments. This legislation remained the basis for Swedish welfare administration for the ensuing forty years. As might be expected, the welfare programs differed widely among the län and were effective only in the larger cities.

The other philosophy of welfare is based on the humanitarian concept that social hazards in modern life may have catastrophic effects on people's lives and security through no fault of their own. This philosophy is reflected in Sweden by the recent adoption of a new phraseology. The terms "social health" and "social welfare" have replaced the term "poor relief" which was characteristic of the first philosophy and carried the connotations of deterrence and a grudging help for the poor. Before the new social welfare law became effective on January 1, 1957, there was a mixture of the two basic concepts of social welfare in various parts of Sweden. The larger cities, such as Stockholm, had already begun to develop programs based on the premises of the new legislation. The Social Assistance Act of 1957 reflects the humanitarian philosophy of welfare administration throughout its provisions and even in its title. The terminology of the law indicates the effort to provide welfare assistance with dignity and consideration. The law of 1957 was based on the extensive work of a Royal Commission on Social Welfare created in 1937. After thirteen years of work, the report of this commission was submitted to the Riksdag. Typical of Swedish legislative deliberation, consultation, and care, the legislation was considered for six years in the Riksdag before approval and there was a delay of one year more before it became effective.

[2] For a detailed outline of Swedish welfare programs in effect in the 1950's see *Social Sweden* and *Freedom and Welfare* (Denmark: Krohns Bogtrykkeri, 1953).

WELFARE AND RELATED PROGRAMS

The report submitted to the Riksdag pointed out the need for general assistance even under a well-developed social insurance system because some people had not been able to adjust even with the help of the insurance programs and others had not been eligible for the insurance benefits. The report also stressed the individual case approach in welfare administration: "Only a general form of assistance based on the determination of individual needs would serve to guarantee that the citizen [would receive] adequate assistance in any state of distress regardless of cause and extent."[3] Since the present administration of public welfare is based largely on the law of 1957, a brief review of the major provisions and changes made by the law will be useful.

The law continued the previous practice of placing initial responsibility for welfare administration on the local governments and referred to three forms of assistance which have traditionally been provided by the local governments. These are (1) assistance to the recipients in their own homes, consisting of either cash allowances or assistance in kind; (2) boarding out with a private family; and (3) care in public institutions such as old-people's, children's, or nursing homes and shelters. The major form of assistance is the first, assistance to the recipients in their own homes. Boarding out with a private family is used only in the rural areas or in special cases (as in foster home care for dependent children). The law also required that local public welfare committees provide medical care for needy people in general hospitals, tuberculosis hospitals, homes for rheumatics, or convalescent homes, or that they reimburse the hospital for this care. However, with the extension of the compulsory health insurance program this phase of the program has lost its significance since hospitalization coverage is practically universal under the Swedish program.

The law of 1957 made five significant changes in the law of 1918. The first is the basic change in terminology which has already been mentioned. The second change concerns the use of the terms "compulsory" and "permissive" in referring to the welfare obligations of local governments. Under the revised law the local government is required to provide assistance in all cases in which other forms of assistance are lacking or inadequate to meet family needs. In either situation, central government grants are provided for the local government expenditures. The

[3] *Report of the Royal Commission on Social Welfare* (Stockholm: Social Welfare Board, 1950), p. 13.

program called Help for Self-Help, while listed as permissive aid, is encouraged by the central government and assisted by financial grants.

A third change made by the law of 1957 is the provision that payments be made in cash whenever possible rather than "in kind," i.e., by food, clothing, or housing as had previously been the custom in many rural areas. The law authorizes local welfare committees to guarantee loans in the self-help program. The revised law also emphasizes the concept of social help by specifically listing areas in which local committees should provide services, such as education, vocational training, and provision of tools.

The fourth major change made by the law is a modification of an old Swedish law which provided that the wife did not have maintenance responsibilities for her husband. Under the law of 1957, both husband and wife have the "unconditional duty" for maintenance of the other.

As a fifth change, the law of 1957 clarified the establishment of legal domiciliary rights including the provisions that a person may move at any age and obtain domiciliary rights in a new community, and that a wife may establish her own domiciliary rights. The law also defined the responsibility for adopted children by removing the previous responsibility of natural parents in case of adoption.

Administration

The administration of public welfare in Sweden is conducted at all four levels of government: the central government, the province or länsstyrelsen, the county or landsting, and, most important, the local.

At the national level, legislation and central government appropriations are the responsibility of the Department of Social Affairs. Under the aegis of this department the National Social Board, a semi-independent agency, has the basic responsibility for supervising the operation of the public welfare programs throughout Sweden. The actual administration of these programs is carried out through public welfare representatives on the staffs of the länsstyrelsen governments. Public welfare representatives stimulate and supervise the administration of public assistance, child welfare, the collection of social statistics, and the special programs for juvenile delinquents and alcoholics. Like the grant-in-aid system in the United States, the National Social Board provides grants and subsidies to local governments for direct payment of social assistance and for the construction and maintenance of institutions.

WELFARE AND RELATED PROGRAMS

The immediate and major responsibility for the administration of the public welfare programs is vested in the local governments. This includes the city, town, and rural kommun governments. Under both the old law of 1918 and the revised law of 1957, every local government is required to have a social welfare and a child welfare committee. These committees are appointed by the city councils or the councils in the local municipalities.

The most extensive public welfare organization is found in the city of Stockholm. The city council appoints a commissioner of social assistance and he appoints four social assistance committees consisting of nine members each. The members of the committees are selected as civic leaders and include those who have had some professional training in law, medicine, nursing, or education. The four committees are called the Social Assistance Committee, the Child Welfare Committee, the Unemployment Committee, and the Temperance Committee. A central admission bureau for the social assistance committees has been established to locate the appropriate office for the particular needs of the applicant.

The Public Welfare Department of Stockholm is administered under a Central Social Assistance Committee (also known as the Social Welfare Board). The commissioner of social assistance serves as chairman of the committee and is aided by an appointed director of social assistance. The staff of this office is organized into the two main branches of home and institutional care. Thirteen social assistance centers have been located in Stockholm, and each social center has a director and several inspectors besides clerical staff and cashiers who handle the actual payment of money. In the institutional care branch there are staff members who supervise homes for the aged, homes for the chronically ill (known as "care homes"), and maintenance homes.

The Public Welfare Department of Stockholm employs approximately 2,100 staff members including those in institutions maintained by the city. Of this staff, only 100 are field workers and of these only one-half have had specific training in social work. The relatively small number of trained social workers in the largest welfare department, that of Stockholm, is typical of the situation throughout Sweden. When the law of 1957 went into effect, it was hoped that the emphasis on individual examination of cases would result in a great increase in the number of trained social workers employed. In practice, however, most local social assistance committees do not rely on a social worker's determination of need but use a scale of amounts of money which are made available in cases of similar need.

There are four schools of social work in Sweden: the Stockholm School of Social Work of the Institute for Social and Political Training, the School of Social Work at Lund, the School of Social Work at Göteborg, and the School of Social Work at Umeå in the north. A training program is conducted in the recently established community school at Sigtuna which is operated by the Association of Rural Areas and used to conduct institutes in social welfare for lay people who are members of local welfare boards.

The training program for a degree in social work at the Stockholm School of Social Work covers a period of two and one-half years. Before admission, students are required to have achieved what is comparable to a liberal arts college degree. The curriculum is much broader than that used in most schools of social work in the United States. Four basic courses are taught: social welfare, local government, public finance, and social philosophy. In their first year, the students are all required to take courses in economics, political science, and sociology; following this, courses in welfare administration, including field work, are given. In the second year, courses in psychology, psychiatry, social medicine, hygiene, and field work are required. The students must take examinations in all subjects and write a thesis.

Statistics

In 1960, 301,962 persons, 4 percent of the population, received social assistance throughout Sweden. This represents a reduction of about 25,000 cases from the previous year. Of the total number receiving assistance in 1960, 89,102 were men, 102,700 were women, and 110,160 were children.[4] Cash assistance was given to 259,700 of these cases. A total of $20,810,800 (104,054,000 kr.) was given for living expenses, $1,768,800 (8,844,000 kr.) was given to 5,630 for hospital care; 59,300 received other forms of relief totaling $2,409,400 (12,047,000 kr.).

In 1960 in the city of Stockholm, under the Stockholm Department of Public Welfare, 11,180 persons received social assistance involving an expenditure of $374,000 (1,870,000 kr.) and the average individual payment was $34 (171 kr.) per month. During the same year, $20,000 was

[4] *Statistical Abstract of Sweden* (1962), p. 231.

spent for social help programs. An average of 30 cases a year are removed from the welfare case load through this program.

An analysis of the cases in 1961 is available and indicates that 75 percent of the recipients designated illness as the chief reason for receiving social help, 79 percent received assistance in their own homes, 35 percent were children under 16 in their own homes, 11 percent were over the age of 67, and the total expenditure for that year amounted to $24,000,000 (120,000,000 kr.).

In 1962, the number of recipients of assistance had dropped to 281,573 persons, or 3.7 percent of the population. Of this number 85,996 were men, 96,809 were women, and 98,768 were children; and 122,439 of these were aided in rural districts and 159,134 in cities and towns. Assistance for living expenses in 1962 was given to 236,800 persons; 6,400 received assistance for hospital care, and 66,000 were given assistance called "other forms of relief." Expenditures in 1962 for these welfare payments totaled $25,974,200 (129,874,000 kr.). Of this amount, $20,748,200 (103,741,000 kr.) was expended for assistance for living expenses; $2,190,000 (10,950,000 kr.) for hospital care; and, $3,036,000 (15,183,000 kr.) for other forms of assistance.

The number of persons receiving social assistance moved gradually downward from 1954 to 1964, as shown in the following list (adapted from the *Statistical Abstract of Sweden*, 1966, p. 254).

Year	Number	Percentage of Population
1954	306,586	4.3
1955	274,917	3.8
1956	287,215	3.9
1957	314,555	4.3
1958	328,937	4.4
1959	326,792	4.4
1960	301,962	4.0
1961	282,813	3.8
1962	281,573	3.7
1963	269,652	3.6
1964	266,783	3.5

By October 1963, the number of recipients in Stockholm had been reduced to 5,900, almost by half, compared with 1960. This reduction may be attributed to the inauguration of the Supplementary Pension program through which actual payments began on January 1, 1963, the

THE SOCIAL PROGRAMS OF SWEDEN

increased amounts of the Basic Pension, the high rate of employment, and the intensive rehabilitative efforts of the welfare departments.

In 1964, the monthly allowance for a single person was $52 (260 kr.), for a single person with one child was $70 (350 kr.), with two children $84 (420 kr.), with three children $96 (480 kr.), with four children $108 (540 kr.), and with five children $120 (600 kr.). To this amount the actual rent as well as allowances for clothing were added. A couple received, apart from the rent, an allowance of $79 (395 kr.). With one child a family received $95 (475 kr.), with two children $109 (545 kr.); $12 (60 kr.) was received for each additional child. These allowances have been increased since July 1, 1964, by $5 (25 kr.) for a single person and $9 (45 kr.) for a couple.

The Swedish public, like the citizenry in the United States, questions the need for large welfare expenditures, particularly in the light of current employment opportunities and the wide coverage of the social insurance programs. Even though there has been a sharp reduction in the number of welfare recipients, in 1962 over 281,000 people were receiving social assistance and this has caused widespread concern. Criticism by citizens, occasionally reflected in letters to newspapers and in some books, indicates the typical taxpayer's objection to the expenditure of public funds for welfare purposes.[5] However, there is a "hard core" of people in Sweden who need assistance and for various reasons are unable to benefit from the eligibility provisions of the social insurance programs, or who are not fully employable because of some mental or physical reason.

The leaders in the Swedish social welfare field searching for causative factors have found that the reasons people need welfare assistance in Sweden are similar to those underlying the establishment of the poverty program in the United States. The principal factors include lack of minimum education, physical handicaps, mental retardation or maladjustment, divorces, broken homes, and alcoholism. Specific programs have been undertaken in each of these areas, particularly in the effort to prevent alcoholism and to rehabilitate alcoholics.

Four case examples, taken from the files of the social assistance branch of the Department of Social Welfare of the city of Stockholm, illustrate the operation of the social assistance and self-help programs.

Nils Johansson Applies for Social Assistance. The first case is that of

[5] See examples given in Wilfrid Fleisher's *Sweden: The Welfare State.*

Mr. and Mrs. Nils Johansson who live in Stockholm. Mr. Johansson was 48 years old and his wife, Brita A., 38. They had five children, four boys and a girl, whose ages were 5, 6, 9, 11, and 13. From 1949 to 1960, Mr. Johansson worked as a night watchman, but he lost his position in March of 1960 when he was found drinking on the job. He was fired with the statement that he was "not dependable." Without special training or satisfactory references Mr. Johansson found it impossible to obtain a job. He applied to the Unemployment Committee of Stockholm but since he had a general reputation of not being a good worker no placement was possible even in a period of high employment.

In October 1960, the inspector assigned to the Johanssons referred the case to one of the four doctors appointed by the Social Assistance Committee of Stockholm, who in turn took Mr. Johansson to a psychiatrist, known in Sweden as a social physician. The doctor and the psychiatrist's report indicated that Mr. Johansson suffered from general inability, bronchial asthma, and some psychological problems. He was diagnosed as having a working ability of 50 percent but since the disability did not appear to be permanent he was not eligible for an advance or disability pension. The doctor also examined Mrs. Johansson and recommended sterilization, to which she and her husband consented. Mr. Johansson applied for public assistance at the social assistance center nearest his home. During 1960, monthly payments of approximately $80 (400 kr.) were authorized in addition to allowances for rent, clothing, and other expenses. At the end of the year the payments were raised to $100 (500 kr.) per month. During December, an additional $100 was supplied for furnishings needed in the apartment, and the following month an extra amount was provided for the children's needs.

Mr. Johansson was placed in a retraining program at Barnangen to improve his skills in metal work. He received a salary of $60 (300 kr.) per month while engaged in this training besides the monthly payments by the welfare department. Mr. Johansson was rated as only a "fair" student and prospects for employment were not considered good.

Sten Bjork Is Helped into a Business. In contrast to the case cited above, the self-help program was successful in the case of Mr. and Mrs. Sten Bjork, also living in Stockholm. Mr. Bjork was 48 years old and his wife 43. They were married in 1942 and had two children, both girls, 12 and 14 years old. Since his youth, Mr. Bjork had worked in a lumber mill in the north of Sweden and was rated an excellent employee. However, he injured his back severely at the mill and, in 1950, became a sailor on a maritime ship. He was promoted in the following year, after an examination, to the rating of engineer. But at the insistence of his wife he left this position and obtained a job as a pipe layer, working mostly outside digging trenches and laying sewer pipe. He received very good wages but the condition of his back kept him from maintaining the pace of the team laying the pipe. He felt it necessary to leave this job and was unable to obtain another one.

In October 1960, he was examined by the doctor at the Southern Hospital in Stockholm who certified that Mr. Bjork was suffering from vertebrae trouble in the lower spine and degeneration of a disc. Mr. Bjork applied to the social assistance center near his home in Stockholm and was referred to the training institute of the Stockholm Department of Public Welfare. The inspector referred him to the Orthopedic Department of the Southern Hospital for further care and treatment. Mr. Bjork strongly insisted that he did not want relief or social assistance. He found a temporary job as a gatekeeper earning $106 (530 kr.) per month, and then the owner of the estate and his neighbors recommended that he start his own business. Mr. Bjork applied to the Department of Public Welfare for a loan of $800 (4,000 kr.) so that he could establish his own pipe-laying company. The doctor approved the request, indicating that he could supervise the work of other men although he could not perform the duties himself. The application was referred to the parish social assistance committee which recommended approval in the amount of $760 (3,800 kr.). Then the application was referred to the central social assistance committee for the city of Stockholm and approved.

In December of 1960, Mr. Bjork opened his pipe-laying business and by May of the next year was making a profit of $2,000 (10,000 kr.) per year. In addition, he built a summer cottage which increased in value and after selling it he was able to pay back the loan from the social committee. No further application for aid has been received from Mr. Bjork and the file lists this case as a successful self-help example. But not all efforts are as successful as the rehabilitation of Mr. Bjork.

Lars Peterson Fails at Chicken Raising. The case of Mr. and Mrs. Lars Peterson is one which has caused a great deal of discussion in the public welfare field in Stockholm because it has been on the social assistance lists for many years. Before presenting his self-help proposal

Mr. Peterson and his family received $140 (700 kr.) per month. The records show that Mr. Peterson had been chronically ill and unable to keep a job more than a few days. However, he and his wife had long desired to operate an egg farm although they had had no previous experience in this field. The plan was presented to the local social assistance committee and upon approval referred to the Public Welfare Department of Stockholm.

Initially, $1,500 (7,500 kr.) was given to Mr. and Mrs. Peterson and they purchased chickens and opened their egg farm. However, Mr. Peterson returned frequently to the social assistance committee in need of new tools, feed, additional hens, and equipment. Up to the present time, the social assistance branch of the Department of Public Welfare has advanced more than $6,000 (30,000 kr.) to the Petersons. Because the egg farm has not been making a profit, it has been necessary for the assistance division to continue to provide living expenses. The egg farm is still losing money and the Department of Public Welfare is discussing the advisability of selling the farm in an effort to recoup some of the funds advanced.

Karl Andersson Is Helped to Own a Newsstand. A case with a happier ending, illustrating the transfer from an invalidity pension and social assistance payments to self-help, is that of Mr. and Mrs. Karl John Andersson. Mr. Andersson and his wife, Louisa, had no children. Mr. Andersson was born in 1901 and his wife in 1892. He had suffered most of his life from diabetes and heart disease, and his wife had heart disease and high blood pressure. Beginning in 1947, the Andersson family received an invalidity pension plus social assistance payments of $1,000 (5,000 kr.) per year for both members of the family.

In 1960, Mr. Andersson applied to the social assistance branch of the Department of Public Welfare in the city of Stockholm for funds to operate a small stand selling tobacco, newspapers, and candy. The application was approved the same year and a stand was opened in a suburb of Stockholm. The Department of Public Welfare guaranteed the loan of $1,000 needed to open the stand. The guarantee was given to the Swedish Press Bureau which places the stands and requires a guarantee before opening a stand. After the first year, the stand operated by Mr. and Mrs. Andersson earned $2,000 net per year. The social assistance committee canceled the advance since this amount was needed to cover living expenses of the family. No additional social assistance has been needed for Mr. and Mrs. Andersson who have become self-sufficient through the operation of their newspaper stand.

Child Welfare

As indicated in Chapter 1, the Child Welfare Act of 1924 required every län to establish a Child Welfare Committee to give special attention to the needs of children. This law was amended by the Child Welfare Act of 1960 which re-emphasized the responsibility of every community with a Child Welfare Committee, also known as a Child Welfare Board. The law of 1960 states that it is the responsibility of each local child welfare board to see the sound development of young people and ensure that they have the opportunity to grow up under favorable conditions. To achieve these aims the local board is required, first of all, to take general preventative measures and, secondly, to carry out individual programs designed to meet cases of need or maladjustment.[6]

In 1962, social assistance grants were provided to 98,768 children. The amount of $17,960,400 (89,802,000 kr.) was expended for assistance for living expenses; $34,400 (172,000 kr.) for hospital care; and $2,200,800 (11,004,000 kr.) for other forms of relief. The amounts expended for assistance are only a small indication of the total care afforded children in Sweden. During the 1930's, the population of Sweden showed a sharp decline with a reduced birth rate and high emigration to other countries. Since that time the Swedish government has sponsored many programs for children.

A general children's allowance, mentioned in Chapter 2, is paid to every family regardless of income or resources for every child up to the age of 16 years. The uniform rate was $140 (700 kr.) per year from July 1, 1964, until 1966, when it was raised to $180 (900 kr.). The allowance is not subject to a means test or taxation. In the 1967–68 fiscal year, $319 million (1,595 million kr.) has been budgeted for children's allowances, making this item second only to the pension programs in the national budget. (*The Swedish Budget, 1967/68*, p. 59.) All children, including children of foreign nationals employed in Sweden, are eligible for this benefit. Children between 16 and 18 continue to receive the children's allowance if they are still in school.

[6] For a comprehensive discussion of this subject, see *Swedish Youth*, James Rössel, *Women in Sweden*, and, Bertil Bagger-Sjöbäck, *Activities for Young People in Sweden*.

WELFARE AND RELATED PROGRAMS

In addition to the regular allowance, special allowances, as previously mentioned, are paid to all children under 16 years of age in cases in which one or both of the parents are dead, the child is not living in the home, the father or mother receive a Basic or Supplementary Pension, or there is need. There is a special children's supplement payable to widows or widowers with one or more children under ten years of age. Also, under the Supplementary Pension, a further benefit is paid for children until the age of 19. Special allowances are also provided under the advance or disability pension when children are living in the home (see p. 25).

The general children's allowances are financed entirely out of national revenue. Special allowances are paid by both the central and the local governments but the local share of these allowances may not exceed one-half of the total cost. Payments for children in both Basic and Supplementary Pension programs are not based on need or an income test but on a mathematical formula that takes into account the number of children in the family.

The present system of children's allowances was established in 1948. From 1917 to 1948, families with children were entitled to a deduction in the government tax assessments similar to that of the federal income tax in the United States. The kommunal income tax system administered at the local level continued the deduction for children until 1952 when the provision for deduction was removed, and the children's allowances paid nationally were increased.

In addition to the actual payments of money, there are a great many programs which relate to almost all phases of life in Sweden and seek to give extra attention to the health and welfare of children. For example, free vacation transportation is provided for children up to 14, when the family meets an income test; there is also provision for free transportation and a modest payment for the guardians of children under the age of 11. Also, vacations are provided at a modest cost, on the basis of an income test, for housewives with 2 children under 15 years of age. Children's holiday camps, particularly for children of low-income families, are available. Special consideration is given to housing loans and applications for apartments when there are children in the family.

A completely free school system has developed as the result of the special attention given to children in Sweden. Since 1946, all primary and elementary school children have been given free lunches, schoolbooks, and writing materials. While the school lunch program is not compulsory, it has been estimated that 700,000 children a year enjoy the free lunches served in the schools. Books and bus travel are also provided for students in the comprehensive (lower grade) schools without charge. All students in the gymnasium, continuation, and vocational schools receive a study grant of $15 (75 kr.) per month, a travel allowance of $6 to $15 (30–75 kr.) per month, a lodging allowance of $20 (100 kr.) per month, and an additional allowance, subject to a means test, of $15 (75 kr.) per month. Children with only one parent may receive a further allowance of $15 (75 kr.) a month, subject to a means test. Students in these schools who have reached the age of 21 receive an augmented study grant of $35 (175 kr.) a month. In addition to these grants, study loans are available for students who need additional amounts to stay in school.

In the higher education schools, students receive a grant and are eligible for a loan with no interest. By statute, every student receives $350 (1,750 kr.) per year and may borrow an additional $1,200 (6,000 kr.) per year, with special allowances for children. Payment of the loan is permitted over a 20-year period and includes an insured protection so that repayment may be postponed or waived in case of unemployment, illness, disability, or other special circumstances.

Central government expenditures for student assistance, known as "study aid," has grown from approximately $4 million (20 million kr.) in 1950 to over $80 million (403 million kr.) in 1966 (*The Swedish Budget, 1967/68*, p. 64).

The government provides for part-time care of preschool children in kindergarten, day nurseries, and "afternoon homes" administered by the municipal social welfare office and the local child welfare boards. Fees are adjusted to the family income. The day nurseries provide full day care for children of working mothers and receive children from 2 to 7 years old. Even in rural areas there are day nurseries for children whose parents are engaged in seasonal farm work. "Afternoon homes" and "walking tours" are provided in many neighborhoods. Under this arrangement one of the women in the neighborhood takes care of the children of employed mothers for the afternoon and, when the weather will permit, takes them on tours.

Since 1944, medical examinations, including innoculations and other services, have been provided for all school children without charge;

medicines are also supplied free. Information on the health of each child is noted on a permanent card which moves with him throughout school. Free dental care has been provided since 1938. Consultation is available at child guidance clinics without charge if there are any indications of maladjustment of the child. Child care officers for assistance to children under 18 are available under the supervision of the local social welfare office and child welfare boards, with the designation of a guardian for each illegitimate child and one for each child whose parents are separated.

There are provisions for older children as well as the younger. As mentioned above, a cash allowance is provided for pupils between 16 and 18 years of age, and since 1946 an extensive system of scholarships and fellowships has been provided for higher education. Interest-free loans for advanced study and board and lodging without charge are available for those who wish to continue their studies but cannot afford to do so. Approximately 5,000 students each year benefit from some type of central government scholarship and the continuation of this program will assist many more students each year.

In 1960, 133,923 children were assigned child welfare guardians throughout Sweden. In the same year, 32,680 children attended free summer camps in more than 580 locations throughout Sweden. During 1960, 48,000 children were referred to local child welfare boards and local care was provided for 24,000. About 7,000 children were under "social protection" in cases of neglect or misbehavior in December 1960.[7] In 1961, there were 51,741 children in day nurseries and after-school homes. In 1962, 47,797 children received special children's allowances because of the loss of one or both parents. The total amount expended in this program was $9,087,600 (45,437,000 kr.).

Care of the Aged

Eleven percent of the population of Sweden is composed of people over 65 years of age as compared with 9 percent in the United States. In contrast with the system of old-age assistance established in the United States, assistance for the aged in Sweden is provided under the general social assistance program. The largest group of recipients under this program has continued to be aged persons. This has resulted, at least in part, from the fact that the Basic Pension payments were below the

[7] *Statistical Abstract of Sweden* (1962), p. 228.

subsistence level in many cases. As the Supplementary Pension program takes full effect, it is anticipated that payments to the aged will decrease.

The Law of Social Assistance of 1957 continued the requirement that each kommun maintain an institution as an old people's home or shelter for the care and maintenance of aged people in need. In earlier years, chronically ill people were also cared for in these homes but recently special provisions have been made for them in connection with the hospitals maintained by the landsting governments. Ninety-six percent of rural and 72 percent of urban institutions consist of homes for the aged.

The Swedish government has shown a great deal of interest in the design and maintenance of homes for the aged. In 1947, a special law was passed by the Riksdag setting up principles governing the construction and operation of homes for the aged. The National Social Board has issued a large number of policy directives, distributed through the provincial governments, that provide advice for the establishment of old people's homes, including architecture and design. National competitions are held to obtain new ideas for design and central government grants are available for the construction or modernization of homes in accordance with the advanced plans.

Between 1947 and 1961 more than 400 new homes for the aged were built.[8] Many more homes were modernized and almost every community has established one or more facilities for older people. At the present time more than 50,000 older people can be accommodated in relatively modern homes. Still, support for the housing program for the aged continues because of the accelerating increase in both the number and the percentage of aged in the Swedish population.

The current program in Sweden represents a reversal of an earlier policy of building large institutions or even villages for older people. In the late 1930's and early 1940's a number of large institutions were built. In 1961, there were 1,350 old-age homes with facilities for about 43,000 people throughout Sweden. In Stockholm, there are now more than 950 old-age home beds and 2,640 nursing-home beds distributed in 11 institutions. The Sabbatsborg home has a capacity of 710, Rosenlund, 750, Stureby 200 old-age home and 890 nursing-home beds, Stadshagsgården 210, Bromma 100, and Spånga-Fristad 50. In addition, the Stockholm Public Welfare Department operates several apartments for the

---

[8] A summary of this program, with photographs, is available in the pamphlet *Homes for the Aged in Sweden Offer Ideas for Americans.*

aged which are called *pensionähemen*. Over 500 apartments are included, with the largest apartment house at Enskede.

At present, instead of building large homes, which become institutional, or old people's villages, modern homes are being built in every kommun which accommodate not more than 40 people in the same building. Emphasis has been given to de-institutionalizing the homes and minimizing the shift from private homes by providing as much privacy as possible. Seventy-two percent of the accommodations in Swedish homes for the aged are single rooms. Double rooms are provided for couples so that they may have a bedroom and a living room; dining rooms are established for limited groups of the residents. Aged people are also located in apartment houses, either regular apartments or those designed for the aged, or permitted to live in their own homes with the provision of home help. Whenever possible, older people are encouraged to stay in their own homes or apartments. This is perhaps a reflection of an old Swedish proverb: "Old people are like Chinese porcelain; let them stay on their shelves and they will not be broken."

The Stockholm Public Welfare Department is making extensive use of the home-help program in which women are employed full or part time to provide home care for the aged and other people in need. This program, initiated in 1951, has about 3,000 home-help women caring for some 8,000 elderly people who cannot cook their own meals or in other ways care for themselves. Special vehicles have been designed to provide service of "Meals on Wheels" to pensioners' homes or flats, and seven specially trained physicians are on call, as well as other doctors and dentists, to serve the needs of aged people. These services enable many aged people to remain in their own homes.

Another reversal in policy concerning homes for the aged is still somewhat controversial. In the early homes for the aged the addition of nursing and infirmary service was considered mandatory. Recently there has been an emphasis on establishment of smaller homes for the aged without medical services in order to "maintain more nearly the home-like atmosphere. . . . There are, at present, two schools of thought in Sweden about whether homes for the aged should admit only the 'normal' aged, persons who, although frail, have no seriously handicapping impairments or whether the homes should also care for persons with long-term illness."[9] This issue is being met by building both

[9] *Ibid.*, p. 12.

types of homes for the aged and ensuring that some medical facilities are readily available to those located in homes without them.

The Swedish experience should be called to the attention of those interested in old-age homes in the United States where there is still the tendency to build communities for the aged or large institutions which tend to segregate people in their declining years. Ironically, several of the projects in the United States have been designed "on the basis of Swedish experience." The planners have presumably not been informed about the change in thinking of most of the Swedish specialists in this field during recent years.

Almost all of the homes for the aged in Sweden have a maintenance charge which is set to fit within the pension income of the older person and leave him the minimum of $120 (600 kr.) per year for personal expenditures specified under existing regulations. This means, of course, that a large amount of the actual cost of construction and maintenance of the homes is still the responsibility of the local community.

Rehabilitation

Today in Sweden a great deal of attention is being given to the field of rehabilitation. The premise underlying the establishment of sickness benefits in the Basic Pension program was that a rehabilitative effort would be made before certification for the advance or disability pension. Under the 1962 law, the advance or disability pension of the Supplementary Pension program requires medical certification indicating the degree of disability and this facilitates early recognition of rehabilitative possibilities. The relatively large amounts of public funds expended in advance pensions makes the expansion of the rehabilitation program good business. In addition, as indicated in earlier chapters, emphasis on rehabilitation and self-help has been stimulated by revisions of the laws and social board regulations in the conduct of the welfare programs.

Historically, progress in the provision of an effective rehabilitative welfare program has been somewhat limited in Sweden partially because the responsibility for this program is divided among several of the national boards. Before the establishment of the National Insurance Board and the administrative consolidation of the pension and health insurance programs, the National Pension Board was responsible for administering medical and rehabilitative service for invalidity pension-

WELFARE AND RELATED PROGRAMS

ers. This board maintained three hospitals specializing in the treatment of arthritis, psychoneurosis, neurology, and comparable diseases and also administered special wards in more than 20 hospitals throughout Sweden. The National Pension Board emphasized the rehabilitation of invalidity pensioners whose disabilities were caused by heart diseases, tuberculosis, arthritis, asthma, and other diseases.

Primary responsibility for vocational rehabilitation has now been delegated to the National Labor Board which has established a division of vocational rehabilitation. The National Labor Board administers the rehabilitation program through this division and the employment service division. The disablement resettlement program, administered through the employment service offices located throughout Sweden, has been delegated the most extensive public activity. Clients are referred to the disablement resettlement offices of the employment service from hospitals, sanatoria, mental hospitals, prisons, social welfare offices, institutions for alcoholics, pension committees, public medical officers, institutions for the blind, deaf, and dumb, or else they come on their own initiative. The program includes occupational therapy beginning in a hospital or nursing institution. St. Göran Hospital and the Karolinska Hospital in Stockholm have established programs of this type.

Besides this occupational therapy the program includes vocational orientation and special counseling for all disabled who visit the employment office; attitude and aptitude tests to determine the capabilities of those who have some limiting physical handicap; work clinics to provide more thorough diagnosis for difficult cases; recuperative training workshops provided by county councils, municipalities, and private organizations with a government subsidy; special placement facilities for the handicapped; semi-sheltered employment in industry with government grants to cover increased expenses resulting from special workshop operation; sheltered employment for severely disabled persons; home work for those in isolated areas or so severely handicapped that they cannot work outside their homes; and financial assistance in the form of a grant or loan without collateral to assist the handicapped person in opening his own small business or activity. Public grants are provided, according to individual needs, for travel to and from the place of training or work, fees for training courses, allowances for materials, medical care, maintenance, and family assistance.

Another public program in the field of rehabilitation is administered by the local county or central public assistance agencies, with support from the National Social Board. Each city, town, and county has a public assistance committee. This committee, especially in the larger cities such as Stockholm, administers the Help for Self-Help program, and seeks to provide a constant review of public assistance cases to determine those which lend themselves to possible rehabilitation. Specially trained personnel are assigned to the selected cases and special efforts are made for placement in cooperation with the local employment offices. In situations where placement is difficult, public assistance recipients are referred to the retraining program of the National Labor Board employment offices. In many cases some physical or mental disability is found to be a factor in the employment difficulty. When this occurs the case is referred to the regular rehabilitation program of the National Labor Board with cash grants for living expenses provided by the local or county public assistance committee.

It is estimated that there are 50,000 to 60,000 handicapped persons in Sweden. With a population of 7,360,000, the number of handicapped represents almost 1 percent of the total population. From the period January 1 to December 31, 1955, 22,950 applications for vocational rehabilitation were received. During the same period 10,675 disabled persons were placed in productive work on the open market through the combined programs. In addition, retraining was provided for 1,050 workers; regular vocational training for 1,540 workers; sheltered employment for 436; and assistance in buying their own business for 347 disabled persons. During 1955, a total of $2,561,000 (12,805,400 kr.) was expended by public agencies for rehabilitation programs. Of this amount, the central government provided $721,000 (3,605,000 kr.); the county councils $840,000 (4,200,000 kr.), for the rural areas; and the cities, $1,000,000 (5,000,000 kr.), half of which was expended by the city of Stockholm.

In addition to the major public programs outlined above, several active private organizations have developed in the field of rehabilitation. This is unusual in Sweden where most programs in health and welfare are publicly operated, but the distinction is not as sharp as it appears on the surface because even these private organizations are financed largely by subsidies from the central government. The Royal Medical Board is the public agency responsible for inspecting the activities of

WELFARE AND RELATED PROGRAMS

the private institutions, particularly with regard to the level of medical care provided, and for reviewing and approving the budgets calling for government grants.

The Institutes for the Care of Cripples in Stockholm, Göteborg, Hälsingborg, and Härnosänd are active in the field of rehabilitation. These institutes, established in 1822, have been organized to provide total care of the cripples. Included in the program of the institutes are elementary schools for crippled children; social service programs maintaining permanent contact with cripples who have left the institutes; services for providing cripples in each district with work and opportunity to sell their products; welfare and work homes for adult cripples who require such care; orthopedic care; and special hospitals and sanatoria for persons suffering from tuberculosis of the bones and joints.

The National Organization of Cripples provides a recreational program for cripples. The Association against Polio, the Association against Rheumatism, and the Swedish Multiple Sclerosis Association also provide some services in this field.

The Swedish Central Committee for the Care of Cripples was founded in 1911 to stimulate programs for the benefit of the disabled and to coordinate the many activities of public and private organizations in this field.[10] The Central Committee seeks to coordinate the work of the institutes for the care of cripples with the public agencies such as the Royal Medical Board and the Royal Labor Board and its employment offices. The National Pension Board and the National Education and Trade Education Boards have special educational programs for vocational training of cripples. Private organizations composing the central committee include: the Norrbacka Institute, Stockholm; the Vocational Schools and Orthopedic Clinic of Änggården, Göteborg; the Institute for Care of Cripples in Hälsingborg; and the Association against Rheumatism. The central committee has five operating branches. These include the negotiating delegations; the technical committee; the research council for prostheses and braces; the educational board for limbfitters and bracemakers; and the committee for care of the cerebral palsied.

Despite the work of the Swedish Central Committee for the Care of Cripples which is effective in some areas, one of the major problems is the difficulty of marshaling the administratively separate rehabilita-

[10] "The Swedish Central Committee for the Care of Cripples" (Svenska Vanforevardens Central kommittee), *Information*, September 1954 and June 1960.

tion facilities, both public and private, to provide maximum service in this field. Little or no effective coordination exists at the present time between the health insurance and the vocational rehabilitation programs. A research program covering five districts with a team composed of medical doctor, rehabilitation specialist, psychologist, and social worker found that only 10 percent of the disabled receiving benefits from the health insurance program had been referred for vocational rehabilitation. Coordination has been sought by the dual assignment of one person to head two boards in this field, by cross attendance between boards at staff meetings, and by other means. However, the result of the scattered responsibility for rehabilitation has been some confusion and duplication of efforts. The creation of the National Insurance Board to administer the Basic Pension, the Supplementary Pension, and the health insurance program should do much to improve coordination of efforts in this significant field. As in the United States, further efforts are needed to organize the many existing but disparate resources to provide maximum assistance in each case.

Another problem in coordination involves the provision of funds for the disabled. Under present regulations, funds for the maintenance of disabled people while they are participating in the various aspects of the rehabilitation program come from several different sources. For example, welfare department payments will frequently be required to maintain a family in which the breadwinner is enrolled in the retraining program. This limits the support of the program by some welfare departments. Similarly, payments of the invalidity pension are continued while a disabled person is participating in the rehabilitation program. Unfortunately this requires the designation of the participant as an invalid to authorize the legal base for the disability pension. Consequently, several administrators have suggested that increased funds for payment of living costs and retraining expenses should be provided under the rehabilitation program rather than calling on other programs to meet subsistence expenses during the period of rehabilitation.

The difficulty of finding cases at a very early stage, preferably upon entrance into the hospital, is another problem which concerns rehabilitation administrators at the present time. The opportunity for a closer relationship with the health insurance program in the new pattern of organization should help in meeting this problem. A recently published booklet, *Social Benefits in Sweden,* should help as well. It lists the offices where disabled persons can obtain assistance. The location of rehabilitation units at all major hospitals, similar to the unit located at the Karolinska Hospital, has been recommended. Another constructive measure which has been proposed calls for the enlargement of educational facilities in the field of rehabilitation for both medical doctors and administrative personnel. Since the first person to see a disabled person is usually a medical doctor, rehabilitation experts recommend that every medical student should be required to have at least one course in rehabilitation in the regular medical school curriculum. In addition, programs should be established in universities to prepare students for careers in rehabilitation as a professional field. The lack of specially trained medical and administrative personnel in this area is one of the major problems.

VI

The Government and the Individual

> "My son, to serve Humanity, Reason,
> the State and enjoy,
> Not only security, but justice also, in
> return,
> Is more, than — at one time — any being
> should demand.
> Three big words, my son, our social
> science adorn,
> Enlightenment, Freedom, Human Right."
> Carl Gustaf Leopold (1756–1829)

AN UNDERSTANDING of the administration of the social programs in Sweden requires some knowledge of the basic concepts, structure, and operation of the government. Most important, this understanding must include a comprehension of the confidence the citizen has in, and his relationship to, the government.

The average Swedish citizen is not afraid of his government. He has what might be called a public philosophy that defines the appropriate role of government in his society and in his life. In this philosophy, which has developed over many years and is deeply woven into the fabric of Swedish tradition and custom, the citizen quite clearly distinguishes between the service or general welfare aspects of government and those involving regulatory powers. He supported a proposal for the nationalization of health insurance, particularly since most of the population was already covered by the voluntary funds and the structure of the funds was retained for administrative purposes. He has no objection to the public ownership and operation of almost all hospitals throughout Sweden because this tradition goes far back into Swedish history. However, he would react quickly and negatively to proposals which permitted the use of wiretapping or any other infringement upon his personal liberties. His philosophy is much more conservative than outsiders might imagine. He does not look with favor on the extension of government into what is generally considered the private sector of the economy. The average Swede is proud that Sweden has an economy based upon free enterprise. He looks on the great cooperatives as privately owned and non-governmental in nature.[1]

The Swedish public philosophy is understood by those in government, the legislative leaders, and administrators. In recent years whenever the government has undertaken a new activity an administrative board has usually been established. The board consists of representatives of all the major parties concerned, including the government, but has legal autonomy and responsibility. For example, to administer the funds established by the National Insurance Act of 1962, the Riksdag established three boards composed of representatives from employers, employees, the government, and, for one of the funds, the self-employed. Similarly, the Regional Sickness Funds were established by the 1962 law as a modified government corporation that is halfway between a regular government agency and a government corporation. The Board of Telecommunications, responsible for the telephone and telegraph services, the Hospital Administration, the State Railways, and the State Waterfalls and Power Administration are controlled by the government but ". . . enjoy a greater freedom of action than regular government agencies."[2] The Sveriges Radio AB is chartered as a limited liability company and is vested by the government with exclusive rights in the production of programs for radio and television broadcast. This agency was set up as a government corporation in 1925 to provide radio broadcasting programs, and in 1957 extended its services to include television programs.[3]

Even in the day-to-day conduct of regular government business the departments of government do not control the administrative activities

[1] Marquis Childs, in *Sweden: The Middle Way*, gives a comprehensive review of the nature and significance of the cooperative movement in Sweden.

[2] *Telecommunication in Sweden* (Stockholm: The Board of Telecommunications, 1962), p. 5.

[3] *Sveriges Radio* (Stockholm: The Swedish Broadcasting Corporation, 1962).

which are under the jurisdiction of semi-autonomous national boards. All of the social programs are conducted by public agencies. Accordingly, an examination of both the structure and the dynamics of the Swedish government is required for an understanding of the health and welfare programs in that country. Certain characteristics of Swedish government have played an important part in the widespread public acceptance of the Swedish health and welfare programs.

A Parliamentary Democracy

An analysis of Swedish government reveals several significant characteristics: (1) It is a democracy both in theory and in practice; (2) public interest and participation exist at all levels of government; (3) it is decentralized, both structurally and geographically; (4) it is staffed by people of ability and prestige; and (5) there are citizen controls of government.

Sweden is a democracy since, according to its Constitution, all basic authority rests with the people. The Swedish Bill of Rights is almost identical to the Oath of Coronation first recorded in the fourteenth century: "The King shall maintain and further justice and truth, prevent and forbid inequity and injustice; he shall not deprive anyone or allow anyone to be deprived of life, honor, personal liberty or well-being, without legal trial and sentence; he shall not deprive anyone or permit anyone to be deprived of any real or personal property without due trial and judgment in accordance with the provisions of the Swedish law and statutes; he shall not disturb or allow to be disturbed the peace of any person in his home; he shall not banish any person from one place to another; he shall not constrain or allow to be constrained the conscience of any person, but shall protect everyone in the free exercise of his religion, provided that he does not thereby disturb public order or occasion general offense. The King shall cause everyone to be tried by the court to the jurisdiction of which he is properly subject."[4]

Except for the Constitution of the United States, the constitutional documents of Sweden represent the oldest written constitution of the nations of the world. Except for the British Parliament, Sweden's Riksdag is the oldest national legislature in the world. The four basic documents of the Swedish Constitution are the Instrument of Government

[4] Amos J. Peaslee, *Constitutions of Nations*, p. 99.

THE GOVERNMENT AND THE INDIVIDUAL

of 1809, the Act of Succession of 1810, the Riksdag Act of 1866, and the Freedom of the Press Act of 1949.[5] The dates given refer to the present, most recently amended form of these documents. Actually, the constitutional relationship of the Swedish citizen to his government is traced back to the fourteenth century. "About 1350 . . . there was drawn up for the first time a law-code for the whole realm. . . . It is thus also a kind of constitution and occupies a place in Swedish history similar to that of *Magna Carta* in the history of England; it defined the ancient rights — for so they were regarded — of the nobility against the king . . ."[6] The Riksdag dates from 1435, although it was not until 1866 that the Riksdag Act was passed stating the principle and functions of the Swedish Parliament.

Swedish political thought was affected by the emphasis on individual liberty and equality stressed by the writers of the French Revolution and by the framers of the Declaration of Independence and the Constitution of the United States. However, it is significant that Montesquieu's concept of a check and balance pattern of the executive, legislature, and judiciary is not emphasized in the development of the Swedish Constitution or government. While the judiciary is clearly independent of both the executive and legislative branches there is a much closer working relationship between them than in the United States. Most new legislation is developed by the ministries of the executive branch and submitted to the Riksdag although significant proposals frequently result from the work of royal commissions of inquiry. A different type of check and balance has been developed in Swedish government. The central government is limited by the national boards, which have relative autonomy and administrative freedom, and by the local governments, which have traditional authority and responsibility.

The Swedish citizen has long been conscious of government under law as sacred both in tradition and in his daily life. The visitor to Sweden will occasionally hear the response *lagom* when a Swede is asked how much cream and sugar he wants in his coffee or his reaction to a par-

[5] A comprehensive discussion of the Constitution, the government, and the Riksdag of Sweden is available in the excellent book by Nils Andrén, *Modern Swedish Government*, printed in Sweden in English, and his *Government and Politics in the Nordic Countries*. See also Ben A. Arnesen, *The Democratic Monarchies of Scandinavia*; and Ingvar Andersson, *Introduction to Sweden*. The dynamics of Swedish government are available in a thoughtful book by Dankwart A. Rustow, *The Politics of Compromise*; see also Herbert J. Shapiro, *Government by Constitution*, pp. 45–48.

[6] Stewart Oakley, *A Short History of Sweden*, p. 50.

ticular article of clothing. The word lagom has come to mean "suitable," "sufficient," "just right," or "appropriate." Literally, lagom means "according to the laws" and the use to which this term is put in daily life may indicate how the average Swedish citizen interprets this essential characteristic of democracy — government under law.

The political scientist would describe Sweden as a constitutional, parliamentary democracy. The king is the symbol of the head of state and this is made clear by the Swedish Constitution. In exercising his constitutional powers the king is required to accept the advice of his ministers. All authority delegated by the people through the Constitution is specifically given to the king-in-council, that is, the king with the heads of the departments, or ministers.

The king is required to select his ministers from the party or coalition that controls Parliament, so the decisive power rests with the party that has won a majority of seats in the most recent election. The operation of this procedure has been described by an official of one of the major ministries: "The King since 1950, Gustav VI Adolf, exerts no political power and takes no part in politics. He represents the nation. According to the Constitution, he is the Head of State. In his capacity as such, he signs all important decisions of the Government. Although formally the King takes the decisions the real responsibility for them rests with his 'Counselors of State' called the Statsråd, the cabinet ministers, who countersign all decisions taken by the 'King-in-Council.'"[7] The king opens the Riksdag on January 11 of each year with a formal address, and even this address usually represents the views of the ministers in power.

The Riksdag may be compared to the Congress of the United States in that it consists of two houses, but there the similarity ends. The Upper House of 151 members is elected by the county councils and the councils of the six major cities which have the status of county boroughs. In a sense, this election gives the county councils the status of an electoral college. Nineteen constituencies have been classified into eight groups which in turn elect one-eighth of the Senate or Upper House each year. This half of the Parliament provides great continuity since its members are elected for a term of eight years with only a fraction of them elected each year. Seats in the Upper House are apportioned every ten years. Elections for all of the members of the Lower House are

[7] Ernst Michanek, *Swedish Government in Action*, p. 2.

THE GOVERNMENT AND THE INDIVIDUAL

conducted every four years although a vote of confidence may be called for on a major issue and then the king must determine the strength of the different parties in Parliament. If the vote is negative the king designates the prime minister to form a new cabinet which will have parliamentary support. If a majority of support cannot be obtained by the party in power and if efforts to form a new cabinet by a coalition of parties are unsuccessful, either or both houses of the Riksdag may be dissolved and a special election called. "If the Upper House is dissolved,

Table 7. Distribution of Seats in the 1967 Riksdag

Party	Lower House	Upper House	Total	Percentage of Seats	Percentage of Votes 1962	1964	1966
Conservatives	35	26	61	15.8	15.5	13.7	14.7
Center Party (Agrarians)	35	19	54	14.0	13.1	13.4	13.7
Liberals	43	25	68	17.6	17.2	17.1	13.9
Social Democrats	113	80	193	50.0	50.4	47.3	42.2
Communists	8	1	9	2.3	3.8	5.2	6.4
Others	1	0	1	.3	0	3.3	1.9
Coalition of Conservatives and Liberals	0	0	0	0			7.2
Total	235	151	386	100.0	100.0	100.0	100.0

SOURCE: *The Swedish Budget, 1967/68*, p. 1.

the new House shall be elected at extra-ordinary sessions of the electing councils. In case of a dissolution of the Lower House, the new House shall be elected on a day prescribed by the King."[8] Table 7 indicates the distribution of seats in the Riksdag as of January 1967.

The Swedish election system provides for proportional representation. The elections for the lower chamber of 235 members are based upon 28 constituencies composed of the counties, the two largest cities, Stockholm and Göteborg, each equaling a constituency, and the third largest city, Malmö, combining with three other cities to form a constituency. Lower chamber seats are apportioned every four years among the constituencies according to their resident population. The number of representatives per district varies from 3 to 24. No official ballots listing the choice of candidates and parties are used. Any piece of white paper may be used as a ballot. In practice, the parties prepare printed ballots which are available to voters, and most voters use one of these. By a complicated formula, the distribution of the number of seats as-

[8] Nils Andrén, *Modern Swedish Government*, p. 51.

signed to each constituency is based upon the vote.[9] Thus, Sweden provides proportional representation by constituency rather than on a national basis.

Public Interest and Participation

The right to vote by secret ballot is important to most Swedes. For many years the Swedish Central Statistical Bureau has published tables showing the voting participation by age, sex, occupational group, and percentage of those eligible to vote.[10] Since most voters do not know the individuals who are listed as candidates for their particular party, except possibly the head of the party listed, voting in Sweden relates much more closely to issues than to individuals. In 1960, a comparison of the number of people on voting registers with those who actually voted in the national election for the Lower House of the Riksdag shows that 85.9 percent of all those entitled to vote cast ballots. In the elections of county councils of 1958, 79 percent of those eligible to vote cast ballots. This pattern of widespread citizen interest and participation in elections is reflected in the votes for municipal and communal councils as well as in the county and national elections.[11]

The figures of 85.9 percent and 79 percent participation in Sweden may be compared with the estimated 60 percent of registered voters who cast ballots in the 1960 general election in the United States. (Even fewer vote in off-year and local elections in the United States.[12]) The significance of the differences between the percentages is especially striking in the light of the fact that all persons over 21 (since 1921 suffrage in Sweden has been universal) who are census-registered are automatically considered eligible to vote in Sweden.

A further demonstration of the Swedes' interest in their government is the widespread use of boards and committees in many fields of government activity at central, province, county, and local government levels. Many people feel that they are part of the governmental process, and in fact they are, as they serve on local pension, welfare, child care, or other committees and boards.

[9] For a detailed description of proportional representation in Sweden, see Dankwart A. Rustow, *The Politics of Compromise*, pp. 123–132.
[10] *Statistical Abstract of Sweden* (1962), p. 360.
[11] *Ibid.*, pp. 362–364.
[12] Jack Walter Peltason and James MacGregor Burns, *Government by the People*, p. 254.

Even the legislative process reflects the desire for widespread participation through the customary use of the remiss system in the consideration of pending legislation. Under this system copies of a proposed legislative bill are sent to all interested groups and organizations together with a request for their comment and evaluation. The replies are printed and attached to the bill as it is considered by the Riksdag and its committees. Since in Sweden almost every person belongs to one or more voluntary organizations, and at least one of the organizations to which he belongs will most likely be consulted in the process,[13] the individual can feel a sense of participation in the legislative process of government. Professor Rustow emphasizes the importance that this organizational tendency has in Swedish life: "A universal inclination to form societies in the pursuit of impersonal objectives provides a salutary complement to individualism. Swedish society is *genomorganiserat* — saturated with voluntary associations. Almost the entire working population is organized according to its function in the productive process . . ."[14]

Not only is the democratic concept of the right of the people to know about governmental affairs recognized in the legislative process, but it is also protected and emphasized in the more mundane administrative machinery. Free access to all government documents is constitutionally guaranteed. The Freedom of the Press Act provides that governmental information must be made available to the press or to a citizen upon request unless it can be proven that it would be clearly against the public interest to provide this information. As a result of this requirement, public information on governmental activities at all levels is readily available and is widely used by newspapers and other communication media throughout Sweden.

Decentralized Government

Swedish government is decentralized both structurally and geographically. This comes as a surprise to the armchair student of Swedish government who has observed that the Swedish Constitution gives all basic authority to the central government. It is by custom and tradition as well as by legislation that the Swedish government is decentralized

[13] Gunnar Heckscher, *Staten och organisationerna* (Stockholm: K. F., 2nd ed., 1951), pp. 22–40.
[14] Dankwart A. Rustow, *The Politics of Compromise*, p. 123.

THE SOCIAL PROGRAMS OF SWEDEN

Administration in Swedish government is based upon semi-independent boards. The departments are significant only in the areas of legislation and appropriations. Since the health and welfare programs, like all other activities of Swedish government, are managed by these governmental divisions, a closer look at the departments and the boards is indicated.

The Departments. There are eleven departments or ministries (the Swedish term is *Departement*) in Sweden: Foreign Affairs; Justice; Defense; Social Affairs; Communications; Finance; Education and Ecclesiastical Affairs; Agriculture; Commerce; Interior (Home Affairs); and Civil Service.

The departments are relatively small in size and each consists of no more than 50 to 100 persons, including the clerical staff. Their functions may be listed as follows: (1) preparing and presenting the proposed laws and budget requests to the Riksdag; (2) issuing basic regulations and general rules for the conduct of the administrative boards; (3) making or recommending the higher appointments in the administration; and (4) receiving and acting on certain appeals from individuals which, according to tradition, are addressed to the king. With the exception of the appeal procedure the departments are not concerned with the details of administration. However, the development of regulations, policies, and procedures by the administrative boards concerning the implementation of legislation or rules may be brought to the departments for consideration and action. The ministers of the departments are often made responsible politically for decisions taken by the semi-independent boards. Frequently a minister does not hesitate to express his opinion as to whether the actions taken by the administrative board are in accordance with the law or the general rules issued by the department.

The Cabinet is composed of the heads of the departments. The 1963 Social Democratic Cabinet included one minister "without portfolio" who inaugurated a program of various kinds of technical assistance for underdeveloped countries. The Cabinet also includes two legal consultants who have the same rank as the department heads and meet with the Cabinet. The members of the Cabinet are selected by the prime minister who is chosen in the following manner: The king requests the leader of the party receiving the greatest vote in the election to serve as prime minister and to form a government. In cases in which one party does not have a clear majority, the speakers of the two houses and the leaders of the political parties will meet with the king and, in fact, make this selection in the king's name. Neither the appointment of the prime minister nor the appointment of the Cabinet members requires formal approval or ratification by the Riksdag as comparable positions would require Senate confirmation in the United States. Cabinet members are usually members of the Riksdag and retain their seats and voting rights while serving as heads of their departments. Even if they are not members of the Riksdag all ministers have the legal right to address both houses of the Riksdag.

The 1963 Riksdag passed a law that changed the functions of the minister of interior and the minister of social affairs. Activities in the field of health, formerly carried out by the Department of Interior, were transferred to the Department of Social Affairs. Activities in labor and housing, formerly assigned to the Department of Social Affairs, were transferred to the Department of Interior. Justification for this change was very similar to that for creation of the Department of Health, Education, and Welfare in the United States; namely, the need to have a close working relationship of officials in health and welfare in the development of legislative proposals and program administration.

The Cabinet as a whole is known as *Regeringen* or *Kunglig Majestat*, the Royal Majesty, and is responsible for all government decisions. Actually, a number of routine matters are decided by individual ministers and only formally confirmed by the total government. However, the principle of collective responsibility is reflected throughout government activity in Sweden.[15] Hundreds of decisions may be taken by the king-in-council, meetings in the Royal Palace presided over by the king and attended by the ministers. This is the top executive agency in Sweden. Individual ministers, before the meetings, make courtesy calls to inform the king of the decisions which are of major importance or in which he has indicated an interest. All important government decisions are subject to discussion by the Cabinet as a whole, and plenary Cabinet meetings under the chairmanship of the prime minister are held usually one to three times a week. These meetings take place behind closed doors and no minutes or reports of these sessions are made public. Cabinet members frequently lunch together at their private restaurant in the Chancery Building where no other guests are admitted, and a great

---

[15] Ernst Michanek, *Swedish Government in Action*, p. 12.

number of decisions are made informally at these luncheons. Also, some matters are referred to the ministers concerned, who make whatever decision they deem best without taking up the time of the entire Cabinet.

As indicated above, it is the Department of Social Affairs which now carries responsibilities in the field of health. Thus, this department is of great interest here. However, some attention to the Department of Interior is necessary since activities in labor and housing have been transferred to it, and the Department of Civil Service will be discussed in the section concerning public administration.

The Department of Social Affairs is one of the earliest departments in the Swedish national government. In 1947 this department was adjudged too large and the Department of Interior was created and took over responsibility for the civil defense, police, fire, public health, and local government affairs. The Department of Social Affairs retained activities related to labor, the large insurance systems, housing, old-age care, children's care, and the alcoholism program.

The Department of Social Affairs is organized into six major divisions: (1) Budget; (2) Legislative Drafting; (3) Public Health; (4) Social Insurance and Workers' Protection; (5) Social Care Activities; and (6) International Relations. All of the branches of the department are required to work closely together. For example, a program of the division of social insurance is likely to have budgetary implications, may require legislative action, or may affect international relations. This coordination of activities is directed by an undersecretary who is called the *Statssekreterare*, translated as secretary of state. The permanent legal secretary of the department, known as an *Expeditionschef*, directly supervises the legal activities of divisions 3 to 5 above and serves as legal adviser to all of them.

In contrast to the United States, and in conformity with the practice generally followed in England, the secretaries and undersecretaries of each department are usually the only political appointees. Even they do not participate actively in party questions or political debate and they are considered non-political officials. Occasionally an undersecretary may be a member of Parliament. If he is not, he is not entitled to speak in Parliament but there is a special listener's seat for him in both houses at the side of the Cabinet bench. The undersecretary represents the department and its minister and he is often named as the chief Swedish delegate to international conferences. A change of the party in office occasions very few changes among the major officials of the department. However, some of the undersecretaries of state are expected to resign and a few political experts who are employed by the departments for indefinite terms of office usually leave. But most of the employees are civil servants and, while they are perfectly free to take part in political activity and to hold political office, their status does not change with the change in political party in power.

The Semi-Independent Boards. The actual administration of central government activities is conducted by a number of central administrative boards known as *Centrala Ambetsverk*. The concept of administration by boards is very old in Swedish government and records have been found which indicate they existed as early as 1634. The Swedish tradition of independent administrative boards is a significant one in the administrative process.

Each board is headed by a director general appointed, for a period of six years, on the recommendation of the minister of the department concerned. Occasionally the director general is chosen on the basis of political activity. The board consists of the director general as chairman and a number of senior officials, appointed by the minister of the department, who serve immediately under the chairman. In addition, laymen representing organizations or sections of the population having special interest in the board are included as members. For example, on the Social Insurance Board, workers and employers as well as owners of small enterprises and farms are included.

The boards meet each week to decide policy in a plenary session. Although the director general has a significant voice in the discussions, it is customary for the bureau heads to vote on the policy to be adopted and the director general in the final action has only one vote. The director general of each board reports only once a year to the minister of the appropriate department. This is done in the process of presenting the budget request for funds for the ensuing year. The review and approval of the proposed budget does give the minister of each department some voice in the over-all policies of each board. However, the committees of the Riksdag call upon the director general to support and defend his budget during their consideration of his request. Thus, the national boards have at least semi-independent status.

The staffs carrying on the day-to-day administrative or specialized activities of the boards are appointed by the board itself. The individual boards cooperate with each other directly and do not go through the departments. Even though the boards are independent in their administrative activities and in their development of rules and regulations within laws that are passed by the Riksdag, the central administrative boards are expected to submit proposals to the government concerning major policies they plan to follow. Boards also propose changes in laws and regulations. By use of the remiss system described above (see p. 99), the opinions of the boards are obtained separately from those of the departments on all matters of proposed legislation, and then presented to Parliament as an identifiable part of the government proposals.

The chief function of the administrative boards has been characterized as ". . . routine administrative work" including inspection and control of subordinate offices, local agencies, and officials.[16] To a certain extent the boards serve as administrative courts of appeal. The work of the boards overlaps that of the departments in some cases and proposals have been developed to consolidate the work of the boards with the departments. Many investigative activities that were formerly performed by the central administrative boards are now handled directly by the departments or by royal commissions established by the Riksdag or the king-in-council for this purpose.

Of particular pertinence to the subject of health and welfare in Sweden are the semi-independent boards of two departments — Social Affairs and Interior. Located within the Department of Social Affairs are the Social Welfare Board, the Social Insurance Board, the Labor Protection Board, and the National Mediation Board; within the Department of Interior are the Labor Market Board and the National Housing Board. The Social Welfare Board, the Social Insurance Board, and the National Medical Board directly administer the social benefit programs discussed in the preceding chapters. The Labor Protection Board, the National Housing Board, and several other boards administer closely related programs. The local, county, and province levels of government participate in the administration of these programs.

Local, County, and Province Government

The Stad and Kommun. The tradition of local government in Sweden has roots which may be traced back for more than a thousand years. As in the United States, the primary responsibility for the provision of

[16] Nils Andrén, *Government and Politics in the Nordic Countries*, p. 113.

services in the field of welfare and public health rests with the *local government*. There are many forms of local government but health and welfare functions are performed mainly by the large cities and the rural governments similar to counties in the United States.

The six largest cities in Sweden, known as *stad*, are Stockholm, Göteborg, Malmö, Norrköping, Hälsingborg, and Gävle. In these cities there is an elected city council and appointive administrative officials. The city council elects a chairman who serves in a position we ordinarily would think of in the United States as that of mayor. The population of the three largest cities in 1964 was as follows: Stockholm, 795,976; Göteborg, 414,466; and Malmö, 241,778. As in the United States, the major cities have developed mainly through the growth of suburban communities. For example, Stockholm has eighteen recognizable suburban communities, ranging in population from Stocksunds with 4,936 to Soln with 54,281. The total population of Stockholm with its suburbs is 1,160,094. Göteborg has thirteen suburbs and Malmö four.

Outside of the major cities, the organization of local government is parallel to the county government of the United States. The local districts called kommuns in Swedish correspond to a community, county, or local district.

The kommun areas were often too small to have enough financial resources to meet their responsibilities, especially in the fields of health and welfare. Until 1952 there were 3,000 kommuns. In the Reorganization Act of 1952, the Riksdag reduced the number of kommuns to 904 and the average population of each kommun was approximately 4,000. By 1964, the number of rural kommuns, known also as *landskommuner*, had been reduced to 777.[17] The kommun is under the direction of a rural council elected by the people in the district for a term of four years. Election is by political party rather than by person. The kommun council elects a chairman called the *kommunalborgmästare*. In contrast to the *borgmästare* of the cities, an official appointed by the king to serve as a major judge, the kommunalborgmästare serves in a capacity similar to that of a mayor in the United States. Kommuns have the right to levy income taxes and receive the revenue of a tax on real estate. They also obtain funds by charging fees for various services. Kommuns provide funds, regulations, and assistance in a number of areas including housing and supplements for housing; roads, sewage systems,

[17] *Statistical Abstract of Sweden* (1964), p. 4.

and water supplies; basic education; public assistance and child welfare. The kommuns represent an extremely important level of government in the administration of health and welfare activities in Sweden. In providing these services, they may originate their own programs but to be eligible for grants-in-aid from the central government, they are required to conform to central government policies and regulations. The pattern is somewhat similar to federal grant-in-aid programs in the United States. The activities of the kommun, particularly in the areas of health and welfare, have continued to increase and there is presently an effort to develop further consolidation along the lines of the unifications achieved in 1952. Such consolidation will serve to increase the efficiency of the kommuns.

Other units of local government include towns, *städer*; boroughs, *köpingar*; rural kommuns, *landskommuner*; towns or cities with limited legal authority, *municipal samhällen*; cooperating cities, *municipalblock*; and cooperating kommuns, *kommunblock*. The accompanying list shows the number of each of the local government jurisdictions in 1966.[18] In addition, there are many special districts established for specific purposes. For example, there are 119 police districts, 156 registration districts, 546 medical officer districts, and 13 social welfare districts.

Jurisdiction	*Number*
Cities, *stad*	6
Provinces, *lanskap*	25
Counties, *län* (including Stockholm)	25
Towns, *städer*	133
Boroughs, *köpingar*	95
Rural kommuns, *landskommuner*	767
Limited towns, *municipal samhällen*	14
Cooperating kommuns, *kommunblock*	282
County councils, *landsting*	25
Dioceses, *stiff*	13
Parishes, *församlingar*	2,568
Judicial districts, *domsagor*	115

The Landsting. The term landsting may be translated as county council. The County Council Law of 1862 provided that each län should elect a county council. The län was established as a major form of local government. The country was divided into twenty-four

[18] *Statistical Abstract of Sweden* (1966), p. 4.

län with an additional län for Stockholm. However, twenty-six landsting have been established since two of the län, one of which was the Stockholm län, were provided with two landsting each because of the large geographic area or population included.

Every four years, the citizens of each län elect approximately fifty *landstingmän* or county councilors. In October of each year, the members of the landsting meet to decide on the administrative program of the län for the year, the budget for the activities of the county government, and the taxes necessary to provide the funds for the services to be performed. "Between the council meetings the work is superintended by central administrative bodies and local boards and committees for the various institutions." [19] Historically, the län had the major responsibility for the construction and maintenance of hospitals and the raising of taxes for this purpose. This is still a responsibility of the län, but many additional important activities are also performed at the county level.

The work of the landsting is divided into six major areas: public health and medical care; education and training; social welfare; education and care of the feeble-minded; roads; and administration. If we use the Uppsala landsting as an example, forty councilors are elected by the 180,000 inhabitants of the län. In 1964, the budget of the Uppsala landsting amounted to $18,000,000 (90,000,000 kr.). The income tax for 1964 was set by the landsting as 6 kronor for every 100 kronor of net, taxable income.

By far the greatest amount of money and activity expended by the landsting is in the areas of public health and medical care. In 1964, 78 percent of the Uppsala landsting budget was spent for these purposes and specifically for the following activities: Treatment of diseases was provided through the general hospitals of the län, including the University Hospital at Uppsala, tuberculosis nursing homes, hospitals for contagious diseases, nursing homes for the chronically ill, nursing homes for the mentally ill, and convalescent homes. Non-institutional health and medical care was provided through the rural district medical officers and the district nursing service; preventive care for mothers and children was provided through maternal and child health clinics, midwives' services, and public dental clinics; general care was received through psychiatric clinics for the treatment of children and adoles-

[19] *The Intellectual Face of Sweden* (Uppsala: Ergo International, 1964), p. 8.

cents, clinics for the treatment of hearing and speech defects, ambulance service, public health education, and occupational therapy and rehabilitation.

Education and training expended 5 percent of the budget for such activities as folk high schools, an agricultural school, a school of rural economics, central vocational schools, nursing schools, scholarship grants for the regular schools, and financial aid for cultural and scientific work.

A separate item in the budget is provided for the education and care of the feeble-minded and 4 percent of the budget in 1964 was expended for special schools for the feeble-minded or retarded, occupational workshops, and nursing homes.

Three percent of the budget was spent for social welfare activities including children's homes, holiday homes, treatment of alcoholics, and the home nursing service.

Seven percent of the budget was expended for administrative expenses including fiscal administration. This item covers the costs of the council offices, council meetings, property management, and expenditures for capital construction.

Three percent of the budget was allotted to a miscellaneous category in the budget including agriculture and forestry activities, an advisory service for trade and industry, and grants for the maintenance of private roads.

The Länsstyrelse. Since many of the län do not have the financial base to raise sufficient taxes to carry out the programs desired by the landsting, grants-in-aid, known as subsidies, are provided by the central government for certain of these functions and administered through central government offices known as länsstyrelse.

The länsstyrelse and the landsting constitute the two main patterns of decentralized structure in public administration in Sweden. Twenty-five länsstyrelse, one for each län, administer many central government activities which otherwise would be regulated from Stockholm. The länsstyrelse are somewhat comparable to the regional offices used by the federal departments and agencies in the United States, with the significant difference that most of the central government activities in a particular län are under the jurisdiction of the one office, while in the United States each department or agency administers its programs through a separate field organization each with its own set of regional or district offices.[20]

Each länsstyrelse is under the direction of a governor known as a *landshovding*. This is a significant and highly respected post in Swedish government. The landshovding is appointed by the king-in-council and is generally under the aegis of the Department of Interior. The landshovding represents the central government in the conduct of government programs in each län and has a wide variety of responsibilities ranging from the calling of elections and custody of ballots to the administration of the highest police authority in each area. His responsibilities have been summarized as follows: ". . . watching and promoting the interests of the county. [He must] . . . supervise and oversee local bodies in the exercise of local self government duties under the law, and receive and examine appeals against the rulings of local bodies or subordinate officials in the county governments. In other words, [the landshovdings] serve also as administrative courts of appeal." [21]

The landshovding office administers the central government programs by providing grants-in-aid or subsidies for health and welfare programs, hospital construction, building and maintenance of major roads, water supply, sewage disposal, and civil defense. It also supervises the maintenance of national standards for the grant-in-aid programs. The landshovding is assisted by a staff of specialists who serve under his direction, including a first medical officer in charge of public health activities, a director of veterinary service, a director of sanitary hygiene, an architect to review housing plans, social welfare and child welfare representatives, engineers, and construction specialists. The landshovding selects the heads of the two major divisions, the administrative branch and the fiscal branch, and with their assistance appoints the staff of specialists.

As indicated above, both the länsstyrelse and the landsting conduct programs in the fields of public health, hospitals, welfare, education, and roads. Consequently, a major problem in coordination of governmental activities exists in day-to-day administration, and some conflicts

---

[20] The disparate nature of the federal field organization in the United States, with the obvious need for greater coordination of federal programs, has resulted in the creation of federal executive boards in fourteen centers of concentration of federal regional and field offices. See Albert H. Rosenthal, *Regional Coordination: The Role of Federal Executive Boards* (Washington, D.C.: American Society for Public Administration, 1963).

[21] Nils Andrén, *Modern Swedish Government*, p. 122.

occur in the same field between the specialists representing the central government and those representing the county government. Another problem of coordination results from the use of separate regional or field offices by the semi-independent administrative boards in areas such as social welfare, social insurance, education, highways, waterways, and public health. In part, this problem is met by the appointment of the landshovding to membership in, or chairmanship of, the special board operating in the area under his general jurisdiction. However, the coordination of the many and varied activities of the central government operating in the field remains an issue calling for further attention in Sweden as in the United States.

The activities of the central government have increased greatly in recent years. This has multiplied the workload of the länsstyrelse particularly in grant-aided programs. As a leading Swedish political scientist has written: "The expansion of the state [national or central government] activities is a characteristic of all modern societies. Practically everywhere the expansion has increased the work of the central administrative authorities, obviously so when the state has taken direct responsibility for a new activity, but to a considerable extent also when the state supports local bodies or private organizations, for support means control and both mean additional work." [22]

As in the United States, local governments criticize the extension of the central government in Sweden. "Central authorities are often overburdened and local authorities are irritated because of the concentration of power in the center. They think that sufficient advantage is not taken of their competence and that matters are handled much more slowly than is necessary." [23] Swedish political scientists are concerned with the issue of decentralization for the same reasons that this subject is under discussion in public administration in the United States. The following question and answer appear to be internationally applicable: "But is it central expert knowledge and uniformity or the local expert knowledge of the matter that should be given precedence? . . . The deciding factor must, however, remain which method of decision is the most rational in every single instance, i.e., the one that gives tolerably good treatment at the lowest expense for the taxpayer." [24]

As indicated earlier, the basic problems of public administration are

[22] *Ibid.*, p. 123.
[23] *Ibid.*
[24] *Ibid.*, p. 125.

much the same in Sweden as in the United States and elsewhere. Two major issues are currently receiving a great deal of attention. The first is related to the inability of local governments to finance the constantly expanding need for additional government services. This is met in Sweden, as in the United States, by grant-in-aid programs financed by the central government utilizing the nationwide tax base. The second area of difficulty arises from the expanding nature of many problems which cut across the jurisdictions of local governments. These include such emerging fields of governmental activity as air and water pollution, roads, zoning, and the like. In the rural areas, efforts to obtain cooperation between kommuns have resulted in the establishment of kommunblocks. In the urban areas, efforts to establish units that would be comparable to metropolitan governments in the United States have been made by creation of municipalblocks. This level of government has been necessary particularly when large numbers of suburban communities are grouped around major cities. The municipalblock is utilized more and more to meet local government responsibilities in such areas as water, sewage, air pollution, schools, and roads.

While the term public administration is rarely heard in Sweden, the activities and concepts it connotes are applied actively throughout many of the government activities in Sweden. The citizens of Sweden are very conscious of the administrative activities at all levels of government, newspapers and journals give extensive coverage of current actions by public agencies, and the officials and employees of the government agencies are afforded status and respect appropriate to those performing an important, even essential, activity.[25]

Civil Service

All positions in the central government, whether located in the government headquarters in Stockholm or as part of the länsstyrelse, are under civil service. The Swedish civil service has three major characteristics: high educational level, tenure, and prestige.

All those selected for the civil service must have a rather extensive education. No formal or written examination system is used, but the requirements call for the completion of a degree comparable to a bachelor's degree in the United States. Almost every civil servant has an aca-

[25] Ernst Michanek describes the dynamics of Swedish government in his *Swedish Government in Action.*

demic degree or its equivalent. "The training of the 'administrative' civil servants is almost without exception an academic degree or similar preparation. The tendency is, however, to avoid any formal requirements of this type. For general administration, a legal training has on the whole always been preferred. It is sometimes said that there is a domination of persons with a law degree, Bachelor of Law — 'Juris Kandidat,' in the administration." [26]

Most positions in the higher civil service in Sweden are filled by graduates of the universities in Stockholm, Uppsala, and Lund. A report in 1964 indicated that 59 percent of a sample of 100 law degree graduates were appointed to civil service positions. Thirty graduates obtained positions in the central government departments and agencies; 23 with the courts, the public prosecutor's office, or the police; and 6 with municipal governments. In recent years, the following degrees and training have been accepted in lieu of, or were preferable to, the Bachelor of Law degree for certain posts: Master of Politics, *politices magister*, Business Administration, *civil-ekonom*, and social work training, *socialinstitut*. All positions are filled on the basis of merit.

Civil service employees serve in one of four classifications: *extra*, *aspiranter*, *extra-ordinarie*, and *ordinarie*. Most civil servants are appointed to the status of aspiranter or extra-ordinarie. These positions are comparable to the probationary appointments in the civil service of the United States, although the classification of extra-ordinarie may also be used to indicate an assignment for a temporary period. After one or two years of satisfactory work these appointments are usually changed to ordinarie, or permanent status. The extra appointments consist of temporary and part-time jobs. In addition, there are posts called "positions of confidence" which may be used by ministers or heads of the boards for the appointment of their personal secretaries and assistants. These positions do not carry or lead to tenure and the incumbents may be dismissed at any time if they become unsuitable.[27]

Appointments and changes of status are made by each national board although, for the higher positions, the minister or undersecretary of the department may take part in or approve the decision. The Department of Civil Service does not participate directly in the employment process. However, it maintains all of the records of the employee and,

[26] Nils Andrén, *Modern Swedish Government*, p. 126.
[27] The Constitution of Sweden, *The Instrument of Government*, Article 36.

by postaudit, approves the selection made by the head of the department or semi-independent board on the basis of the academic background of the candidate. The same methods of recruitment and classification of status are used for the state business enterprises, and government-owned corporations, as for the regular departments and agencies.

The rules of tenure make arbitrary dismissal or dismissal for political purposes virtually impossible. The permanence of government appointments in Sweden deserves emphasis: "The security of tenure, which almost all civil servants enjoy, is an important feature. They are appointed for their life-time and can be removed before their retirement age only as a result of legal procedure due to breach of duty or criminal offense. This means that a civil servant can be held legally responsible for the way in which he holds his office before a court of law, rather than before his superior."[28]

Personnel hired without a royal letter of appointment, which accompanies selection to ordinarie status, may be dismissed at any time as long as notice is given. In cases in which employees have attained permanent status charges must be brought and the burden of proof is on the supervisor. Few dismissals have been made and then only in clear cases that an employee has been guilty of a major crime or gross negligence. The royal letters of appointment, *Kunglig fullmakt*, have been used in studies of tenure in civil service to illustrate the ultimate in job protection. According to the *Instrument of Government*, a public servant appointed by royal letter may not be dismissed or even transferred against his will (Article 26). He can, however, give up this right by accepting new salary provisions.

The Department of Civil Service had only 299 employees in 1964 and is not comparable in size, organization, or function to the Civil Service Commission of the United States. No standard, written specifications have been developed for positions. The job classification system in which the grade of a position is determined by the duties performed and is based largely on a position description rather than on the qualifications of the occupant, remains unique with the United States.

Statistics are available for employment in the Swedish civil service in 1963. Ordinarie status was held by 36.8 percent of all government employees; 34.8 percent held extra-ordinarie appointments; 18.3 per-

[28] Ernst Michanek, *Swedish Government in Action*, p. 10.

cent had aspiranter or extra posts; and 10.4 percent were classified as "other." [29] There were 250,943 government employees in Sweden. Of these, 165,583 were men and 85,360 were women.[30] Employment was divided as follows between the regular departments, including the administrative boards, and the state-owned business enterprises: 134,727 men and women were employed by the regular departments, and 116,216 by the state-owned businesses. Employment of men is nearly double that of women. Table 8 indicates employment by department, including their administrative boards, and the type of status held by employees. Table 9 gives figures for the employment of personnel in each of the state business enterprises and the relative status of employees.

Table 8. Civil Service Employee Status in 1963, by Department

Department	Ordinarie	Extra-Ordinarie	Aspiranter and Extra	Other	Total
Justice	1,622	1,714	2,349	68	5,753
Foreign Affairs	404	353	174	136	1,067
Defense	17,202	14,205	8,119	1,898	41,424
Social Affairs	7,557	6,208	9,284	305	23,354
Communications and Transportation	1,425	3,431	2,821	860	8,537
Finance	3,629	1,490	998	367	6,484
Education and Ecclesiastical Affairs	8,379	8,174	5,244	3,152	24,949
Agriculture	1,574	2,275	1,455	633	5,937
Commerce	275	499	488	277	1,539
Interior and Health	3,862	5,678	3,946	875	14,361
Civil Service	43	146	75	35	299
Staff of Riksdag	215	448	116	244	1,023

SOURCE: *Statistical Abstract of Sweden* (1964), p. 217.

Table 9. State Business Enterprise Employee Status in 1963, by Enterprise

Enterprise	Ordinarie	Extra-Ordinarie	Aspiranter and Extra	Other	Total
Post Office	11,530	6,548	5,907	14,833	38,618
Board of Telecommunications	7,299	12,056	2,894	1,186	23,435
State Railways	25,746	17,526	976	963	45,211
State Power Administration	90	4,666	422	232	5,410
State Forest Service	722	823	192	9	1,746
Other	34	1,284	399	79	1,796

SOURCE: *Statistical Abstract of Sweden* (1964), p. 217.

[29] *Statistical Abstract of Sweden* (1965), p. 217.
[30] *Ibid.*, p. 214.

THE GOVERNMENT AND THE INDIVIDUAL

Local government employees, because they are not directly under the Department of Civil Service and do not have the protection of that office, have developed organizations which seek to protect their interests. They belong to one of forty-two constituent unions of the *Landsorganisation*, the Swedish Federation of Trade Unions, or one of thirteen unions of the *Tjanstemannens centralorganisation*. A Swedish political scientist has written: "The rapidly increasing body of local government employees has also won a security by this means which is scarcely inferior to that of state civil servants."[31] Government employees may not strike, but they have the right to negotiate with the government at all levels, concerning the conditions of employment, promotion, and work, vacation periods, and, more recently, salaries.

Prestige is an important element in the obtaining of highly qualified employees for public employment in Sweden. The salaries of civil servants are not exceptionally high — they are described as "small but safe" — and several writers on this subject point out the traditional advantage of ". . . giving a certain social prestige" to those who hold positions in the civil service. However, the fact that Sweden has almost full employment has been a factor in improving salary level for civil servants.

Each position in civil service is given a number in the official scale of salaries. The salaries are regulated by a statute, the *General Salary Regulations of the State*, administered by the Department of Civil Service. There are automatic salary increments within an established scale.

The Swedish central government salary scale is composed of two tables: *Löneplan A* and *Löneplan B*. Löneplan A gives the monthly salaries in groups by geographic location for lower grade employees and Löneplan B for higher grade employees. The lower grade scale consists of thirty levels for each of three geographic locations. For the geographic location with the highest salaries, the scale ranges from $168 a month for those in salary class 1 to $760 a month for those in salary class 30. The scale of higher salaries consists of ten classes, ranging from $829 a month to $1,564 a month. Representative salaries taken from the Swedish and American civil service payment plans, show, as indicated in the following list, that salaries for public employees in Sweden are generally quite comparable at the lower grades, although lower than those in the United States at the higher grades.

[31] Nils Andrén, *Modern Swedish Government*, p. 127.

	Sweden	United States [32]
Lower Grades [33]		
Grade 1 (GS 1)	$ 168	$ 300
Grade 14 (GS 3)	328	355
Grade 20 (GS 6)	447	488
Grade 23 (GS 8)	552	589
Grade 30 (GS 11)	760	768
Higher Grades [34]		
Salary Class 1 (GS 12)	829	910
Salary Class 4 (GS 13)	959	1,072
Salary Class 6 (GS 14)	1,088	1,250
Salary Class 9 (GS 16)	1,409	1,672
Salary Class 10 (GS 18)	1,564	2,157

A rather complicated plan has been established for sick pay. In principle, the formula calls for the payment of an amount which consists of the daily salary, less a fixed amount, plus a sickness allowance. The amount deducted ranges from $2.80 per day (14 kr.) to $4 per day (20 kr.) depending upon the salary level of the employee. The sick pay allowance added ranges from approximately $2.40 (12 kr.) per day, which is paid from day 184 to day 733 of illness, to $4 per day, which is paid from day 4 to day 183.

The salary plan for government employees includes a provision for recompensing employees who are temporarily placed in a position of higher responsibility. A special table which is called *Vikariatsersättningar*, Additional Payment for Higher Temporary Assignments, provides for additional amounts to be paid, adjusted to the salary class of the employee, for the time periods he is on temporary assignment.

As in the United States, a per diem allowance is provided for employees while they are traveling. This plan also uses a graduated salary scale so that higher income employees are given a higher per diem to maintain their standard of living while traveling.

All public employees with some form of tenure also receive a service pension and a family pension. The service pension is about 65 percent of the annual average salary of the last five years of service.

Because of the differing government structures and classifications of

---

[32] U.S. Civil Service Commission, Classified Employees Salary Table, amended by P.L. 89-504, July 18, 1966.
[33] Salary Plan A, 1963, for Location 5.
[34] Salary Plan B, 1963.

what is or is not public employment, precise comparisons between the number of people employed by the government in Sweden and the number employed by the United States government are quite difficult to make. As indicated above, 250,943 men and women were employed in the Swedish central government service in 1963, with 1,023 employees of the Riksdag and 116,216 employees in the state business enterprises which are comparable to government corporations in the United States. The enterprises include the Post Office, the Telecommunications Board, the State Railways, the State Power Administration, and the State Forest Service. However, the Swedish statistics do not include the employees in the quasi-official occupations such as clergymen, teachers of primary and infant grades, policemen, and members of the county agricultural committees and regional forestry boards, who are also considered public employees in Sweden. In 1961, 63,468 people were employed by the Swedish government in these categories.

Comparison of 250,000 central government employees to the total employment in Sweden of 3,244,084 provides a ratio of 73 per 1,000. In the United States there are 2,358,000 federal government employees of a total employment of 68,809,000, or a ratio of 34 per 1,000.[35] Superficially, it would appear that Sweden has twice as many central government employees as the United States. However, this comparison is highly questionable, not only because of the differing definitions of public employment but also because employees of the central government in Sweden perform many duties through the länsstyrelse offices, duties that are performed by state governments in the United States.

Citizen Controls of Government

An administrative system that includes permanent tenure for civil servants is faced with the problem of control over, and the responsiveness of, the civil servants. This is particularly true in a democracy. In Sweden, this issue is brought into even sharper focus because of the relative independence of the national boards which head the administrative structure for most activities of the central government.

There are at least five major ways in which extensive control is exercised over the work of the civil servant or public official in Sweden: (1) review and discipline by superiors; (2) an intensive finance au-

[35] *Employment and Earnings*, Bulletin of the Bureau of Labor Statistics, Department of Labor, p. 2.

dit; (3) an efficiency audit; (4) the right of appeal of Swedish citizens in relation to all actions by public agencies; and (5) the operation of the office known as the *Ombudsman.*

The disciplinary control and review of the work of individual civil servants is very much the same in Sweden as in the United States and in Great Britain. The head of a particular office, branch, section, division, or unit supervises the individual civil servant to see that he performs his activities in accordance with the stated laws, rules, regulations, and policies. As in the United States, if a supervisor has complaints concerning discourtesy or illegal action by one of his employees, an official warning is given first and, under the Swedish civil service rules, the employee may be suspended from work and salary for a limited period. If there is a graver offense or an alleged criminal action, the agency will take an employee into a court of justice.

Swedish law places a penal responsibility upon higher administration officials. "The law prescribes that if a judge or civil servant out of neglect, ignorance, or want of skill, disregards what is incumbent upon him in conformity with law, instructions, or the nature of his office, he shall by court be condemned to a fine or to suspension. This wide area of penal responsibility, combined with the obligation to compensate for damage caused by an error, has restrained the officials from submitting to any undue interference or to neglect the rights of the citizens."[36] The regular courts of law are used for this procedure rather than the administrative tribunals. The administrative tribunals consider questions of law and fact in the decisions made by administrative agencies rather than the conduct of the officials themselves.

A further protection afforded the Swedish citizen against the abuse of authority by officials is provided by the office known as the *justitiekansler,* or chancellor of justice (known in Sweden as the JK). This office, comparable with that of the Attorney General in the United States, was established in the Constitution of 1809, paragraph 27, but has its roots in the creation of an office with the same name in 1719. The Constitution states the duties of the office and the qualifications of the officeholder. He occupies the Principal Law Office of the king, repre-

[36] Statement by Alfred Bexelius, Ombudsman of Sweden, in *Hearing before the Subcommittee on Administrative Practice and Procedure of the Committee on the Judiciary,* United States Senate, March 7, 1966 (Washington, D.C.: U.S. Government Printing Office, 1966), p. 13.

sents the crown in legal cases, supervises the administration of justice, and takes action against officials or judges in cases of dereliction of duty.

The justitiekansler's duties have been specifically stated in an Instruction issued by the king-in-council in 1947. They are classified into four fields of jurisdiction: to act as the principal legal adviser of the government; to represent the government in cases affecting the state's interest; to supervise on behalf of the crown all public servants and to take action in case of abuse; and to carry out specific duties to accomplish these responsibilities.[37] In some ways, the justitiekansler performs duties quite similar to those of the ombudsman, described below. "Ever since the JK's office came into existence, the supervision of public servants has had the leading role among the various functions of the office. This particular function is performed in a manner and form corresponding to the Ombudsman's equivalent functions. . . ."[38]

A further control of administrative officials and agencies is the periodic audit of all financial actions. This is conducted regularly by the Public Accounting Office for Civil Administration, a special audit department of the Department of Defense, and the auditing staffs of each department and board. These reviews seek to ensure the appropriate expenditure of all public funds.

There is also what might be called an efficiency audit, although the term itself is not generally used. This review of the work of central government offices is performed by the auditors of the Riksdag, who have a function similar to that of the General Accounting Office of the United States. The Office of the Paymaster General, *Statskontoret*, also performs an efficiency audit, particularly concerning the preparation of payrolls. The reports of the paymaster general frequently include recommendations for greater economy, especially in the number of employees required to administer a new or changed function.

The semi-independent administrative boards are audited by an agency called the High Auditors, *Överrevisorer*. There is a permanent commission for efficiency audit and administrative supervision, which is known as the *Statens Sakrevision*. The purpose of this agency is to ensure that full value is received and that bids are called for, in all purchases, by government agencies. There is also a government office

[37] Sten Rudholm, "The Chancellor of Justice," in Donald C. Rowat, *The Ombudsman*, pp. 18, 19.
[38] *Ibid.*, p. 19.

similar to an organization and methods office, in Swedish the *statens organisationsnamnd*.[39]

The right of the citizen to appeal to higher authority or to special administrative courts is a striking characteristic of the Swedish system of public administration and permeates every level and phase of the administrative programs in Sweden. Where an appeal is submitted depends largely upon the subject matter. If it is a question of the appropriateness or equity of a decision, it may ultimately go to the king-in-council. A question about the legality of a decision may go finally to the Supreme Administrative Court. On matters involving money, appeals may be made to the finance court, called the *kammarrätten*. Major matters, involving legal questions, are submitted to the Supreme Administrative Court known as the *regeringsrätten*. The right of appeal is very frequently used and ". . . the Swedish appeal system enjoys the confidence of the general public."[40]

As discussed in the preceding pages, the Swedish citizen is not confronted with a monolithic government. The decentralization of government, both at the national level and throughout the country, has been achieved by the widespread use of the semi-independent administrative boards, the local authority of the landsting, and the decentralized operation of the länsstyrelse. In addition, administrative control is afforded by recourse to supervisors in each administrative agency, by financial and efficiency audits of all activities, and by an extensive system of appeals to the administrative system and to the courts.

The Ombudsman. Throughout the world a great deal of attention is currently being given to the Swedish office called the ombudsman. This interest is not simply in an additional service provided by the Swedish government but, more significantly, in the Swedish approach to meeting the problems developing from the increasing size, authority, relative independence, and possible unresponsiveness of government today.

Democratic constitutional systems are premised on the principle of ultimate control over government by the people. A system of periodic elections affords opportunity for the expression of popular will in the legislative area; presidential elections give the electorate the same type of control over the top executive. However, the administrative area,

---

[39] Nils Andrén, *Modern Swedish Government*, p. 131.

[40] *Ibid.*, p. 132. See also Brian Chapman, *The Profession of Government: Public Service in Europe*, p. 245.

THE GOVERNMENT AND THE INDIVIDUAL

with its increasing authority over, and impact on, the individual, includes no comparable system of control. The problem is intensified by the security of tenure and the independence of the administrative agencies.

The present ombudsman has described the need which his office seeks to meet: "During the last few decades, the development of society has made it necessary to extend the activity of the Government to new fields. To an ever increasing extent, society has been forced to interfere in a regulating manner in activities in which previously the citizens might engage unrestrictedly. The citizens have become increasingly dependent on public agencies. The need for a body independent of the bureaucracy for controlling the growing administration has therefore become more and more evident."[41]

Consequently, the eyes of political scientists and of many thoughtful citizens throughout the world have turned to the Swedish office of the ombudsman and the concept which produced it. Similar offices, but with variations, have been created in Denmark, Finland, Norway, and West Germany. New Zealand established a Parliamentary Commissioner in 1962.[42] Great Britain has adopted and is in the process of installing a similar office, with the same name, in the British administrative system. In Israel the function is performed by the state controller. Perhaps the world's newest ombudsman is in Tanzania where a Permanent Commission of Enquiry was created in October 1965 with the stated objective ". . . to safeguard human dignity, freedom and rights."[43] The Swedish title of ombudsman has been adopted in many countries where a similar office has been established.

What is the ombudsman? ". . . The *Ombudsman* is a law officer, appointed by a national parliament for the task of supervising the activities of certain categories of public service and of public authorities. His main concern is with the rights and liberties of citizens. The supervision of the activities under his control has, on the whole, the observance of the laws as its primary objective, not the general suitability

[41] Statement by Alfred Bexelius, Ombudsman of Sweden, in *Hearing before the Subcommittee on Administrative Practice and Procedure of the Committee on the Judiciary*, United States Senate, March 7, 1966, p. 17.
[42] An excellent review of ombudsmen in several countries is available in Donald C. Rowat, *The Ombudsman*, and in Walter Gellhorn, *Ombudsmen and Others*.
[43] Winston Makamba, "Tanzania's Own Ombudsman — An Answer to Critics," *Tanzania Sunday News*, June 26, 1966, p. 4.

of decisions."[44] A recent official Swedish document states: "The Ombudsmen are the watchdogs of the Riksdag over the civil service." (*The Swedish Budget, 1967/68,* p. 16.)

The word ombudsman means in Swedish simply "one who represents someone." It is used quite frequently in many aspects of Swedish life. It may refer to an elected member of the Riksdag or to the representative of special organizations, such as trade unions and political parties. It is used in labor organization like the term "shop steward" in the United States — an ombudsman will call upon an employee to point out that certain practices are not in accordance with an agreement. It is used also in local government and in semi-public organizations to refer to the official who watches over the legal interests of a particular public authority.

The concept and position of the ombudsman, as it operates in the administrative system of Sweden today, was established by a Swedish constitutional document, the *Instrument of Government* of 1809. The Instrument was amended in 1915 to establish an ombudsman for military affairs, the *Militieombudsman*. This divided the functions of the office as it had been initially established and the ombudsman was no longer responsible for *all* government affairs. Article 96 of the revised Instrument stated that ". . . the Riksdag shall appoint two citizens of known legal ability and outstanding integrity, the one as *Ombudsman for Civil Affairs* and the other as *Ombudsman for Military Affairs,* to supervise the observance of the laws and statutes in the capacity of representatives of the Riksdag, according to instructions issued by the Riksdag . . . The *Ombudsman* of Civil Affairs should supervise the observance of laws and statutes as apply to all other matters (except the Military) by the courts and by public officials and employees." The full name of the ombudsman is *Justitieombudsman.* Since most titles are abbreviated or given a nickname, throughout Sweden the justitieombudsman is known as the "J.O." and his counterpart for military affairs is known as the "M.O." According to the Riksdag Act of 1866, the ombudsman and his deputies are appointed for a period of four years by a committee of 48 members chosen from the Riksdag. The committee members are equally divided among the two chambers.

[44] Nils Andrén, "The Swedish Ombudsman," *Anglo-Swedish Review,* p. 3. Professor Andrén provides a detailed outline of the development of the concept of the ombudsman in Sweden and many examples of its operation.

THE GOVERNMENT AND THE INDIVIDUAL

In brief, the Swedish ombudsman is charged with the responsibility of receiving and hearing citizen complaints and of instituting proceedings before the appropriate court against any public official or employee who, in the execution of his official duties, has been found to have acted illegally or has failed to perform his duties in an appropriate manner. This may include what would be called nonfeasance or malfeasance in office by an administrative or elected official in the United States. The Swedish ombudsman is required to follow the same legal procedure as prescribed for all public prosecutors in both civil and criminal courts and follows the same rules of legal procedure in the courts.

A question frequently asked is "Why is the ombudsman necessary when the Swedish citizen himself has the right to appeal to the courts or to higher executive officials?" The Swedish historian Alexanderson has stated the essential value of the office in comparison with use of other legally established appeals: "This [ombudsman] is also an expression of the idea that the private citizen would, with greater confidence and frankness, dare to present his legal worries if he could turn to a guardian of the rights and liberties of the individual, appointed by the popular representatives and outside the bureaucracy, than if he had to go to a high officer appointed by the crown." [45]

An article appearing in the *American-Swedish Monthly* is significantly entitled "But the *Ombudsman* Thought Otherwise." [46] The author describes how a student editor appealed to the ombudsman because he had been punished with a low mark for a story appearing in the student newspaper that the faculty did not approve of. The ombudsman investigated the matter and ruled that the laws which guarantee freedom of the press in Sweden apply to all publications, even to a school publication, and therefore the student was not required to clear the story in advance. The ombudsman wrote a letter rebuking the faculty for infringing upon Sweden's freedom of the press laws and requested that the grade of the student be reconsidered. Because of the status of the ombudsman, it was generally understood that the student's grade would be corrected to a more favorable one.

In practice, the ombudsman uses three sources of information, among other things, in performing his functions: (1) the receipt of complaints

[45] Nils Andrén, "The Swedish Ombudsman," *Anglo-Swedish Review*, p. 3.
[46] Karl Olof Bolang, "But the *Ombudsman* Thought Otherwise," *American-Swedish Monthly*, p. 22.

from citizens; (2) articles which appear in the public press or reports from organizations or groups concerning a problem in a governmental organization or activity; and (3) his personal attendance at any public deliberations or decisions, including the meetings of the Supreme Court and the Supreme Administrative Court.

The ombudsman may investigate complaints concerning officials at local, regional, or central levels of administration. He is empowered to request the assistance of all public officials in his investigation and he has access to all files and documents in the course of his inquiry. He may initiate the prosecution of any administrative official or judge, and he reports both to the Riksdag and to the king any deficiencies in existing legislation. He may use the techniques of warning officials or requesting corrective action, rather than prosecutions, if in his judgment this would be more appropriate in the light of the facts of a particular case.

The citizen does not need legal counsel or advice in filing a complaint with the ombudsman. All complaints are investigated, regardless of the form, as long as they are signed. Prompt preliminary consideration is given — often on the same day the complaint is received. About one-third of the complaints are dismissed without investigation, if it is found upon review by the ombudsman or his deputy that they are directed against the king, the Riksdag, or a private citizen and are thus outside his jurisdiction. If a complaint belongs to another office it is forwarded to the appropriate place. When a case is accepted for investigation, the ombudsman requests the official concerned to file an explanation promptly. In about one-half of the cases reviewed in 1960 — one-third of all cases filed — the explanation was deemed satisfactory. That is, the ombudsman found that under existing laws and regulations the official could not have acted otherwise. In some cases the law or regulation may not have been understood by the citizen concerned and when this occurred the citizen was notified that his complaint had been investigated but that no action could be taken. In the remaining one-third of the cases filed in 1960, the ombudsman continued his investigation and determined that action should be taken. Most of the cases were decided within 90 days from receipt of the complaint.

The ombudsman may be satisfied if corrective action is taken by the official concerned, or he may decide that the case calls for the filing of a prosecution. Warnings and reminders are more frequent than prosecutions. In 1960, of approximately 1,200 complaints received or cases reviewed, 8 court actions were filed and 271 corrections obtained by the ombudsman. Of these cases, 674 concerned actions of the law courts and 91 involved mental hospitals or authorities. Sixty percent of the work of the ombudsman is concerned with administrative matters. In 1960, prosecutions included such cases as these: a police officer who neglected official duties and insulted citizens; a judge who was cited for criticizing a legal representative of a client in a court case; a forest supervisor charged with receiving bribes; and a regional assessment official who had decided an assessment for a case in which he had previously been an interested party.

In 1964, 1,429 cases were received by the ombudsman. Of these, 1,239 were complaints from citizens, 179 were initiated as the result of investigations and inspections instituted by the ombudsman, and 11 resulted from items or information appearing in the press. Of these cases, 381 were dismissed without further action for such reasons as not coming within the authority of the ombudsman, misunderstanding of the law by the complainant, and similar reasons. The complainants withdrew 12 cases. After inquiry, 722 cases were dismissed. This disposed of 1,115 cases. Action by the ombudsman on the remaining cases resulted in 283 admonitions, 3 referrals to other authorities for action, 2 prosecutions, and 7 recommendations for new legislation or regulations. Eighty-three percent of the cases were disposed of within a period of six months after their receipt.

The cases reviewed by the ombudsman in 1964 included the following areas: the judiciary, public prosecutors, police, prisons, care of alcoholics, mental and other hospitals, state business enterprises, church authorities, child welfare, schools, tax authorities, central government agencies, and municipal administration.

In 1965, the Ombudsman opened the year with a workload of 1,859 cases. Of these, 1,217 were complaints submitted by private individuals, 190 were developed on the initiative of the Ombudsman, 5 were filed by the government or the Riksdag, and 447 had been pending from the previous year. No formal action was taken for 1,127 cases, 7 were transferred to other government agencies, 5 brought disciplinary actions, and in 3 cases formal statements were issued. Three cases resulted in prosecution in the courts, 7 in the formulation of proposals to the government, and over 400 formal admonitions or criticisms were issued to officials. At the end of the year 307 cases were pending. It is significant that there are few cases filed in relation to the total population. In 1965 Sweden had a population of approximately 7,800,000 and only 1,859 cases were considered—less than .02 percent of the population. (These figures are adapted from Table 322 in the *Statistical Abstract of Sweden*, 1966, p. 281.)

One of the greatest values of the ombudsman may be psychological—simply the fact that such an office exists and government officials are conscious of its existence. This office may be part of the reason the Swedish citizen has so much confidence in his government. The present ombudsman stresses the implicit contribution made by his office: "This provides a constant and healthy influence on the manner in which public servants exercise their duties."[47] The same point has recently been emphasized in a statement made in the United States: "In summing up the work of the Ombudsman's office for the advancement of security under the laws, it should perhaps first be emphasized that the office by its mere existence counteracts tendencies to transgressions of authority and abuse of power."[48]

In the United States, almost every administrative agency which makes decisions concerning the rights of the individual has an appeals system. All decisions concerning the social security benefits and other health and welfare benefits do provide for appellate procedures. In addition, the General Accounting Office provides a very close and careful review of expenditures, both for conformity to existing laws and for the use of proper procedure and intelligent judgment. Because the General Accounting Office reports directly to the Congress it, in one sense, may be considered parallel to the position of ombudsman in Sweden. However, there may still be a need for the establishment of an additional agency or office which would make it easy for the "man on the street" to file questions or complaints concerning the appropriateness of an action taken by a member of the bureaucracy at the federal, state, or local level. In the United States, constitutional considerations would require the establishment of an ombudsman for each level of government, since, for example, a federal ombudsman could not legally have jurisdiction over the actions of state officials.

There is currently a widespread interest in the establishment of such

[47] Nils Andrén, "The Swedish Office of the 'Ombudsman,'" *Municipal Review*, p. 821.

[48] *Hearing before the Subcommittee on Administrative Practice and Procedure of the Committee on the Judiciary*, United States Senate, March 7, 1966, p. 17.

an office in the United States. Bills for this purpose have been introduced in both houses of Congress and in several state legislatures. In 1963, Henry Reuss introduced a bill in the House of Representatives to provide for an administrative counsel of the Congress to recognize and help remedy a condition stated in the introduction of the bill: ". . . that the increasing complexity of the Federal Government has created difficulties on the part of private citizens in dealing with the government . . ."[49] In 1965, Senator Claiborne Pell introduced an identical bill in the Senate.[50] Senators Edward V. Long and Warren Magnuson have jointly introduced a bill to establish tax ombudsmen in each of the ten Internal Revenue Districts. With the title of small tax commissioners, the tax ombudsmen would represent taxpayers who, in Senator Long's words, ". . . are harassed, annoyed, threatened, and often must pay hundreds of dollars to a lawyer, not only to protect their constitutional rights, but also to explain the vast complexities in our tax laws."[51]

Several cities and some county governments have established information and complaint offices with attendant publicity indicating that these offices are similar to the ombudsman of Sweden. Most of these offices bear little resemblance to the ombudsman in that they have no authority independent of the administrative branch and are performing the functions of providing information and receiving complaints – a process quite customary in the normal routine of government or business in the United States. Consequently, the term ombudsman is used erroneously for most of these agencies, because they do not have the same standards of independence and authority to take disciplinary or corrective action characteristic of the Swedish position.

The newly established parliamentary commissioner in England and the legislation proposed by Congressman Reuss differ significantly from the Swedish ombudsman in the manner of channeling complaints and requests for action. In Sweden, the citizen deals directly with the ombudsman. In Congressman Reuss' proposal, the citizen would make his complaint to a congressman who may turn it over to the office of the administrative counsel. The British plan also involves a member of the House of Commons in dealing with the parliamentary commissioner.

[49] H.R. 7593, House of Representatives, 88th Congress, First Session, July 16, 1963, Section 2. Re-introduced as H.R. 4273 in the 89th Congress, First Session.

[50] S. 984, 89th Congress, First Session, February 3, 1965.

[51] " 'Ombudsman,' Citizen's Friend Comes to the U.S.," *The National Observer*, Vol. 5, No. 3 (June 6, 1966), p. 14.

These plans are open to the possibility of politically motivated action rather than the completely nonpolitical action of the Swedish system.

The case for the ombudsman in the United States has been eloquently stated by Congressman Reuss: ". . . I have been impressed by the job that is being done in behalf of the average citizen in his relations with the bureaucracy by the Scandinavian *Ombudsman*. This political innovation acts as an administrative Robin Goodfellow to see that the citizen obtains the individual rights from his government to which he is entitled." [52] Another favorable response is found in a paper, prepared for hearings before the Subcommittee on Standing Rules of the United States Senate, which recommends consideration of the ombudsman approach: "An essentially different approach to the problem of controlling the administrative machinery is practiced in Scandinavia, and the Swedish and Danish experiences seem particularly relevant to an appraisal of U.S. methods." [53]

However, there are those whose response is less favorable. A restrained view is provided in an article which states: "The establishment of the Ombudsman would aggravate this trend toward weakening of the presidency and diffusion of control." [54] The author adds that antagonism toward the executive would be intensified should the ombudsman be created as a creature of Congress. He suggests the use of this device at state and local levels instead of at the federal level, since states and local units would more closely approximate the size and scope of the Scandinavian countries where the institution developed.[55]

Despite these and other questions, the establishment of an ombudsman in the United States would afford a concept of protection for the citizen in relation to the bureaucracy. It could provide a step in the development of a sound public philosophy toward government, particularly in social fields. It would seem that the most important value of the concept is the citizen's knowledge that he is not helpless before the

---

[52] Henry S. Reuss, *Congressional Record*, 88th Congress, First Session, February 11, 1963, pp. 2193–2194. See also Clayton Fritchey, "Citizen Needs 'Shield' From Uncle Sam," *Minneapolis Tribune*, May 24, 1966, p. 5.

[53] *Hearings before the Subcommittee on Standing Rules of the Senate*, 88th Congress, First Session, June 27 and 28, 1963, paper by Professors Thomas J. Bennett and Q. L. Quade, pp. 114ff. See also Nils Andrén, *Modern Swedish Government*, p. 141, and Brian Chapman, *The Profession of Government: Public Service in Europe*, p. 241.

[54] Samuel Krislov, "A Restrained View," in Donald C. Rowat, *The Ombudsman*, p. 252.

[55] *Ibid.*, p. 254.

large, impersonal, and complicated administrative machinery which stands between him and the accomplishment of some of his purposes. Perhaps the psychological values alone involved in the existence of this office warrant careful consideration of the possibility of establishing a similar office in the United States.

The Tax System

A pattern of decentralization is followed in the collection of taxes as well as in the administration of government programs in Sweden. An official document of the Ministry of Finance summarizes the tax structure briefly: "The functional decentralization, that is a leading feature of public administration in Sweden, is a characteristic also of the tax administration. Thus, the Ministry of Finance has practically no day-to-day administrative functions in the field of taxation. Instead the executive work of tax administration lies with government agencies and special boards such as the Provincial Governor's Offices, *Länsstyrelsen*, the National Board of Excise, *Kontrollstyrelsen*, and the National Board of Customs, *Generaltullstyrelsen*. These bodies act independently within the limits laid down in the tax laws and in supplementary regulations and instructions issued by the Government." [56]

The concept of decentralization is further carried out in actual administration in that, particularly for income and capital taxes, administrative work is performed almost entirely at the level of the regional or province government. The 26 regional länsstyrelsen administer this program under the regional governors. Each regional governor's office has a department of finance headed by a tax superintendent. The tax superintendent serves in a position parallel to that of the district director of Internal Revenue Service in the United States. He periodically institutes tax audits, performed by accountants on sample cases, or investigates complaints in the geographic area of the län. Approximately 1,000 persons are employed on the staffs of the regional tax offices.

A further administrative device is the use of assessment districts, each with an assessment board, *taxeringsnämnd*. There are about 3,000 assessment districts in Sweden and each board is responsible for the assessments of 1,500 to 3,000 taxpayers. The chairman of each board is appointed by the regional governor. The board consists of from three to twelve members who are elected by the municipal councils of the

[56] *The Swedish Budget 1963–64*, p. 8.

municipalities included in the district. All members of the boards work without compensation and are appointed annually. The regional tax superintendent reviews the assessments made by the boards within each province, and may appeal any assessment to the Provincial Appeal Board, *Prövningsnämnd*. The taxpayer, if he is not satisfied with the assessment, may also appeal to the appeal board of the region in which he lives. Further appeal may be made to the national Court of Fiscal Appeal, kammarrätten, and, under certain conditions, final appeal may be made to the Supreme Administrative Court, *regeringsrätten*.

A National Tax Board, *riksskattenämnden*, was established in 1951 to coordinate the work of the assessment boards for uniform application of taxation in Sweden. The board has advisory and coordinating responsibilities, but does not directly supervise the work of the province and district tax agencies. In 1960, when a general sales tax was introduced, similar responsibility for it was assigned to the board. The board provides advisory determinations to forecast tax liabilities.

In addition, there are 120 tax offices located throughout Sweden to determine the tax to be levied on each taxpayer on the basis of the assessments made. The tax offices estimate the preliminary tax, which is the advance payment of income tax in the year in which the income is received. Employers withhold the preliminary tax, similar to the withholding tax in the United States, for their employees on the basis of tax tables provided by the tax offices. Self-employed people must arrange for their own prepayments of estimated tax.

The tax rates in Sweden are relatively high. Both local and national taxes are collected. Examples of total taxes for a married couple are illustrated in Table 10. The local government collects property and income taxes. The local income tax law authorizes Swedish local governments to tax individuals and corporations residing within their jurisdiction, as well as those who reside elsewhere but who own property or conduct a business within that jurisdiction. The local income tax is the major source of revenue for the local government. It is a proportional tax levied at a rate fixed by the local council for the ensuing year. In addition to the municipalities, cities, towns, church districts, and rural kommuns, the landsting governments are given taxing authority by the local tax law. The combined average rate of all local taxes for the whole of Sweden in 1963 was 15.47 percent of taxable income, that is, assessable income after standard deductions. The average tax rate for

THE GOVERNMENT AND THE INDIVIDUAL

Table 10. Examples of Total Taxes for a Married Couple

Income	Marginal Rate*	Total Tax†	Percentage of Net Income
$ 1,000 (5,000 kr.) ...	4	$ 36 (180 kr.)	3.6
1,200 (6,000)	26	82 (410)	6.8
1,400 (7,000)	26	134 (670)	9.5
1,600 (8,000)	26	186 (930)	11.6
1,800 (9,000)	26	238 (1,190)	13.2
2,000 (10,000)	26	290 (1,450)	14.5
2,400 (12,000)	26	390 (1,970)	16.2
3,000 (15,000)	26	550 (2,750)	18.3
3,600 (18,000)	24	706 (3,530)	19.6
4,000 (20,000)	32	804 (4,020)	21
5,000 (25,000)	41	1,136 (5,680)	22.7
6,000 (30,000)	47	1,554 (7,770)	25.9
7,000 (35,000)	47	2,026 (10,130)	28.9
8,000 (40,000)	47	2,500 (12,500)	31.2
9,000 (45,000)	52	3,008 (15,040)	33.4
10,000 (50,000)	52	3,522 (17,610)	35.2
12,000 (60,000)	56	4,616 (23,080)	38.4
15,000 (75,000)	56	6,290 (31,450)	41.9
20,000 (100,000)	61	9,324 (46,620)	46.2
30,000 (150,000)	65	15,642 (78,210)	52
40,000 (200,000)	70	22,340 (111,700)	55.8

SOURCE: *Sweden, Its Private Insurance and Social Security* (Stockholm: Association of Swedish Insurance Companies, 1963), p. 51.
*Percentage of income tax that is applied to highest part of income.
†Includes local and national taxes as well as Basic and Supplementary Pension fees. The health insurance premium is not considered a tax. The local tax is calculated at 15 percent since 15.4 was the national average in 1963.

municipalities was 11.09 percent, for church districts .80 percent, and for the county districts 5.05 percent.

The central government also has tax authority and receives its greatest revenue from the national income tax. The national income tax applies to all individual and legal entities residing in Sweden or, with a few exceptions, deriving income from sources in Sweden. The legal provisions for the computation of income, standard deductions, and allowances are almost identical for national and local income taxes. There is a basic deduction of $450 (2,250 kr.) for a single person and $900 (4,500 kr.) for a married couple. In addition, the local income tax paid for the previous year is deducted from the taxable income for the central government income tax. There is a maximum deduction of $400 (2,000 kr.) for a wife's earned income. As mentioned before, in 1948 tax deductions for children were replaced by a system of children's allowances which provide cash grants for every child under 16. An additional deduction of up to $900 (4,500 kr.) per year may be claimed on demonstrated grounds of continued illness, heavy family responsibilities, or other special burdens.

In addition to the national income tax, all citizens pay a tax called the Basic Pension premium. This is levied at the flat rate of 4 percent of taxable income up to $3,000 (15,000 kr.) per year before deductions of the basic allowances. Companies and most other corporate bodies pay tax at the flat rate of 40 percent of their taxable profits for that year. The winners of Swedish lotteries pay a flat rate of 30 percent of their winnings in lieu of the regular income tax for this amount.

There is no capital gains tax system in Sweden but there is what is called a capital tax, which is an annual levy on the net value of capital assets which exceed $16,000 (80,000 kr.) for each individual. Taxable capital assets include real estate, stocks, bonds, bank deposits, automobiles, and the like. This tax is set at the rate of .5 percent for the first $4,000 over $16,000 in capital assets, .8 percent of the next $10,000, and 1 percent of the next $10,000. The gains from the sale of real property are included as income, in both the central and local government income taxes, except that the amount of the tax on sales of real property varies with the length of time the property has been held. Real property owned for a period exceeding ten years is exempt from tax on gain resulting from the sale. A substantial inheritance tax also provides revenue for the central government. This tax is doubly progressive in that the rate increases both with the size of the inheritance and with the distance of the relationship between the deceased and the beneficiary.

A general sales tax or, as it is popularly called in Sweden, the turnover tax was established on January 1, 1960. This tax is levied on the sale of goods to consumers, but is also applied to the import of goods by consumers and the provision of certain services. Exports are excluded from the tax. This tax is normally collected at the retail level at the flat rate (since July 1965) of 9.1 percent on the transaction, including the tax. The 1967 Finance Bill proposes to raise the general sales tax to 10 percent of the value of the goods or services. Because the tax is included in the valuation, the tax rate would actually be 11.1 percent. Other sources of revenue include taxation on liquor, tobacco, motor vehicles, substantial special sales taxes on motor vehicles, taxes on energy consumption, and a relatively low set of customs duties.

Still other sources of income for the central government include the revenue from public enterprise funds which are the surpluses or profits primarily from the Board of Telecommunications and the State Power Board. Additional amounts are received from interest on government funds.

Both the Supplementary Pension plan and the health insurance program are considered self-supporting in that special premiums are paid by those covered for the benefits to be received. The Supplementary Pension program is wholly financed by contributions from employers, with self-employed persons paying their own contributions. During the initial period of operation of this program, additional amounts were collected to build up a reserve fund known as the National Pension Insurance Fund, *Allmanna pensionsfonden*. The fund actually consists of three distinct accounts each administered by a separate board: one for employee premiums paid by employers in large companies; one for employee premiums of small companies and the self-employed; and the third for premiums paid by public authorities and organizations. As of January 1961, the Supplementary Pension funds had in reserve $95.6 million (478 million kr.). In January 1963, the amounts in the reserve funds had grown to $590 million (2,950 million kr.). By January 1965 the amounts in the reserve funds were $1,300 million (6,500 million kr.). By January 1967, the pension funds had grown to $2,920 million (14,600 million kr.). These amounts are invested in bonds issued by mortgage companies, government bonds, and loans to local authorities. Investment in privately owned business is specifically prohibited. Under certain conditions a contributor may reborrow up to one-half of his contributions. The following tabulation, taken from p. 52 of *The Swedish Budget 1967/68*, shows, in millions of kronor, how the pension funds were invested as of December 1966.

Investment	Kronor	Percentage of Investment
Government bonds	1,211.3	8.3
Housing credits	6,599.2	45.2
Agriculture	474.6	3.2
Local authorities	1,963.5	13.5
Industry	3,350.3	22.9
Foreign bonds	59.0	.4
Loans to contributors	953.6	6.5
Total	14,611.5	100.0

THE SOCIAL PROGRAMS OF SWEDEN

The health insurance program, while supported by premiums collected from the insured, employers, and the government, is also supported indirectly by the local governments since these governments pay most of the cost of hospital care provided by the program.

For 1966, the distribution of sources of income for the health insurance program was approximately one-half from the premiums of the insured, one-third from the fees of employers, and one-fifth from central government subsidies, based on general taxation. The amounts received in 1966 included: premiums from the insured, 1,140 million kronor; fees from employers, 800 million kronor; and subsidies from the central government, 440 million kronor, for a total of 2,380 million kronor, the cost of the program for the year. (See *The Swedish Budget, 1967/68*, p. 52.) The health insurance program pays about 4 percent of the actual costs of hospitalization, the remaining 96 percent being paid by regional governments with central government subsidies.

In the Swedish central government budget for 1967–68, the proposed expenditures included the following: $1,060 million (5,300 million kr.) for Basic Pensions; $58 million (290 million kr.) for the Supplementary Pension; $476 million (2,380 million kr.) for the health insurance program; $519 million (2,595 million kr.) for general children's allowances; and $45 million (225 million kr.) for the housing allowances which are provided at the local level, on the basis of an income test, and reimbursed by the central government through subsidies to the local governments. This budget also provides for special subsidies of $160 million (800 million kr.) to underwrite the increased costs for the regional governments when they assumed responsibility for the mental hospitals.

This list [57] shows receipts from taxes and social security as percentages of gross national product for Sweden and the United States.

Receipts	Sweden	United States
Direct tax		
Corporations	2.5	4.3
Individuals	15.1	9.9
Indirect taxes	11.7	9.5
Social Security contributions	3.1	4.2
Total	32.4	28.9

[57] *The Swedish Budget, 1963–1964*, p. 7. See also *Taxation in Sweden*.

VII

Program Comparisons Sweden and the United States

"But you must give Truth its right, even if it
   is in bad company;
And you can hardly say too many harsh things
   about a Spirit of Age
Which, if it would have worked without a counter-
   balance, would have rooted
Man on the ground, and plundered the eternal,
   the treasures of his heart."

Esasis Tegner (1782–1846)

As INDICATED in the Preface, this study represents an endeavor to provide a relatively brief survey of the social programs of Sweden and of the philosophy, structure, and dynamics of the government through which they operate. Some American observers who have traveled briefly abroad return to their own country enthusiastically supporting adoption of one or more Swedish programs in the United States. No drastic or dramatic transplants are proposed here. The system of government in Sweden and the social programs of that country have developed from the traditions, interests, needs, resources, and, possibly, politics of that country. While the observer is struck by marked similarities between Sweden and the United States, in a democratic way of life, free enterprise, and a modern society, thoughtful reflection points up significant differences: in size of both land and population, homogeneity, traditions, and maturity of political institutions.

However, the advantages in considering Sweden as a "social laboratory" for study of issues and problems that are also of concern in the United States should not be overlooked. The social scientist should seek to ascertain specific areas and techniques in which progress has been made in other countries. One of the architects of Swedish social policy in its formative years, C. E. Strang, Minister of Social Affairs in 1952 when the book *Social Sweden* was published, stated in the Preface to that book: "Knowledge of measures taken by other nations and exchange of experiences in the important field of social reform is one of the most essential aspects of positive international collaboration."

Sweden is not a welfare heaven. There has been some misunderstanding about this in the United States and other countries, but Swedish leadership is frank and forthright on this point. Ernst Michanek, the former undersecretary of the Department of Social Affairs, who was highly instrumental in designing the recent expansion of the social security program, has written: "The preceding . . . may have given the impression that Sweden has solved the problems of old age. This is not true."[1] Again, this author writes: "We have not yet reached our goals. On the contrary, there are many things that cause us discontent — but a discontent that is constructive in nature."[2]

The administrators of the social insurance and welfare programs in Sweden are beset by the same problems confronting social planners in the United States. Charges of misuse of welfare funds, although based upon examples representing only a minute fraction of the total case loads, cause the same public criticism in Sweden as in the United States. Both countries are concerned about second-generation welfare recipients and are undertaking extensive programs of education and retraining to alleviate poverty that occurs in the affluent society of the United States and the full employment economy of Sweden. Juvenile delinquency, crime, alcoholism, desertion, divorce, illegitimacy, and similar social problems are of great concern today in both countries. "The fact remains that Sweden, despite her cradle-to-the-grave welfare programs, is racked by the same problems that confound other highly industrialized, urbanized societies."[3]

However, both Sweden and the United States have made great progress in the past thirty years in meeting the financial and health needs

[1] Ernst Michanek, *Old Age in Sweden*, p. 36.
[2] Ernst Michanek, *For and Against the Swedish Welfare State*, p. 44.
[3] John H. Stassen, "Serpents Spoil Sweden's Eden," *Minneapolis Star*, p. 13A.

of their citizens and, through the social security programs, in protecting against the social hazards of death of the breadwinner, disability, and retirement. Sweden, where older citizens constitute a higher percentage of the population, was concerned much earlier with the need to plan and provide adequate housing and a constructive life for older citizens. However, if the activities of not only the federal government but state and local governments and private organizations in the United States are taken into account, this country is not far behind. The care of children, highly emphasized in Sweden, is given equally great attention, although less publicity, in the United States through the extensive child health and welfare programs of the Children's Bureau working through state and local governments and supplemented by private organizations. Millions of needy citizens in the United States are helped through the large grant-in-aid programs of the federal government with aid to dependent children, to the blind, and to the permanently and totally disabled. However, actual administration of these programs rests with the state and local governments. These needs could not possibly be met through state and local financial resources alone.[4]

Amendments to the Social Security Act beginning in 1962 emphasize extended social services and the development of a positive approach toward welfare administration. Such concepts were adopted much earlier, and are still being developed, by the Swedish welfare programs. The social security program, with practically universal coverage, is an accepted institution in the United States. Current proposals call for a general increase in benefits. This, if adopted, could bring the United States system closer to the Swedish program, which ultimately will provide retirement benefits of almost 60 percent of previous annual earnings.[5]

The adoption of a health insurance program for people sixty-five years of age or older by the Social Security Amendments of 1965 represents a movement, however modest and limited, toward filling the largest single gap in the social programs of the United States in comparison with those of Sweden. An examination of the similar social programs in the two countries indicates a striking, and to some observers surprising, similarity in both stated objectives and accomplishments. A closer look, program by program, is provided in the following pages.

[4] Daniel Elazar, *The American Partnership*, p. 337.
[5] *Status of the Social Security Program and Recommendations for Its Improvement*, Report of the Advisory Council on Social Security, p. 10.

THE SOCIAL PROGRAMS OF SWEDEN

The Social Security Programs [6]

Until January 1963, the Swedish Basic Pension, with its identical block payments to all recipients, was more comparable to the state old-age assistance payments than it was to the United States social security program. The major difference was that the Basic Pension was paid to every person at age 67, regardless of income and need, while the old-age assistance payments were paid only after determination of need and with amounts that differed widely among the states, based upon that need. Currently, with the initiation of the Supplementary Pension program, the social security systems of Sweden and the United States, except for the benefit amounts, are practically identical. Both programs, providing retirement, disability, and survivor's benefits related to previous earnings, mitigate the financial problems of old age for most employed people. However, a problem remains in both countries with regard to the low-income or part-time worker whose previous earnings are so low that retirement, disability, or survivor's benefits are not large enough to provide minimum subsistence.

Coverage comparisons must recognize the dual nature of the Swedish program. Everyone is covered by the Basic Pension (see pp. 13–14). While the Supplementary Pension is also universal in coverage, the application of a minimum amount of earnings in crediting pension points limits the coverage of this program to about nine out of ten working people. The coverage ratio [7] of the Social Security program in the United States is approximately the same.

Both programs cover the self-employed. However, the Swedish program from the beginning made no exceptions in coverage in contrast to the exclusion of medical doctors in private practice from the social security program of the United States until the 1965 amendments. Full benefits are paid in the United States at age 65 and in Sweden at age 67. Both programs provide for earlier payments at reduced amounts, in Sweden four and in the United States three years before retirement. Both systems are based upon average earned income. The benefit structure in the United States is slightly more generous at present although

---

[6] A comparative summarized review of the major characteristics of the social security programs in Sweden and the United States as well as other countries is provided in a report of the Department of Health, Education, and Welfare, *Social Security Programs throughout the World.*

[7] *Your Social Security,* Department of Health, Education, and Welfare, p. 3.

SWEDEN AND THE UNITED STATES

the Swedish program will provide greater benefits after it is in full operation.

The Swedish Supplementary Pension is based upon an adjusted average of the highest fifteen years of a twenty-year period of earnings. The United States social security program uses a fifteen-year base with a "drop out" provision for exclusion of the lowest five years of earnings. The Swedish program uses a minimum of $960 per year with a maximum earnings of $7,200 per year for accumulation of pension credits, while the United States social security program uses a minimum of $200 per year, $50 per quarter, and a maximum of $6,600 effective in 1966. An increased payment in the United States system began in 1964, since the credit for earnings up to $4,800 started in 1949 and the maximum payment covers employment for a fifteen-year period. The full payment in the Swedish system will begin in 1981 when beneficiaries born in 1914 or later will have achieved the age of 67. The maximum payment in the United States based on maximum earnings of $6,600 will not be effective for retirement at full amounts until 1976, ten years after the effective date of 1966 (fifteen years less the "drop out" of the low five years). An outline of comparative benefits of the American social security and the Swedish Supplementary Pension is presented in the accompanying tabulation.

Comparative Benefits of the Two Pension Systems

Sweden	United States
Coverage	
Universal.	Almost universal.* Covers 90 percent of all gainfully employed.
No citizenship requirement.	No citizenship requirement.
Includes government employees who have own retirement system, which is coordinated with the Supplementary Pension system.	Excludes federal government employees who have own retirement system. State and local employees included by agreement.
Includes self-employed.	Includes self-employed.
Eligibility	
Based on 15 highest earning years of a 20-year earning period.	Based on year of birth and uses 15 years highest employment income with "drop out" of five lowest earning years after 1950.

THE SOCIAL PROGRAMS OF SWEDEN

Provisions

Reduced amounts permitted by 1/20 for each year not covered in installation of program. Pension credits require minimum of $800 to maximum of $7,050 per year.

Coverage must equal one quarter of social security tax paid for each year after 1950, or age 22 if later, to year of death or attainment of retirement age (62 for women, 65 for men) with a minimum of 6 quarters. Most benefits based on years after 1950, or age 22 if later, less 5 years, to year of death or year of attaining retirement age. Lower eligibility requirements for older population during installation of program. Benefit credits accrue for minimum of $50 per calendar quarter to maximum of $6,600 per year effective in 1966.

Restrictions

No earnings restrictions for full eligibility at age 67.

Retirement test requires substantial retirement from gainful employment from age 65 to age 72.

Age

For full benefits, 67 years; for reduced benefits, 63; for increased benefits, after 67.

For full benefits, 65 years, with application of retirement test. Reduced benefits at age 62.

Benefits

Retirement, disability, and survivor's benefits.
Ranges from $6.40 per month plus Basic Pension of $98.30 to $312 a month plus Basic Pension of $98.30 when plan is in full operation.

Retirement, disability, and survivor's benefits.
Ranges from retirement benefits of $44 per month at age 65 to $168 with maximum family payment of $368 per month effective in 1976.

Cost of Living Adjustment

Annually adjusted to cost-of-living index.

No adjustment but frequent revision of benefit schedule by Congress.

Wife's Benefit

Benefit provided by Basic Pension. No special provision under Supplementary Pension.

Additional amount of 1/2 husband's benefit provided for wife 65 years of age or older. Reduced benefit at age 62.

SWEDEN AND THE UNITED STATES

Widow's Benefit

Widow receives 40 percent of benefit if no children. Basic Pension provides additional payment of 90 percent of the base amount.

Widow under 62 will receive 3/4 of benefit amount if she has a child under 18.† Widow over 62 will receive 82 1/2 percent of benefit amount within maximum.

Children's Benefit

Covers children under 19. One survivor‡ receives 40 percent of pension, 2 survivors 50 percent, and 3 survivors 60 percent.

Covers unmarried children under 18.§ Increased by number of surviving children to family maximum. Each child, as a survivor, receives 3/4 of wage earner's benefit. Upon retirement child, like wife, receives 1/2 of benefit within maximum.

Burial Benefits

None.

Three times monthly benefit with maximum of $255.

---

* The Social Security Amendments of 1965 extended coverage to self-employed physicians of medicine and interns after December 31, 1965.
† Proposed amendment would provide reduced benefits at age 60.
‡ Under 19 years of age.
§ Proposed amendment would retain eligibility to age 22 if child is still in school.

Currently, the Supplementary Pension benefit in Sweden begins at $6.40 (32 kr.) per month for a pensioner born in 1896 whose average income was $2,000 per year compared with a recipient under the United States social security program who, at age 65 or later, will receive $84 per month on the basis of an average earned income of $2,400 a year. However, the Supplementary Pension in Sweden automatically includes the addition of the Basic Pension which in 1964 added $98.30 per month for a married couple and eligibility for the municipal housing allowance, based upon an income test.

The maximum payment under the Swedish Supplementary Pension program is $3,744 a year which together with the Basic Pension will provide a benefit of $4,924 per year for a pensioner and wife born in 1914 or later with average earnings of $7,200 per year or more. Under the United States social security program, the maximum payment in 1966 was $1,490.40 per year for a single pensioner at age 65 who had earned $4,200 per year or more. The maximum earnings creditable for social security in the United States are $3,600 for 1951–54; $4,200 for

1955–58; $4,800 for 1959–65; and $6,600 starting in 1966. Table 11 gives the range of benefits and examples of typical monthly cash benefit payments in the United States program. Table 12 provides comparative examples of benefit payments of the Swedish Supplementary and Basic Pension and the United States social security program.

Table 11. Examples of U.S. Social Security Monthly Payments, According to Average Earned Income after 1950

Example	$800 or less	$1,800	$3,600	$4,200	$4,800	$5,400	$6,600
Retirement at 65 with disability benefits	$44.00	$78.20	$112.40	$124.20	$135.90	$146.00	$168.00
Retirement at 63	38.20	67.80	97.50	107.70	117.80	126.60	145.60
Retirement at 62	35.20	62.60	90.00	99.40	108.80	116.80	134.40
Wife's benefit at 65 or with child in her care	22.00	39.10	56.20	62.10	68.00	73.00	84.00
Wife's benefit at 62	16.50	29.40	42.20	46.60	51.00	54.80	63.00
One child of retired or disabled worker	22.00	39.10	56.20	62.10	68.00	73.00	84.00
Widow 62 or over	44.00	64.60	92.80	102.50	112.20	120.50	138.60
Widow under 62 and 1 child	66.00	117.40	168.60	186.40	204.00	219.00	252.00
One surviving child	44.00	58.70	84.30	93.20	102.00	109.50	126.00
Two surviving children	66.00	117.40	168.60	186.40	204.00	219.00	252.00
Maximum family payment	66.00	120.00	240.00	280.80	309.20	328.00	368.00

SOURCE: *Your Social Security*, Social Security Administration, (Washington, D.C.: U.S. Government Printing Office, 1965), p. 21.

Several aspects of the Swedish pension programs deserve consideration for possible application to the social security program in the United States. The addition of cost-of-living adjustments, long an integral part of the Basic Pension and utilized also in the recently established Supplementary Pension in Sweden, would provide for the United States social security program an adjustment of benefits essential in an inflationary period. Some state pension programs in the United States include a cost-of-living adjustment in the administration of the old-age assistance program, and consideration is being given to the adjustment of benefit payments of the social security program in the United States. President Lyndon Johnson, in his State of the Union Message to Congress in 1967, recommended: "We should raise Social Security payments by an over-all average of 20 per cent — adding $4.1 billion to Social Security payments in the first year."[8] The present United States old-age and survivor's insurance program provides benefits related to dollar earnings at the time wages were earned rather than on the basis of the purchasing value of these amounts at the time benefits are paid. Automatic adjustment of future benefits, according to the price index, and rising or falling with the cost of living, is unquestionably a more equitable and

Table 12. Comparative Examples of Monthly Benefit Payments by the Swedish Supplementary and Basic Pension Programs and by U.S. Social Security, According to Average Annual Income after 1950

Income	Retirement*	Disability	Wife's Benefit	No. of Surviving Children under 18 One	Two
United States					
$1,800	$ 78.20	$ 78.20	$39.10	$ 58.70	$117.40
3,000	101.70	101.70	50.90	76.30	152.60
4,800	135.90	135.90	68.00	102.00	204.00
6,600	168.00	168.00	84.00	126.00	252.00
Sweden					
$2,000	72.20†	117.00	35.40‡	49.60§	83.20
3,000	80.60	168.40	. . .	70.20	108.80
5,000	97.20	270.60	. . .	111.20	160.00
7,000	109.60	367.20	. . .	149.80	208.00

* In United States at age 65; in Sweden at age 67.
† Data given are for an unmarried man, born in 1897.
‡ Income-tested; Supplementary Pension regarded as income.
§ Data given are for a child under 16; both parents dead.

desirable feature in an insurance program designed to provide financial protection for the future.

A second feature of the Swedish social security system that is applicable to the United States is the designation of an account number for each citizen. As indicated before (see pp. 19–20), the Swedish plan has an effective system of vital statistics. The simplicity of this system, where each person must remember only his birthdate plus one to four digits, means that almost everyone knows his social security number. The same number is used in Sweden for other related social programs. The completeness of the vital statistics program provides for current and automatic proof of the applicant's age. In the United States program, at the time of eligibility and filing his claim, the applicant must present proof

[8] Text of President Johnson's State of the Union Message, *Minneapolis Tribune*, January 11, 1967, p. 6.

of age, such as a birth certificate or other documents. In the administration of the Supplementary Pension in Sweden, this information is maintained in the basic file of each person. Although the applicant may be asked to submit additional evidence of age at the time of application, the task is greatly simplified.

The benefit formulas of social security in both countries are complicated, with the Swedish pension points plan being more complex. The simplification of these formulas would be desirable in both countries to enable citizens, with relative ease, to calculate their future benefits and the extent of protection for themselves and their families. While the social security program in the United States has been quite effective in providing a financial floor for the retirement of most citizens, and has been a model program administratively, there remains the problem of developing a systematic, long-range plan of adjusting benefits as provided in the Swedish program. Numerous proposals for increasing social security benefits are regularly introduced at each session of the Congress.

The Health Programs

The most significant difference in the social security programs is related to the extensive Swedish health insurance program. The adoption of a comparable program for the general population in the United States has been blocked because of the polarization of two groups: the government officials and the organized medical profession.

No one argues against the need and value of health insurance as a means of meeting the hazards of illness, particularly chronic illness.[9] The issue has been resolved almost entirely except for the role government should play in the provision of this insurance. The Swedish experience, in which the large public health insurance program was based upon traditional institutional development over a period of time, may provide a pattern for constructive action in the United States.

As indicated in the opening chapter, the Swedish health insurance program was developed on the basis of nonprofit sickness funds established in all parts of Sweden and audited by government agencies. Later, government subsidies were provided for these funds and when a large percentage of Swedish citizens had been covered by the volun-

[9] For an authoritative and objective treatment of this subject in the United States, see Herman and Anne Somers, *Doctors, Patients, and Health Insurance*, particularly pp. 502–534.

tary funds, the program finally was nationalized. However, it is significant that the actual administration of the Swedish program remains with the regional insurance boards composed of representatives of all groups concerned. In addition, the Swedish plan includes the deduction principle to keep costs low and provides for practically free choice of doctors and pharmacists. The Swedish health insurance program is not considered socialized medicine in Sweden. A distinguished professor of medicine at the Karolinska Institute has written: "I do not think that Swedish doctors generally feel socialized." [10]

A period of dissatisfaction of the medical profession has not been observed in the Scandinavian countries as it has been in England, France, Italy, Austria, Belgium, and Germany. "Only Scandinavia escaped this phase. The explanation does not seem to lie primarily in the organization of programs — in Sweden, Norway and Denmark; it is rather that, in the view of one Norwegian social security expert, Scandinavian doctors are well paid and know it. Also doctors and patients alike accept the necessity of governmental action in many areas of modern life, including health." [11]

A comparison of the recently adopted Medicare program in the United States with the practically universal Swedish health insurance program points up the gaps in the United States program. The Social Security Amendments of 1965, which established a program of hospital and medical insurance for people 65 or older, represent an initial step rather than a complete system of health insurance.

Coverage. The most significant difference between the health insurance program in Sweden and that of the United States relates to the limited coverage of the United States program. The latter program emphasizes the relatively greater medical needs of the older population. Sufficient congressional support for a general health insurance program has not been obtained mainly because of the highly organized opposition by the American Medical Association.

The United States program of Health Insurance for the Aged consists of two related health insurance programs for people 65 and over: (1) a hospital insurance plan providing for partial payment of hospital costs for a limited period; and (2) a voluntary medical insurance plan which

[10] Gunnar Biörck, *Trends in Swedish Health and Welfare Policy,* p. 10.
[11] Anne Ramsey Somers, "The European Experience," *New Republic Supplement,* p. 33.

calls for a payment of $3 monthly by the insured with the federal government paying an equal amount of the cost.

It is estimated that by July 1, 1966, 19,011,000 people over 65 were covered by hospital insurance under social security and 17,300,000 under the voluntary medical insurance program.[12] In other words, almost all people in the United States over 65 are now covered by hospital insurance. The only exceptions to universal coverage of this age group are those covered by the federal civil service hospitalization program and members of subversive organizations who were unable to sign the disclaimer provided in the law. In November 1966, a special three-judge Federal Court in Los Angeles declared this disclaimer provision unconstitutional and, early in January, 1967, the solicitor general of the United States sent a memorandum to the Supreme Court stating that the Justice Department will not appeal that decision.[13] Consequently, this provision cannot be enforced and will very likely be deleted by a future Congress. Approximately 91 percent of those over 65 have indicated their desire to have $3 deducted from their monthly social security payments and have obtained coverage under the medical insurance feature of the law.

Since the population of the United States was 196,842,000 on July 1, 1966, the United States Medicare program provides coverage for approximately 10 percent of the population in contrast to the Swedish program with its practically universal coverage.

The Health Insurance for the Aged program was established by legislation in 1965 which added a new Title XVIII to the Social Security Act.[14] At the same time, Congress added a new Title XIX as an amendment to the Social Security Act and this legislation established federal grants for state programs which provide medical assistance for recipients of any of the public assistance programs: Old Age Assistance; Aid to Families with Dependent Children; Aid to the Blind; and Aid to the Disabled. In contrast to the insurance program for those over 65 (Medicare), the medical assistance program, known as Medicaid, is

[12] *Medicare Newsletter* of the Department of Health, Education, and Welfare, No. 16, August 10, 1966.

[13] "Getting Rid of Medicare Loyalty Oath," *Minneapolis Tribune* editorial, Jan. 10, 1967.

[14] An excellent summary description of the Medicare program is provided in *Health Insurance under Social Security*, Department of Health, Education, and Welfare, and *Health Insurance for People 65 or Older*, Department of Health, Education, and Welfare.

limited to those in need or who would be in need of public assistance if they had to meet health care costs. State limitations of assets and income differ widely. In New York State, a family with four or more children may have an income of $6,000 per year and still be eligible, while in Minnesota the maximum income allowable for eligibility is $2,200 for a married couple plus $400 for each dependent. Services in most states under this program are comprehensive and include hospital care, nursing home care, physicians' services, outpatient and clinic care, home health care, private nurses, physical therapy, dental care, laboratory and X-ray services, drugs, eye glasses, dentures, prosthetic devices, diagnostic screening, and preventive services. All treatment must be provided by a licensed practitioner or a recognized vendor of health care services.[15] Thus in contrast to the complete health insurance coverage in Sweden, medical care in the United States remains a matter of personal or family responsibility except for those over 65 years of age or those determined to be in need on the basis of the state laws in their place of residence.

Benefits. As presented in some detail in Chapter 3, the Swedish health insurance program provides a comprehensive system of benefits including hospital care, physicians' services, medicines, cash benefits, maternity care, and travel costs related to hospital and medical care. The following pages compare the relative benefits of the Swedish and American health insurance programs.

The costs of hospital care in Sweden are as follows: Free hospitalization is provided in wards; unless medically required, there is a $4 (20 kr.) per day charge for a semi-private room and a $7 per day (35 kr.) charge for a private room. This hospitalization covers the costs of operations, medical treatments, hospital tests, blood transfusions, X-ray examinations, and all medicines. In the United States, effective on July 1, 1966, after a deduction of the first $40, the insurance pays the cost of up to 60 days of a "spell of illness." After 60 days, the beneficiary pays $10 daily for the services during the next 30 days, with the insurance paying the remainder. No limit is set on the number of "spells of illness" of up to 90 days each but a lifetime limit of 190 days is established for treatment in mental hospitals. This hospitalization includes the cost of a semi-private room (2–4 beds in a room), hospital nursing service,

[15] The Minnesota Medicare program is described in *Minnesota Medical Assistance Program.*

appliance and equipment, blood transfusion except for the first three pints of blood in each illness, medical social service, therapeutic services such as X-ray or radium treatments, operating room, drugs furnished by the hospital, diagnostic services such as blood tests and electrocardiograms, and services of hospital residents and interns in approved training programs.

The costs of medical care in Sweden can be outlined as follows: The doctor's bill is reimbursed to the patient up to the amount of three-fourths of the fee schedule for the care received. This includes cost of X-ray examinations and X-ray and radium treatment, and travel expenses of doctors. The patient may call on the doctor of his own choice, the outpatient department of a hospital, or the district public health doctor. All medical care in the hospital is provided by doctors on the staff of the hospital at no additional cost to the patient. In the United States, for those who have agreed to pay the voluntary assessment of $3 per month, the medical insurance program assists in paying the cost of physician services by the following formula: After a deduction of the first $50 of medical expenses each year, the medical insurance pays 80 percent of the cost of all additional covered services for that year. This includes medical and surgical services by a physician wherever they are furnished, diagnostic tests, and major dental surgery.

Medicines in Sweden are provided according to the following plan. The health insurance program pays one-half the amount in excess of the first $.60 (3 kr.) for ordinary medicines prescribed by the doctor. The full cost of drugs or medicines is paid in cases of chronic diseases requiring such drugs as insulin, cortisone, and related medicines. In the United States no provision is made for the cost of medicines except for drugs routinely provided in the hospital or nursing home and administered by a physician as part of his treatment.

The cost of transportation to and from the doctor's office or hospital is reimbursed in Sweden for amounts exceeding a range of $.80 (4 kr.) to $1 (5 kr.). The transportation costs of a relative or companion are also paid when necessary because of the patient's condition. There is no provision for transportation costs in the United States but the cost of certain ambulance services when medically necessary is reimbursed.

A daily cash allowance is paid under the Swedish plan from the fourth day of each illness. Supplementary cash allowances are paid for those who have a higher income and who pay premium payments. The

SWEDEN AND THE UNITED STATES

daily payments range from $1 (5 kr.) to $5.60 (28 kr.). In the United States no provision for cash allowances is included.

Maternity benefits in Sweden are generous. All costs of medical care, hospital treatment, and travel related to pregnancy and childbirth are reimbursed to the mother under the same standards followed with general illness. In addition, a maternity cash allowance of $180 (900 kr.) is paid at the birth of each child. No provision is made for maternity benefits in the United States because the health program is limited to the elderly.

All costs of nursing home care, as required following hospital care, are paid by the health insurance program in Sweden. In the United States as of January 1, 1967, the hospital insurance program assists in paying for up to 100 days of extended care in a participating facility by paying for all covered services for the first 20 days and all but $5 daily for the next 80 days.

Home health benefits are available in Sweden and an unlimited number of home visits are made as medically required following discharge from a hospital or nursing home. The hospital insurance program in the United States pays for up to 100 home health visits for one year following discharge from a hospital or extended care facility.

Outpatient diagnostic and treatment care by doctors in the outpatient departments of public hospitals is provided in Sweden with reimbursement to the patient of three-fourths of the fee schedule. In the United States when diagnostic services are declared necessary by a doctor, such services may be obtained from the same hospital for a period of 20 days. The beneficiary pays the first $20 and the hospital insurance plan pays 80 percent of the remaining costs of diagnostic services. These payments are limited to diagnostic services only.

The costs of the Swedish health insurance program are paid by employees, employers, and the central government. Premiums for medical care including hospitalization are paid by all employed and self-employed persons at amounts ranging from $12 (60 kr.) to $15 (75 kr.). Separate premiums are paid for the daily cash allowances ranging from $11 (55 kr.) to $14 (70 kr.). Employer contributions were based at 1.5 percent of wages up to annual earnings of $4,400 (22,000 kr.) for the year 1963. The subsidies of the central government in 1963 amounted to 50 percent of the expenditures of the health insurance funds. The American hospital insurance program is financed by required contributions from employees, self-employed persons, and employers. The contribution is collected along with regular social security payments. In 1966 the amount was one-third of 1 percent up to $6,600 of earnings, for 1967 one-half of 1 percent; periodic increases will be made until 1987 when it will reach eight-tenths of 1 percent on the first $6,600 of earnings. The medical insurance program is financed by the payment of $3 per month by each participant matched by a payment of $3 a month by the federal government.

Three major problems confront the operation of the health insurance programs in both Sweden and the United States. The first problem is the shortage of hospital beds in certain locations in both countries. Second, both countries are troubled by the rising costs of hospital care, construction, and maintenance. Third, the programs in both countries call on the doctors to maintain reasonable fee schedules on a voluntary basis. The practice of some doctors of raising fees to the extent of the health insurance coverage negates the value of the insurance to the patient. Attention is being given to this problem in both countries.

The Welfare Programs

As indicated earlier, the welfare programs in Sweden and the United States have much in common. Despite the expansion of the social insurance programs in Sweden and of the social security program in the United States, there are still welfare cases to be dealt with. These are cases in which the welfare recipient has not held a job or worked long enough to obtain sufficient credits for the insurance program.

Concern in Sweden, as in the United States, is expressed for the second generation of welfare recipients. Both countries are presently seeking to break this chain by focusing attention upon economically distressed areas. For many years Sweden has sought to provide retraining and resettlement for those unemployed because of a deteriorating industry located in a particular section of the country. For example, in the 1940's the closing of mines in the north of Sweden was followed almost immediately by a program of retraining and government-paid transportation of workers to the shipyards at Göteborg.

In the United States, the programs proposed by Presidents Kennedy and Johnson to eliminate pockets of poverty in certain geographic sections of the United States rest upon a similar philosophic base. The Economic Opportunity Act, passed by Congress on August 20, 1964, was

SWEDEN AND THE UNITED STATES

enacted "To mobilize the human and financial resources of the Nation to combat poverty in the United States."[16] The Social Security Act Amendments of 1963, emphasizing social service and rehabilitation of welfare recipients, rather than the continuation of routine welfare payments, represent a philosophy parallel to the Swedish emphasis on Help for Self-Help. Also, the Public Works and Economic Development Act of 1965 has the purpose of establishing long-range economic planning by the federal and state governments working through Regional Action Planning Commissions to reduce unemployment and underemployment.[17]

Both Sweden and the United States give great emphasis in their social programs to the provision of services for children. Under the expanded programs of the Children's Bureau in the United States, there are few areas in the country where an infant crippled at birth cannot receive corrective surgery and other assistance if the family cannot afford these services. Similarly, in both countries, an expansion of children's services is in progress, including the establishment of foster homes, improved adoption procedures, and day nurseries for working mothers. Both Sweden and the United States are still searching for a more effective way of administering welfare programs. At present, the administration of these programs in both countries is conducted at the local level with subsidies from the central or federal government. The director of the Welfare Department of Stockholm has written: "It is considered the duty and privilege of the municipalities to take care of their inhabitants, and they also pay most of the costs for the social welfare activities."[18]

In the United States the use of trained social workers is required for state eligibility for federal grants. In Sweden, the use of social workers has not been as extensively established although the facilities for the training of social workers are increasing as well as the number of graduates.

The welfare programs in Sweden and in the United States are comparable in their objectives, the quality of administration, and the efforts to make welfare recipients self-sufficient. Even Sweden's traditional leadership in providing model homes for the aged is being rapidly challenged by the United States, although on a less uniform geo-

[16] Public Law 88-452, 88th Congress, August 20, 1964.
[17] Public Law 89-136, 89th Congress, August 26, 1965.
[18] Letter from Mr. Helge Dahlström to the author, March 23, 1964.

graphic basis. The problems in both countries are also comparable. The difficulty of coordinating social programs confronts Sweden and the United States because programs which are developed by disparate pieces of legislation must be focused upon the whole person in his total family and social setting. Both countries are having difficulty in administering welfare programs with emphasis upon the rights, dignity, and rehabilitation of the recipient. In the United States, as in Sweden, malingerers and fraudulent applicants represent a very small percentage of the welfare cases. However, this is a very troublesome percentage, particularly because of the negative public reaction which results from the disclosure of each fraudulent case. The striking reduction in the number of Swedish welfare cases, as indicated in Chapter 5, is due not only to the Help for Self-Help and rehabilitative efforts of the social assistance agencies, but also to the full employment situation in Sweden and the extensive health insurance and expanded Supplementary Pension program. These preventative programs serve as a means of meeting social needs without recourse to the welfare programs.

There are very different definitions of welfare used in the two countries. For example, the Basic Pension in Sweden is not classified as a welfare program while the Old Age Assistance Program in the United States is. Comparative statistics must be viewed in the light of the differing classifications of welfare programs used in the two countries as well as the federal-state character of the major programs in the United States. However, statistics indicate that 3.5 percent of the Swedish population receive welfare in comparison with 4.1 percent of the American population. The following lists compare the number of welfare recipients in the two countries. The first shows the number of men, women, and children receiving social assistance in Sweden, and the second gives figures for individual programs in the United States.

Sweden 1963 [19]

Recipient	Number
Men	81,137
Women	91,465
Children	94,181
Total	266,783

[19] *Statistical Abstract of Sweden* (1966), p. 254.

SWEDEN AND THE UNITED STATES

United States 1965[20]

Old-age assistance	2,149,186
Medical assistance for the aged	264,402
Aid to the blind	95,349
Aid to the permanently and totally disabled	555,465
Aid to families with dependent children	4,429,044
Total	7,493,446

[20] *Annual Report*, Department of Health, Education, and Welfare (Washington, D.C.: U.S. Government Printing Office, 1965), p. 119. Does not include general assistance which is financed and administered by state and local governments.

VIII

Freedom in the Secure Society

MANHEM
"There was a time when lived in the North
A noble lineage ready for peace as war.
Then, no man's slave and no man's master either
Every rustic was a man of his own.

He himself his own defense
He knew to protect others,
And sons of kings were raised in his cottage."
                    Erik Gustaf Geijer (1783–1847)

SWEDEN has established an extensive system of social programs, administered at all levels of government, to meet the needs of its citizens from prenatal care through survivor's benefits. Even though there are some relatively minor gaps in the network of programs it may be said that the Swedish citizen is quite thoroughly protected against the major known hazards of life. In contrast to the United States where there is a vast complex of private charitable organizations, almost all of the funds and services for the Swedish health, hospital, and social programs are provided through public agencies. However, there are a few private charitable organizations in Sweden for health, welfare, children's, and rehabilitation services.[1]

The impact of this secure society upon the rights and incentives of the individual may be partly ascertained by posing several basic ques-

[1] Such as *De Fyras Bod*, the "Fours Shop," which sells goods made by disabled people and the "Children's Day" organizations which raise money for children's services through carnivals.

tions: (1) To what degree have individual liberties been reduced in Sweden as a result of the establishment of the secure society? (2) Is there a relationship between the Swedish acceptance of extensive government activities, particularly in social fields, and certain characteristics of Swedish government designed to build confidence and respect for government? (3) Has the extension of government into the social insurance and welfare areas been reflected in a loss of free enterprise? (4) Has the development of the secure society caused a concomitant loss of incentive among young people for obtaining and continuing their education and among businessmen for saving money and expanding their businesses and exports? (5) Is the cost of the Swedish program so prohibitive that the tax structure is in effect confiscatory and reduces the motivation of businessmen and investors? (6) Has the development of the secure society been a causative factor in the lowering of moral standards, leading to promiscuity, illegitimacy, abortions, alcoholism, and suicides?

Individual Liberty

Most political scientists and constitutional lawyers would agree that the Constitution of Sweden provides strong protection for the individual liberties of Swedish citizens. Some writers put this Constitution first on the list among constitutions of the world that provide the most specific protection of individual freedom. For example, as we have noted, one of the constitutional documents of Sweden, the Freedom of the Press Act, guarantees any citizen access to public information. The Instrument of Government in the Swedish Constitution restricts the powers of government as does the Bill of Rights in the United States Constitution, and any action by the government to deprive a citizen of life or personal liberty without legal trial and sentence is prohibited. Honor and well-being are among the personal freedoms protected. The respect for the dignity of the individual is reflected in the laws and procedures of the insurance and social assistance programs.

The entire governmental structure and procedure emphasize the importance of the individual citizen and the service role of government. Sweden originated the office of the ombudsman which added, to the legal protection of the Swedish citizen, a built-in mechanism in the administrative structure to guard against arbitrary or capricious action by the bureaucracy. Most important, freedom and personal independence

THE SOCIAL PROGRAMS OF SWEDEN

are part of the way of life of the Swedish citizen. Even with recent disclosure of espionage in high government circles, no responsible political figure has suggested the loosening of restrictions against wiretapping as a means of law enforcement.

The measurement of individual freedom is a very complicated matter that includes psychological as well as legal factors. However, most political scientists would agree that the legal protections of civil liberties and of individual freedom have not in any way been weakened in Sweden.[2] Indeed, some argument has been advanced that the freedoms of the individual have been extended by the establishment of the social programs which give almost every individual in Swedish society the opportunity for good housing, adequate food and clothing, necessary health services, and education on the basis of ability rather than financial resources.

As exemplified in the Swedish experience, freedom and the provision of economic security are not antithetical. In fact, a compelling case is made that freedom in modern society requires the opportunity for good health, education, and productive employment for all citizens. An American political scientist has written about the extension of individual freedoms: "These new freedoms are rights of an economic and social character which characteristically involve collective and more especially governmental effort. Among them are the right to social security, to work, to rest and leisure, to education, to an adequate standard of living, to participation in cultural life, and even to an international order ensuring these rights."[3] These personal liberties are also discussed by a justice of the Supreme Court of the United States: "Today one measure of liberty is the extent to which the individual can insist that his government live under a Rule of Law. Another is the immunity of the individual when he shakes his fist at the authorities and defies them if they fail to follow the supreme law. Still another measure of liberty is the degree to which society affords the individual an opportunity to develop as an integrated human being, healthy in body and soul, with a mind unfettered, with ideas, conscience, and belief inviolate from governmental interference, with a chance to individual preferment and opportunity."[4]

[2] Ingvar Andersson, *Early Democratic Traditions in Scandinavia*, p. 12.
[3] Carl Friedrich, "Rights, Liberties, Freedoms: A Reappraisal," *American Political Science Review*, Vol. 57, No. 4, p. 842.
[4] William O. Douglas, *The Anatomy of Liberty*, p. 1.

FREEDOM IN THE SECURE SOCIETY

There is no evidence in Sweden today that the development of the social programs has lessened the freedom of the individual. Even the political opposition does not make this charge. The Swedish social planners "believe that a welfare state, such as [they] have tried to build . . . provides the best foundation for cultural, technical and economic development and progress."[5] The prime minister of Sweden from 1933 to 1946, when many of the social programs were initiated, stated: "The good home is characterized by equality for all, charitableness towards and concern for the well-being of others . . . We are trying to turn Sweden into that kind of home for all its citizens . . . We think that to do so is Democracy in the best sense of the word — and we want to prove that Democracy is the best way of life."[6]

The Role of Government

A major issue today in the United States and several other countries is the appropriate role of government in meeting the social needs of its citizens. In Sweden most citizens and the political parties no longer argue the basic question of the government's role in providing the social insurances and health and welfare programs. This does not mean that there has always been unanimous support for the social programs. In 1948, the leader of the Conservative party in Sweden, while not directly opposing the social programs, gave major credit to the growing economy rather than to the social programs as the causative factor of Swedish progress. "As a matter of fact, it may well be that the successful solution of a number of difficult problems in the 1930's was the result less of superior wisdom or of the excellency of a social system than of favorable economic conditions."[7]

Many Swedes, particularly in the upper economic classes, have expressed the view that the social programs and the need to submit business or construction proposals for government approval have limited individual and corporate freedom. However, election statistics indicate that most Swedish citizens have supported for over thirty years the party which established the social programs. The votes do not reflect any fear of governmental influence over the individual through the ex-

---

[5] Ernst Michanek, *For and Against the Welfare State: Swedish Experiences,* p. 43.

[6] *Ibid.*, p. 44.

[7] Gunnar Heckscher, "Pluralist Democracy, The Swedish Experience," *Social Research,* p. 461.

THE SOCIAL PROGRAMS OF SWEDEN

tensive social programs. In 1964, the Social Democratic party received 2,006,923 votes, 47.3 percent of the votes cast in the general election. The nearest opposition party was the Liberal party which received only 723,988 votes, or 17.1 percent of the total.[8] In the municipal elections on September 19, 1966, a voting turnout of 78.7 percent of Sweden's 5,500,000 registered voters gave the Social Democratic party local candidates 42.8 percent of the vote. The Liberal party received 16.5 percent of the vote.[9]

What is the relationship of the widespread acceptance of the role of government in Sweden to the unique characteristics of Swedish government and administration? The Swedish public philosophy has many roots, including the long tradition of respect for law, the homogeneity of the population, and the responsive nature of the parliamentary system which requires the support of the electorate on major issues for a party to stay in power. Also, the executive branch is headed by the leaders of the party given legislative control by the electorate. Consequently, the parliamentary system makes it impossible to have a situation which can occur in the United States in which the head of the government, the President, and a majority of the legislature represent different political parties.[10]

As indicated in Chapter 6, many facets of Swedish government and administration give day-to-day meaning to the constitutional protections of personal freedom in relation to government activity. These include the office of the ombudsman, providing a psychological as well as a legal protection for all citizens in their relationships with the bureaucracy; the use of semi-independent boards rather than a monolithic hierarchical organization for central government administration; the widespread participation of organizations and citizens in the administrative process; the decentralization and coordination of central government activities through the use of the offices of the province governors; the emphasis and strengthening of local government in the administration of health, welfare, and other programs through central government subsidies and grants-in-aid; the prestige of the civil service; and the constitutional requirement for access to information about all government activities. All of these characteristics, designed to build confidence in government, unquestionably have played a part in the development

[8] *Statistical Abstract of Sweden*, (1965), p. 388.
[9] *Minneapolis Star*, September 19, 1966, p. 13A.
[10] James MacGregor Burns, *The Deadlock of Democracy*.

of the public philosophy of Sweden. The citizen has no hesitation in calling upon his government to provide the means for meeting his health, social security, and welfare needs. There is little question that most Swedish citizens expect rather than fear the provision of service activities by their government agencies.

Free Enterprise

The status of free enterprise or private business in Sweden is often bluntly questioned by those who ask: "Is Sweden socialistic?"

A recent book, *Product of Private Enterprise*, helps answer this question. The Preface states: "Sweden's material progress has all along been the product of private enterprise." [11] The book gives detailed information, industry by industry, and points out, in summary, that 93 percent of all business in Sweden, measured by value of production, is conducted today by private enterprise. Swedish business, measured by number of employees, is 91 percent private enterprise, 5 percent government, and 4 percent cooperative. Most political scientists would define socialism as the government ownership of the means of production and distribution. On the basis of this definition, the Swedish economy cannot accurately be labeled socialistic. Table 13 summarizes the extent to which private enterprise, the government, and cooperatives, con-

Table 13. Percentage of Private, Public, and Cooperative Enterprise in Swedish Industry

Industry	Private	Public	Cooperative
Forest	95	3	2
Iron mining	62	38	0
Steelmaking	93	7	0
Power	58	42	0
Metalworking	98	1	1
Electrical manufacturing	92	6	2
Shipbuilding	99.8	0.2	0
Chemical	92.2	2.5	5.3
Construction	80	16	4
Food	86	0	14
Wholesaling	90	0	10
Retailing	86	0	14
Banking	94	6	0

SOURCE: *Product of Private Enterprise* (Stockholm: Stockholm Chamber of Commerce, 1956), p. 60.

[11] *Product of Private Enterprise* (Stockholm: The Chamber of Commerce, 1956), p. 1.

Table 14. Expenditure and Investment in the Public and Private Sectors of Swedish Economy

Sector	Expenditure Millions of Kronor	Percentage	Investment Millions of Kronor	Percentage
Public				
Central government	7,800	10	7,700	20
Regional and local government	10,700	13	6,400	17
Private	62,500	77	24,000	63
Total	81,000	100.0	38,100	100.0

SOURCE: *The Swedish Budget, 1967–1968*, p. 48.

duct business in Sweden, and Table 14 indicates expenditure and investment in the three major sectors of the economy.

There are those who use terms as convenient labels regardless of their accuracy, and this has caused some confusion. A recent article appearing in the United States was entitled "How Swedish Free Enterprise Co-Exists with Socialism." The content of the article belies the use of "Socialism" in the title because it points out that 92.4 percent of manufacturing and 99 percent of wholesaling ". . . remain firmly in the private sector. It is free enterprise that had made Sweden a major world exporter of paper, wood products, steel, shipping, and automobiles."[12] A more legitimate point of confusion may result from the extensive use of privately owned cooperatives in Sweden and the similarity in translation of "social" and "socialism."[13] Sweden may well be characterized as "social" in the sense that Swedish people rather proudly emphasize the importance of the social programs as a distinguishing feature of their way of life. This is exemplified by the book *Social Sweden*, published by the Social Welfare Board of Sweden in 1936, which describes in some detail the social programs of Sweden at that time.

The director general of the Federation of Swedish Industries, a leading organization of private business in Sweden, sums up the current situation: "It is not unusual for foreign observers with some knowledge of the Swedish governments of the last thirty years to imagine Sweden as a socialist country. The assumption may sound plausible enough but, in fact, the Swedish economy is governed by the market, and private

[12] *Fortune*, p. 80. See also "Socialism Goes Tame in Sweden," *Business Week*, p. 77.
[13] Marquis Childs, *Sweden: The Middle Way*.

industry is the firm basis of the country's economic life. . . . As in other Western countries the profits account is the criterion of financial efficiency. There is no general management by the government, and the thesis of the incentive value of competition is still alive although humanized and influenced by experience gained during this century." [14]

Loss of Incentive

It is frequently charged that the establishment and the extension of the secure society will almost automatically result in the loss of incentive among young people for continuing their education and among businessmen for saving money, developing investments, formulating new inventions, extending exports, and in other ways seeking to increase the profit of their corporations.

A brief examination of objective statistical information suggests an answer to the question of incentive in Sweden. In the middle 1950's, western Europe produced 60 percent more goods than before World War II. In Sweden, the increase was more than 87 percent. The same ratio is reflected in the development of new inventions, the increase in export trade, and similar measurements. The annual rates of growth of the gross national product, per employed person for the period 1950–60, averaged 3.3 percent for Sweden compared to 1.9 percent for the United States.[15] The annual percentage of growth of the gross national product increased 2.8 percent in the period 1950–60 compared to 1.1 percent in the United States.[16] The average yearly rate of growth in gross national product in Sweden, during 1960–65, exceeded that of the United States, Great Britain, and West Germany. In the same period a similar pattern is found in the average yearly rate of growth of gross national product per inhabitant and of industrial production as shown by the following figures (adapted from the table on the back cover,

	G.N.P.	G.N.P. per Inhabitant	Industrial Production
Sweden	5.0	4.3	7.1
U.K.	3.4	2.6	3.0
U.S.A.	4.7	3.2	5.7
France	5.1	3.7	5.1
West Germany	4.8	3.5	5.7

[14] *Labor Peace and Full Employment in Sweden*, p. 25.
[15] *Ibid.*
[16] *Ibid.*

THE SOCIAL PROGRAMS OF SWEDEN

The Swedish Budget, 1967/68). The gross national product of Sweden in 1962 still was lower than that of the United States. During that year, expressed in billions of United States dollars, the gross national product of Sweden was 192.4 compared with 556.2 for the United States. In 1965 the G.N.P. per inhabitant was $3,560 in the United States and $2,550 in Sweden. Both countries exceeded Great Britain, France, and West Germany in this measurement. But Sweden is ahead of each of these countries, including the United States, in the rate of growth in gross national product and in industrial production. Clearly, the high rate of growth of business and industry in Sweden indicates a very high degree of incentive by businessmen and investors. The relationship between this growth and the social programs is conjectural although the continued income provided by the large social insurance programs tends to result in a continuing consumer purchasing power.

With respect to the incentive for young people, the number of students beginning study in higher secondary schools of Sweden has shown a tremendous increase. In 1931, 4 percent of all 17-year-old or college-age young people in Sweden entered school. In 1961, this had increased to 21 percent and in 1962 to 23 percent. Preparation is being made for an enrollment of from 32 to 42 percent of all 17-year-olds by 1970.[17] In 1960 more than 1,179,054 students were enrolled in public primary, secondary, and vocational schools, people's colleges, and institutions of higher education.[18] Of this number, 36,909 were enrolled in institutions of higher education, 3,813 in vocational schools, and 49,426 in people's colleges.[19] By 1965, the number of students enrolled for higher education had increased to 68,992. In 1950, there were 385,000 adults enrolled in the study circles of the National Popular Study Association. In 1962, it is estimated that more than 1,000,000 students were enrolled in this program for continuing education.[20]

Critics of the social insurance programs have also charged that they will result in a reduction in savings and in private insurance programs as a form of protection and savings. The statistics reflect the opposite. Sweden ranks first among all countries in Europe today in the amount

[17] Ernst Michanek, "For and Against the Welfare State," lecture given in Berlin in October 1963, p. 25.
[18] *Statistical Abstract of Sweden*, (1962), p. 267.
[19] *Ibid.*
[20] Ernst Michanek, "For and Against the Welfare State," lecture given in Berlin in October 1963, p. 25.

of actual ownership of private life insurance and ranks third among the countries of the world.[21]

The growth of individual life insurance has resulted in the doubling of the amounts of insurance written in the period from 1950 to 1961. In 1950, there was $2,251,200,000 (11,256,000,000 kr.) of individual life insurance in Sweden. The amount of $4,415,600,000 (22,078,000,000 kr.) had been written in 1961.

The need for private group life insurance was recognized in the collective agreement in 1962 between the Swedish Employers Federation and the Federation of Swedish Trade Unions. It is estimated that 2,000,000 employed people are covered by the new type of group life insurance. Similarly, there has been an increase in private health and accident insurance even though all people in Sweden are covered by the national health insurance program. By 1961, more than 5,600,000 health and accident policies had been written in comparison with the 4,000,000 policies which were in force in 1956.[22]

Costs of the Social Programs

Those who are concerned about the increase of government activity in social fields often raise the problem of prohibitive costs. Unquestionably, the extensive social programs of Sweden are expensive and these costs are reflected in both the general taxes of Sweden and the required contributions (see pp. 17, 46–48, 130–134).

A comparison of expenditures for social programs in Sweden with those in the United States indicates that a larger percentage of the gross national product is expended for these programs in Sweden. Sweden expends 32.4 percent of its gross national product for social programs measured by the total taxation and the social security contributions budgeted for these programs. The United States expends 28.9 percent of its gross national product for social programs on the basis of the same measurement.

The social programs in 1962 cost the central government of Sweden a total of $1,331,000,000 (6,655,000,000 kr.) for the Basic and Supplementary Pensions, health and industrial injury insurance, unemployment insurance, and subsidies to local and regional governments for these programs. The major expenditures for social welfare purposes are

[21] *Sweden: Its Private Insurance and Social Security*, p. 9.
[22] *Ibid.*, p. 19.

the benefits paid under the Basic Pension program. These costs, as reflected in the budget for 1963–64, total $622,000,000 (3,110,000,000 kr.). The second largest item provides for the payment of general children's allowances totaling $189,400,000 (947,000,000 kr.). The following list includes the amounts in millions of kronor, budgeted in 1962, 1963, and 1966 for the Basic Pension, health insurance, and general children's allowances.

	1962	1963	1966
Basic Pension	2,985 kr.	3,110 kr.	5,300 kr.
Health insurance	1,185	1,370	2,380
General children's allowances	955	945	1,595

The costs of the social programs are great in relation to the total Swedish budget but these programs rest on the premise that meeting social needs is expensive in any case. If payments are not made to widowed mothers and children to enable them to remain together in their homes then institutions for children, such as orphans' homes, must be constructed and maintained. Similarly, the repetitive payments to welfare recipients, even though these be kept at minimum subsistence level, can total astronomical figures. If, as the records show, in Sweden as in the United States, the growth of social insurance and other preventative programs results in the reduction of welfare payments, might it not be also said that these programs are "good business"?

Moral Standards

Some critics of the social programs of Sweden have sought to relate the establishment of the extensive insurance and welfare programs to such social problems as promiscuity, illegitimacy, abortions, alcoholism, and a relatively high suicide rate.

The social attitudes and mores in Sweden toward sex are quite different from those generally prevalent in the United States. Rather frank courses on sex are provided in high schools in mixed classes and information concerning birth control methods is provided in the schools and is readily available without any legal restrictions.[23] While illegitimacy is not looked on favorably, it does not result in social ostracism as in the United States. The general, but by no means universal, Swedish attitude toward premarital sex relationships has been stated as: "We would prefer that you have no sex relations until you marry. But if you choose

[23] "Swedes Debate Sex Hysteria," *Washington Post*, p. E4.

to have sex relations, you should use birth control. If you get pregnant nevertheless, you are always welcome here, and we will support you." (Birgitta Linner, "Sexual Morality and Sexual Reality: The Scandinavian Approach," *American Journal of Orthopsychiatry*, July 1966, Vol. 36, No. 4, p. 690.) Birth certificates do not distinguish between illegitimate and legitimate babies, and all public benefits are available to every child. No evidence is available showing a cause and effect relationship between the social programs and the freer pattern of sex mores.

As indicated in Chapter 4, the Swedish laws and administration concerning abortions are widely misunderstood outside of Sweden. There were 112,903 live births in Sweden in 1963 and 3,528 legal abortions,[24] a ratio of 1 abortion to every 32 live births. While adequate statistics are not available in the United States since abortions are illegal, an informed observer estimates that one million abortions were performed in the United States in 1966 — a ratio of 1 to every 4 live births.[25] In 1964, there were 16,117 illegitimate births in Sweden of a total of 122,644 live births, a ratio of 1 illegitimate birth to every 8 live births.[26] While this represents a 50 percent increase since 1957, a parallel increase is estimated for the United States.[27]

In 1964, an informed American observer pointed out that no relationship between the increase in illegitimacy and the social programs could be found. "Sweden does have a high rate of suicide, a major problem of alcoholism, a disturbing rate of children born out of wedlock. But I could find no evidence that the problems are because of security against joblessness, catastrophic illness, and poverty. Most likely reasons could be the emotional frustrations of long, hard winters, crowded cities and isolated rural areas."[28] A distinguished Swedish writer has stated: "There is one type of foreign visitors, journalists or authors which has become extremely common here.... For the most part, they have a thesis that welfare is not enough, that welfare leads to boredom and hysteria, which in turn lead to sexual promiscuity, alcoholism, a high frequency of suicide and juvenile delinquency. In my most suspicious moments, I think they are out to prove that it doesn't pay to have any kind of democratic and socially active policy. Their fanaticism is so

---

[24] *Statistical Abstract of Sweden* (1965), p. 265.
[25] Walter C. Alvarez, "Some Sex Views Outmoded," *Minneapolis Tribune*, p. 12.
[26] *Statistical Abstract of Sweden* (1965), p. 50.
[27] Alvarez, op. cit., p. 12.
[28] Sylvia Porter, "Welfare State Psychology," *Denver Post*, p. 42.

great that you might take them for propagandizers for medieval society." [29]

Alcoholism represents a major social problem in Sweden. However, both the local and central governments are providing clinical service and educational programs in the effort to reduce alcoholism. Laws are strictly enforced concerning drunk driving to the point where most Swedish citizens will not drive if they have taken a drink. The standard penalty for driving with even a minimum of alcohol content in the blood includes a mandatory jail sentence. Any connection between alcoholism and the social programs is purely conjectural. Observers relate the present alcoholism problem to the long, dark winters, the Viking tradition, the psychological make-up of the Swede, and many other factors.[30] It should be noted that in 1962 Sweden ranked eighth in the international comparisons of consumption of alcohol in all forms — spirits, wines, and beer. France, Italy, Switzerland, West Germany, the United States, Great Britain, and Denmark had a higher per capita consumption. However, a great deal of attention is being given to the problem of alcoholism in Sweden and several extensive programs including education and treatment, with government financing and support, are in operation.

The suicide rate in Sweden has been listed for several years as among the highest in the world. This is often explained in part by the fact that morbidity and mortality statistical reporting in Sweden has been developed over many years into almost an exact science. In Sweden all suicides are reported as such. This is not the case in many jurisdictions in the United States and in other parts of the world. In the effort to clarify the possibility of any relationship between the social programs of Sweden and the suicide rate, the statistics on the causes of death were reviewed for the past 50 years. In the period 1901–10, before the establishment of the social programs, there were 15.1 suicides per 100,000 inhabitants. By 1961, the rate had increased only slightly, to 16.9.[31] These statistics indicate that the relatively high suicide rate cannot be ascribed to the secure society. In 1961 Sweden was listed as eighth among the nations of the world in number of suicides. Hungary had the highest number of suicides, 25.4 per 100,000 inhabitants.

[29] Lars Gustafsson, *The Public Dialogue in Sweden*, pp. 16–17.
[30] *The Alcohol Question in Sweden*, p. 21. This pamphlet also gives the historical background of public and private efforts to combat alcoholism in Sweden.
[31] Reduced from 19.8 in 1957. *Statistical Abstract of Sweden* (1963), p. 266.

FREEDOM IN THE SECURE SOCIETY

A report, "Suicide and the Welfare State," presented at the Annual Congress of the American Psychological Association held in Philadelphia in 1963, based on nine different studies, indicated no observable relationship between suicide and the social programs. In fact, the speaker giving the report commented to the press that his findings would seem to imply that a more extensive welfare system would lead to a decrease in the suicide rate:[32] ". . . the Swedes are characterized by a high degree of incentive, throwing themselves into their jobs with perhaps a greater intensity than Americans. . . . The welfare state has little impact on self-destruction and, if anything, may serve to reduce the rating."[33] Another authority, in a study of psychological stress, points out that differences in belief systems concerning death have much to do with differing cultural and national patterns of suicide. He writes: "Attitudes toward suicide and death differ (for example, suicide is much more acceptable in Denmark than in Norway) and . . . explain the higher incidence in the former of this solution to life stress." (Richard S. Lazarus, *Psychological Stress and the Coping Process*, p. 136.)

A thorough study of the subject of suicide in the Scandinavian countries was recently made by a leading psychiatrist in the United States, a member of the faculty of the Columbia University Psychoanalytic Clinic, who flatly rejects a correlation between the so-called welfare state, bad weather, or accurate statistical recording and the relatively high Swedish and Danish suicide rates. He points out that while Norway has an advanced social welfare program, equally bad weather, and an accurate statistical system, its suicide rate is only a third as high as those of Sweden and Denmark. The author develops the thesis that there is a closer causative relationship between personal factors involved in Sweden's rapid industrialization and suicide. As he explains: "Much of the attention which the high Danish and Swedish suicide rates have received is a consequence of the social welfare measures applied in the two countries. Both inside and outside Sweden and Denmark, opponents of economic planning and social welfare measures have attempted to explain the suicide rate as a consequence of character defects produced by these measures. But the Danish suicide rate has been higher than those of most other European countries for the last hundred years. The Swedish suicide rate has climbed since the turn of the century, and a

[32] Maurice L. Farber, "Suicide in the Welfare State," p. 3.
[33] "Socialism and Suicide," *Scandinavian Times*, p. 3.

better case could be made for relating this rise to Sweden's late but fast developing industrial capitalism than can be made for relating it to the relatively recent social welfare measures."[34]

In brief, Sweden is troubled by the same kinds of problems that concern all urbanized, industrial societies. There is little objective evidence that these problems have developed from the secure society. Indeed, the relative security of the society may point up the existence of these problems. "Life in a welfare society also has its moral aspects. . . . that both foreign and domestic political tranquility and favorable conditions have turned us into a comfortable country, with great material security and an unusual degree of that kind of freedom that material security can give. It would be a doubtful statement to say that such a situation creates new problems. It rather makes other problems clearer."[35]

A Public Philosophy for the United States

The general acceptance of government and the clearly defined and established public philosophy of Sweden underlie much of the success in the adoption and administration of the Swedish social programs. This represents the most striking difference between Sweden and the United States.

As indicated in the preceding chapter, the social programs of the United States, with the exception of health insurance, compare quite favorably with those of Sweden. The major distinction lies in the willingness of the Swedish citizen to rely on public rather than private agencies to meet social needs, and the effectiveness and responsiveness of the Swedish public agencies which perform this task. The citizen in the United States does not accept with confidence the enlarging role of government in the social fields.

The question of the appropriate role of government, particularly in the health and welfare fields, is of concern to many thoughtful people in the United States, and reflected in the current political dialogue. This concern over the expansion of government activities at all levels may be partly explained by the rapidly increasing federal, local, and state taxes and public indebtedness. No thoughtful person favors the leviathan of big government. Few people overtly favor centralized government. However, many citizens are seeking the provision of services

[34] Herbert Hendin, *Suicide and Scandinavia*, p. 4.
[35] Lars Gustafsson, *The Public Dialogue in Sweden*, p. 12.

which require a financial base beyond the resources of private agencies or local governments. One fact is clear, whatever the reason: Most citizens in the United States have not determined with any degree of consistency the role that they want their government to play in their lives.

The appropriate role of government, a fundamental question in the issue of security and freedom, has been debated throughout the history of political philosophy. In the United States, the debates reflected in the *Federalist Papers* have been repeated through the years as new functions of government have been proposed. The decisions of the Supreme Court have played a significant part in determining the constitutional functions of government, particularly those of the federal government, in the United States. The powers of the federal government in the promotion of the general welfare have been defined by the Supreme Court in the cases of *United States v. Butler, Helvering v. Davis,* and *Carmichael v. Southern Coal and Coke Co.*, and in the *Steward Sewing Machine Company* case, among many others. In *Helvering v. Davis*, decided in 1937, Justice Cardozo, an appointee of President Hoover, wrote in upholding the constitutionality of the Social Security Act of 1935: "Congress may spend money in aid of the general welfare . . . There have been great statesmen in our history who stood for other views. We will not resurrect the contest. It is now settled by the decision . . . Nor is the concept of the general welfare static. . . . Needs that were narrow and parochial a century ago may be interwoven in our day with the well-being of the nation. What is critical or urgent changes with the times . . . states and local governments are often lacking in the resources that are necessary to finance an adequate program of security for the aged." [36]

A few contemporary writers have seriously sought to bring light rather than political partisanship or emotion to bear on this question. Walter Lippmann addresses himself to this subject in his book *Essays in the Public Philosophy* and, concerned about the "functional derangement of the relationship between the mass of the people and the government" suggests the determination of the appropriate role of government is fundamental to the development of a public philosophy which would state, with some degree of consistency and rationality, the citizen's relationship to his government and the government's relationship

---

[36] Helvering v. Davis, 301 U.S. 619, 672, No. 910 (1937).

to the citizen.[37] More recently, Herbert Block of the *Washington Post*, in presenting the Elmer Davis Memorial Lecture at Columbia University, pointed out that many citizens of the United States look at government as an "enemy" rather than as a "servant," and that this is particularly true of the general image of the federal government. "Many sections of the press, including some of our most widely-read national magazines, have fostered the idea that the United States Government somehow does not belong to the people but is the enemy. Not corruption, injustice or inequities in representation, but the federal government itself, and most particularly the Executive and Judicial branches, is made out to be some kind of enemy. The local government may do things for you — like paving roads, even though this is generally done mostly with federal funds — but those 'bureaucrats' in Washington take from you. And the bureaucrats who supposedly take from you your money and your good old-fashioned rights are generally conceived of as wastrels in a city of complete confusion. I think a part of the press — and a part not by any means confined to the South — which constantly pictures the Executive and Judicial branches of government in Washington not as public servants or protectors, or even as people we may consider unwise and wrong-headed, but as enemies, might ask themselves if they are not promoting something more akin to anarchy than to American conservatism."

A similar observation concerning the fear of Americans, particularly those in the West, about the activities of the federal government has been pointed out by the secretary of the interior who is perplexed because, as he indicates, the history of the West has been largely underwritten by the federal government. "However, it is more difficult to explain the anti-federal government movement in the West, for our region has always had a special — and uniquely profitable — relationship with the government in Washington. . . . The 'new wave' anti-federalists of the West have, I fear, misread the political history of their region, and have failed to grasp the central significance of the conservation policies hammered out by Powell, by Pinchot and by the two Roosevelts. . . . Yet, despite all this, the anti-federalists in our midst have identified the growing national government of a growing Nation as the paramount threat to our way of life. ('Fear Washington more than

[37] Walter Lippmann, *Essays in the Public Philosophy*, p. 19.

Moscow' some of them say.) To hear these men tell it, government action and individual freedom are irreconcilable opposites."[38]

Antagonism toward the federal government is particularly sharp and vocal in the public welfare and social insurance areas. Here the charge is frequently made that the provision of security by the federal government will result in the loss of individual freedom. The reasons for the relationship of security to authoritarianism are not usually given, although occasionally there is a reference to communism which includes security for all people as one of its major goals.

In Sweden, the acceptance of government activity in social fields did not develop in a vacuum. As indicated before, the respect for law, inherent in Swedish tradition and custom, has played a part in the present prestige of government service and respect for governmental institutions. In addition, the basic concepts and dynamics of Swedish public administration may have played a significant role so that the average Swedish citizen does not fear his government. The structure, design, and day-to-day operation of government in Sweden rest upon the basic premise of concern for the rights and dignity of the individual citizen and his relationship to the bureaucracy.

A positive definition of freedom, in a democracy, requires not only the provision of protection against authoritarianism, but also the recognition of the dignity of each individual in the day-to-day administration of government programs. The attitudes and competence of the personnel administering social programs are extremely important in ensuring that the dignity and the independence of the individual are maintained in the process of meeting his social needs. One of the early leaders[39] in the development of public welfare concepts in the United States has written: "Laws and the rights and equities they established are not self-operative. They exist only if they are administratively maintained. This is particularly true of a program which not only proposes to offer the individual the opportunity and the means of sustaining his income when it is interrupted by the contingencies of life, but which also seeks in do-

---

[38] Stewart L. Udall, John Field Simms Memorial Lecture, University of New Mexico, Albuquerque, February 6, 1964.

[39] Karl de Schweinitz, *People and Process in Social Security* (Washington, D.C.: American Council on Education, 1948), p. 205. See also David Lilienthal, *This I Do Believe* (New York: Harper and Row, 1949); Mary Follett, *Creative Experience* (New York: Longmans, Green and Company, 1924); and Herbert A. Simon, Donald W. Smithburg, and Victor A. Thompson, *Public Administration* (New York: Alfred A. Knopf, 1959).

ing this to protect his initiative and his spirit of independence. The goal of a basic security with a maximum of personal freedom cannot be achieved through statute alone. Its attainment depends upon the competence and philosophy of the men and women who administer its benefits and services." It would seem that in the United States increased attention to those aspects of administration which lead to greater public confidence, understanding, and respect would contribute significantly toward the development of a sound and meaningful public philosophy in the United States.

Perhaps the most significant lesson in the Swedish social laboratory for the United States is the perception of the carefully nurtured values of government which underlie the Swedish citizen's confidence and participation in, and support of, his government and the public programs, both of which are designed to afford him the opportunity to develop to his maximum capacity as an individual and to contribute to society in an environment that is both secure and free.

With strong interest in individual freedom and with concern for making the basic concepts of democracy meaningful to all citizens, both Sweden and the United States are seeking to say with Carl Sandburg: "The People — Yes."

BIBLIOGRAPHY AND INDEX

Bibliography

Books

Albinsson, Gillis. *Public Health Services in Sweden.* Halmstad: Meijels Bokindustrie, 1963.
Andersson, Ingvar. *A History of Sweden.* London: Weidenfeld and Nicolson, 1956.
Andrén, Nils. *Government and Politics in the Nordic Countries.* Stockholm: Almqvist and Wiksell, 1964.
———. *Modern Swedish Government.* Stockholm: Almqvist and Wiksell, 1961.
Arnesen, Ben A. *The Democratic Monarchies of Scandinavia.* Princeton, N.J.: Van Nostrand, 1949.
Burns, James MacGregor. *The Deadlock of Democracy.* Englewood Cliffs, N.J.: Prentice-Hall, 1963.
——— and Jack Walter Peltason. *Government by the People.* Englewood Cliffs, N.J.: Prentice-Hall, 1963.
Chapman, Brian. *The Profession of Government; Public Service in Europe.* London: Allen and Unwin, 1959.
Childs, Marquis W. *Sweden: The Middle Way.* New Haven, Conn.: Yale University Press, 1947 (rev. ed., 1960).
———. *This Is Democracy.* New Haven, Conn.: Yale University Press, 1938.
Douglas, William O. *The Anatomy of Liberty.* New York: Trident Press, 1963.
Eckstein, Otto, ed. *Studies in the Economics of Income Maintenance.* Washington, D.C.: The Brookings Institute, 1967.
Elazar, Daniel. *The American Partnership.* Chicago: University of Chicago Press, 1962.
Engel, Arthur. *The Swedish Regionalized Hospital System.* Stockholm: National Board of Health, 1960.
Evang, Karl. *Medical Care and Family Security.* Englewood Cliffs, N.J.: Prentice-Hall, 1963.
Fleisher, Wilfrid. *Sweden: The Welfare State.* New York: John Day Co., 1956.
Friis, Henning, ed. *Scandinavia — Between East and West.* Ithaca, N.Y.: Cornell University Press, 1950.
Geijerstam, Gunnar af. *Den Sexuella Samlevden.* Stockholm: The Swedish Institute, 1965.
Gellhorn, Walter. *Ombudsmen and Others.* Cambridge, Mass.: Harvard University Press, 1966.
Gendell, Murray. *Swedish Working Wives.* Totowa, N.J.: Bedminster Press, 1963.

Hartz, Louis. *The Liberal Tradition in America.* New York: Harcourt, Brace and World, Inc., 1955.
Harvard Law School. *Taxation in Sweden.* Cambridge, Mass.: Harvard University Press, 1959.
Heckscher, Gunnar. *The Swedish Constitution 1809–1959: Tradition and Practice in Constitutional Development.* Stockholm: Svenska Institutet, 1959.
Hendin, Herbert. *Suicide and Scandinavia.* New York: Grune and Stratton, Inc., 1964.
Herlitz, Nils. *Sweden: A Modern Democracy on Ancient Foundations.* Minneapolis: University of Minnesota Press, 1939.
Hinshaw, David. *Sweden: Champion of Peace.* New York: Putnam, 1949.
Larsson, Tage. *Mortality in Sweden,* rev. ed. New York: S. Karger, 1965.
Lippmann, Walter. *Essays in the Public Philosophy.* Boston: Little Brown and Co., 1955.
Marsh, David C. *The Future of the Welfare State.* London: C. Nicholls & Co., Ltd., 1964.
Michanek, Ernst. *Swedish Government in Action.* Stockholm: The Swedish Institute, 1962.
Myers, Robert J. *Social Insurance and Allied Government Programs.* Homewood, Ill.: Richard D. Irwin, Inc., 1965.
Norr, Martin, and Claes Sandels. *The Corporate Income Tax in Sweden,* 2nd ed. Stockholm: AB Egnellska Boktrycheriet, 1963.
Oakley, Stewart. *A Short History of Sweden.* New York: Praeger, 1966.
Peaslee, Amos J. *Constitutions of Nations.* Concord, N.H.: The Rumford Press, 1950.
Richardson, John Henry. *Economic and Financial Aspects of Social Security: An International Survey.* Toronto: University of Toronto Press, 1960.
Rowat, Donald C. *The Ombudsman.* London: Allen and Unwin, 1965.
Rustow, Dankwart A. *The Politics of Compromise.* Princeton, N.J.: Princeton University Press, 1955.
Schottland, Charles I. *The Social Security Program in the United States.* New York: Appleton-Century-Crofts, 1963.
Schweinitz, Karl de. *People and Process in Social Security.* Washington, D.C.: American Council on Education, 1948.
Shapiro, Herbert J. *Government by Constitution.* New York: Random House, 1959.
Somers, Herman, and Anne R. Somers. *Doctors, Patients, and Health Insurance.* Washington, D.C.: The Brookings Institute, 1961.
Strode, Hudson. *Sweden: Model for a World.* New York: Harcourt, Brace and World, Inc., 1949.
Titmuss, Richard M. *Essays on "The Welfare State,"* 2nd ed. London: Allen and Unwin, 1963.
Vasey, Wayne. *Government and Social Welfare.* New York: Henry Holt and Co., 1958.
Wendt, Paul F. *Housing Policy — The Search for Solutions.* Berkeley, Calif.: University of California Press, 1962.
William-Olsson, William Fritz, ed. *Sweden and Finland: Statistical Data for Counties, Provinces, and Statistical Regions.* Stockholm: Almqvist and Wiksell, 1964.

Pamphlets

Nelson, George R., ed. *Freedom and Welfare — Social Patterns in the Northern Countries of Europe.* Copenhagen: Krohns Bogtrykkeri, 1953.
Organization for Economic Cooperation and Development. *Economic Survey: Sweden.* Paris, 1966.
Social Benefits in Sweden. Stockholm: Framtiden Insurance Co., 1964.

BIBLIOGRAPHY

Sweden: Its Private Insurance and Social Security. Stockholm: Association of Swedish Insurance Companies, 1963.

United Nations. Department of Economic and Social Affairs. *Study of Legislative and Administrative Aspects of Rehabilitation of the Disabled in Selected Countries.* New York: United Nations, 1964.

Government and Institute Publications

SWEDEN

Alcohol Question in Sweden, The. Stockholm: The Swedish Temperance Education Board, 1960.

Amilon, Clas. *The Swedish Correctional System.* Stockholm: The Swedish Institute, 1965.

———. *Youth Prison: A Swedish Form of Treatment for Young Offenders.* Stockholm: The Swedish Institute, 1965.

Andersson, Ingvar. *Early Democratic Traditions in Scandinavia.* Copenhagen: The Danish Institute, The Norwegian Office of Cultural Relations, and The Swedish Institute in Cooperation with the American-Scandinavian Foundation, 1958.

———. *Introduction to Sweden.* Stockholm: The Swedish Institute, 1962.

———. *Swedish History in Brief.* Stockholm: The Swedish Institute, 1962.

Bagger-Sjöbäck, Bertil. *Activities for Young People in Sweden.* Stockholm: The Swedish Institute, 1962.

Bexelius, Alfred. *The Swedish Institution of the Justitieombudsman.* Stockholm: The Swedish Institute, 1965.

Biörck, Gunnar. *Trends in Swedish Health and Welfare Policy.* Stockholm: The Swedish Institute, 1963.

Bolin, Lars. *Measures to Combat Juvenile Delinquency in Sweden,* rev. ed. Stockholm: The Swedish Institute, 1965.

Bruun, Ulla-Britta. *Nursery Schools in Sweden.* Stockholm: The Swedish Institute, 1965.

Carlsson, Sten. *History of Modern Sweden.* Stockholm: The Swedish Institute, 1963.

Central Bureau of Statistics. *Socialvården 1962* and *1963.* Stockholm: Kungl. Boktryckeriet, 1964 and 1965.

Cost and Financing of the Social Services in Sweden in 1963. Stockholm: Central Bureau of Statistics, 1965.

Dental Education in Sweden. Stockholm: The Swedish Institute, 1962.

Development of Sweden in Figures. Stockholm: The Swedish Institute, 1962.

Eltz, Sylvia. *Health and Pension Insurance in Sweden.* Stockholm: The Swedish Institute, 1964.

———. *Housing for the Aged and the Disabled in Sweden.* Stockholm: The Swedish Institute, 1963.

Facts about Sweden. Stockholm: The Swedish Institute, 1962.

Gustafsson, Lars. *The Public Dialogue in Sweden.* Stockholm: Norstedt/The Swedish Institute, 1964.

Heckscher, Gunnar. *The Swedish Constitution.* Stockholm: The Swedish Institute, 1961.

———. *Swedish Public Administration at Work.* Stockholm: The Swedish Institute, 1961.

Hessler, Tore. *Survey of the Swedish Vocational School System.* Stockholm: The Swedish Institute, 1962.

Hook, Erik. *The Changing Face of Sweden's Economy.* Stockholm: The Swedish Institute, 1963.

Iveroth, Axel. *Private Enterprise in Sweden: Industrial Peace and Prosperity.* Stockholm: The Swedish Institute, 1963.

THE SOCIAL PROGRAMS OF SWEDEN

Kalvesten, Ann-Lisa. *The Social Structure of Sweden.* Stockholm: The Swedish Institute, 1965.
Labor, Peace and Full Employment in Sweden. Stockholm: KVE Institut for Informationsmethodik, AB Direktkopia, 1962.
Langenfelt, Per. *Local Government in Sweden.* Stockholm: The Swedish Institute, 1962.
―――. *Principles for a New Division of Sweden's Municipalities.* Stockholm: The Swedish Institute, 1962.
Linner, Birgitta. *Society and Sex in Sweden.* Stockholm: The Swedish Institute, 1965.
Michanek, Ernst. *For and Against the Swedish Welfare State.* Stockholm: The Swedish Institute, 1963.
―――. *For and Against the Swedish Welfare State: Swedish Experiences.* Stockholm: The Swedish Institute, 1963.
―――. *Old Age in Sweden.* Stockholm: The Swedish Institute, 1962.
―――. *Sweden's New National Pension Insurance.* Stockholm: The Swedish Institute, 1962.
―――. *Swedish Government in Action.* Stockholm: The Swedish Institute, 1962.
―――. *The Right to Security.* Stockholm: The Swedish Institute, 1965.
Michanek, K. G. *Social Insurance in Sweden.* Stockholm: The Swedish Institute, 1962.
Ministry for Foreign Affairs. *The Constitution of Sweden.* Stockholm: Ivor Haeggströms Boktryckeri HB, 1954.
Ministry of Finance. *Swedish Budget 1963–64, 1964–65, 1965–66, 1966–67, 1967–68.* Stockholm: Isaac Marcus Boktryckeri HB, 1963–67.
National Labour Market Board. *Modern Swedish Labour Market Policy.* Falköping: Gummessons Boktryckeri HB, 1966.
National Insurance Act, May 25, 1962. Stockholm: Ministry of Social Affairs, 1963.
Orring, Jonas. *The School System of General Education in Sweden.* Stockholm: The Swedish Institute, 1964.
Osvald, Olof. *The Swedish Public Dental Health Service.* Stockholm: The Swedish Institute, 1962.
Pers, Anders. *Newspapers in Sweden.* Stockholm: The Swedish Institute, 1963.
Persson, Konrad. *Social Welfare in Sweden.* Stockholm: National Pensions Board, 1961.
Right to Security. Stockholm: The Swedish Institute, 1965.
Rössel, James. *Women in Scandinavia.* Stockholm: The Swedish Institute, 1965.
Savings Banks in Scandinavia. Stockholm: NCSD, 1956.
Schmidt, Folke. *Introduction to the Law of Labour Relations in Sweden.* Stockholm: The Swedish Institute, 1963.
―――. *Negotiation and Mediation in Sweden.* Stockholm: The Swedish Institute, 1963.
―――. *Organization and Jurisdiction of the Labour Court in Sweden.* Stockholm: The Swedish Institute, 1963.
Social Welfare Board. *Social Sweden.* Stockholm: Gernandts Boktryckeri, 1952.
Stahre, Sven-Arne. *Adult Education in Sweden.* Stockholm: The Swedish Institute, 1965.
Statistical Abstract of Sweden. Stockholm: Central Bureau of Statistics, 1962–1966.
Swedish Youth. Stockholm: The Swedish Institute, 1964.
Tegner, Göran. *Social Security in Sweden.* Stockholm: The Swedish Institute, 1956.
Therapeutic Abortion and the Law in Sweden. Stockholm: The Swedish Institute, 1964.
Wiman, Anna. *Vocational Training for Adults in Sweden.* Stockholm: The Swedish Institute, 1962.

BIBLIOGRAPHY

UNITED STATES

BUREAU OF THE CENSUS:

———. Foreign Demographic Analysis Division. *Bibliography of Social Science Periodical and Monograph Series: Denmark.* Washington, D.C.: 1964.

———. Foreign Demographic Analysis Division. *Bibliography of Social Science Periodical and Monograph Series: Norway, 1945–1962.* Washington, D.C.: 1964.

———. Foreign Demographic Analysis Division. *Bibliography of Social Science Periodical and Monograph Series: Sweden, 1950–1963.* Washington, D.C.: 1964.

———. Foreign Manpower Research Office. *Bibliography of Social Science Periodical and Monograph Series: Iceland, 1950–1962.* Washington, D.C.: 1963.

CONGRESS:

———. Joint Economic Committee. *European Social Security Systems.* Economic Policies and Practices Paper No. 7. 89th Congress, 1st Session, 1965.

———. Joint Economic Committee. *Unemployment Programs in Sweden.* 88th Congress, 2nd Session, 1964.

DEPARTMENT OF HEALTH, EDUCATION, AND WELFARE:

———. *A Brief Explanation of Medicare: Health Insurance for People 65 or Older.* Washington, D.C.: November 1965.

———. Children's Bureau. *Reduction of Infant Mortality, Selected Countries, 1950–1962.* Washington, D.C.: August 25, 1963.

———. Office of Education. *Sweden – Educational Data.* Washington, D.C.: 1965.

———. Social Security Administration. Division of Research and Statistics. *Social Security Programs throughout the World.* Washington, D.C.: 1964.

———. Social Security Administration. *Health Insurance under Social Security.* Washington, D.C.: 1966.

———. Social Security Administration. *If You Work While You Get Social Security Payments.* Washington, D.C.: April 1966.

———. Social Security Administration. Office of Administration and Statistics. *Sweden's Social Security System: An Appraisal of Its Economic Impact in the Postwar Period.* Washington, D.C.: 1966.

———. Social Security Administration. *Your Social Security.* Washington, D.C.: November 1965.

DEPARTMENT OF LABOR:

———. *Employment and Earnings.* Bulletin of the Bureau of Labor Statistics, Vol. 10, No. 7, January 1964.

Furman, Sylvan S. *Community Mental Health Services in Northern Europe.* Public Service Publication No. 1407. Bethesda, Md.: National Institute of Mental Health, 1965.

Holmes, Ann C. *Living Conditions in Sweden.* Washington, D.C.: U.S. Government Printing Office, 1962.

King, Margaret L., and George A. Male. *Sweden: Educational Data.* Washington, D.C.: U.S. Government Printing Office, 1965.

Minnesota Medical Assistance Program. St. Paul, Minn.: Department of Public Welfare, 1966.

President's Council on Aging. *Homes for the Aged in Sweden Offer Ideas for Americans.* Washington, D.C.: 1965.

President's Panel on Mental Retardation. *Report of Mission to Denmark and Sweden.* Washington, D.C.: 1963.

Rosenthal, Albert H. *Regional Coordination: The Role of the Federal Executive Boards.* Washington, D.C.: American Society for Public Administration, 1963.

THE SOCIAL PROGRAMS OF SWEDEN

Schnitzer, Martin. Joint Economic Committee. *Unemployment Programs in Sweden.* Economic Policies and Practices Paper No. 5. 89th Congress, 2nd Session, 1964.
Status of the Social Security Program and Recommendations for Its Improvement. Report of the Advisory Council on Social Security. Washington, D.C.: 1965.

Articles and Periodicals

Alvarez, Walter C. "Some Sex Views Outmoded." *Minneapolis Star*, May 16, 1966, p. 53.
Anderson, S. V. "Scandinavian Ombudsman." *American Scandinavian Review*, December 1964, pp. 403–409.
Andrén, Nils. "The Swedish Ombudsman." *Anglo-Swedish Review*, May 1962, p. 3.
———. "The Swedish Office of the 'Ombudsman,'" *Municipal Review*, 33 (No. 396):821 (December 1962).
Bengston, Sven F. "Social Policy in Sweden – A Survey." *Free Labour World*, January/February 1962, pp. 22–25.
Bexelius, Alfred. "The Swedish Institution of the Justitieombudsman." *International Review of Administrative Sciences*, November 3, 1961, pp. 243–256.
Bixby, Lovell. "Penology in Sweden and Denmark." *American Journal of Correction*, May/June 1962, pp. 18–25.
Bolang, Karl Olaf. "But the Ombudsman Thought Otherwise." *American-Swedish Monthly*, July 1963, p. 22.
Cramond, R. D. "Housing Without Profit." *Public Administration*, Summer 1965, pp. 135–154.
Favre, George H. "Ombudsman Ends Year in N.Y. Area." *Christian Science Monitor*, July 19, 1967.
Friedrich, Carl. "Rights, Liberties, Freedoms: A Reappraisal." *American Political Science Review*, 57:842 (1963).
Fritchey, Clayton. "Citizen Needs 'Shield' from Uncle Sam." *Minneapolis Tribune*, May 24, 1966, p. 5.
Hazlitt, H. "Progressive Taxation." *Newsweek*, May 13, 1963, p. 88.
———. "Taxes in Sweden." *Newsweek*, October 29, 1962, p. 78.
"Health Care For All." *Scandinavian Times*, News Magazine, May 1965, pp. 3–8.
Heckscher, Gunnar. "Pluralist Democracy, the Swedish Experience." *Social Research*, 15 (No. 4): 461 (December 1948).
Higuchi, T. "Old-Age Pensions and Retirement." *International Labour Review*, October 1964, pp. 333–351.
Hirsch, P. "How the Swedes Do It." *New Republic*, July 20, 1963, p. 9.
"Housing as a Social Problem (Sweden)." *Architectural Record*, April 1964, p. 162.
"How Europe Deals with Medical Care." *U.S. News and World Report*, July 30, 1962, p. 46.
"How Medicare Works in Europe." *Realities*, January 1965, pp. 66–69.
"How Sweden Keeps the Labor Peace." *Business Week*, October 20, 1962, p. 158.
"How Swedish Free Enterprise Co-Exists with Socialism." *Fortune*, May 1962, p. 80.
"How the Swedes and Danes Do It." *Economist*, May 1965, pp. 1042–1043.
Hutton, Graham, "America – Beware of the Welfare State." *Reader's Digest*, October 1961, pp. 84–87.
"If You Think Welfare Costs Are High in America: Here Is What's Happening to Costs and Coverage Abroad." *U.S. News and World Report*, March 1, 1965, pp. 101–102.
"If You Wonder Where Welfare Is Heading: U.S. vs. Sweden." *U.S. News and World Report*, July 19, 1965, pp. 86–87.
"Infant Mortality: No Change." *Time*, September 6, 1963, p. 48.
"Inflation in Utopia." *Time*, April 15, 1966, p. 97.

BIBLIOGRAPHY

"Jungles of Bureaucracy." *St. Paul Pioneer Press*, January 19, 1967, p. 6.
Letofsky, Irv. "Danes Are Sexually Free." *Minneapolis Tribune*, April 20, 1966, p. 13.
Lundquist, Gunnar. "Treatment of Alcoholism in Sweden." *British Journal of Addiction*, January 1962, pp. 4–12.
Martin, K. "Are the Swedes Happy?" *New Statesman*, October 11, 1963, p. 480.
Myrdal, Gunnar. "Swedish Way to Happiness." *New York Times Magazine*, January 30, 1966, p. 144.
"New Social Insurance Code in Sweden." *International Labour Review*, May 1963, pp. 489–491.
Plumb, Robert K. "U.S. Health Care Is Found Lagging." *New York Times*, November 6, 1963.
Porter, Sylvia. "Welfare State Psychology." Denver *Post*, December 3, 1964, p. 42.
Quade, Quentin L., and Thorman J. Bennett. "Shield for the Citizen: the Ombudsman of Scandinavia." *Modern Age*, Fall 1964, pp. 377–388.
"Recommendation on Swedish Wage Policy." *Monthly Labour Review*, February 1963, pp. 171–172.
Rehn, Gosta, and Erik Lundberg. "Employment and Welfare: Some Swedish Issues." *Industrial Relations*, February 1963, pp. 1–14.
Rosenthal, A. H., and D. C. Rowat. "An Ombudsman for America?" *Public Administration Review*, December 1964, pp. 226–233.
Russel, F. "Sweden: That Middle Way." *National Review*, October 6, 1964, pp. 877–878.
Seldowitz, Estelle, and Agnes W. Brewster. "Sweden's Health and Cash Sickness Insurance Program." *Public Health Reports*, September 1964, pp. 815–822.
Snider, Arthur J. "Scarcity of Hospital Beds: Real Problem," *Minneapolis Star*, July 27, 1967, p. 15B.
"Social Security Programs of Foreign Countries." *Social Security Bulletin*, September 1964, pp. 16–26.
"Socialism and Suicide." *Scandinavian Times*, September 10, 1963, p. 3.
"Socialism Goes Tame in Sweden." *Business Week*, July 14, 1963, p. 72.
Somers, Anne Ramsey. "The European Experience," in "Health: Are We the People Getting Our Money's Worth?" *New Republic Supplement*, November 9, 1963, p. 33.
Starnes, Richard. "Sweden: Paradise or Pipe Dream?" *Rocky Mountain News*, February 28, 1965, p. 24A; March 1, 1965, p. 18; March 2, 1965, p. 17; March 3, 1965, p. 31; March 4, 1965, p. 23.
Stassen, John H. "Serpents Spoil Sweden's Eden." *Minneapolis Star*, August 26, 1966, p. 10A.
"Sweden: The Uneasy Paradise." *Realities*, English ed., August 1962, pp. 18–23.
"Sweden's Way: A Survey by the Economist." *Economist*, March 30, 1963, pp. 1231–1265.
"Swedes Debate Sex Hysteria." *Washington Post*, February 23, 1964, p. 12C.
Swerdloff, S. "Sweden's Manpower Programs." *Monthly Labour Review*, January 1966, pp. 1–6.
Tammelin, Paul. "Rationalization in Swedish Public Administration." *International Review of Administrative Sciences*, Vol. XXVIII, No. 4, 1962, pp. 415–418.
"Tantalising." *Economist*, June 7, 1958, pp. 877–878.
"The Swedish Justitieombudsman." *American Journal of Comparative Law*, Spring 1962, pp. 225–238.
"Thirty Years Without Recession: How Sweden Does It." *U.S. News and World Report*, November 23, 1964, p. 100.
Tomasson, R. F. "Swedes Do It Better." *Harper's*, October 1962, pp. 178–180.
"Unindignant Swedes." *Economist*, May 31, 1958, pp. 805–806.

Vicker, Ray. "Sweden Versus Unemployment." *Wall Street Journal*, March 28, 1962, p. 10.
"When You Abolish Poverty — Here's What Life Is Like: The Swedish Utopia." *U.S. News and World Report*, March 16, 1964, pp. 61–64.
Wurinen, J. H. "Socialized Medicine in Sweden." *Current History*, June 1963, pp. 333–338.
Zanker, A. "Life in a Great Society: What One Country Finds." *U.S. News and World Report*, February 7, 1966, pp. 58–60.

Index

Abortions, 54, 63–67, 155, 164: regulation of, 60, 63–64, 64–65, 66; foreigners seeking, 60, 66; sex education about, 61; reasons for, 63–64, 64, 65, 66; number of in Sweden, 65, 165; number of in U.S., 165
Act of Succession (*1810*), 95
Advance pension, *see* Disability pension
Aged: plans to aid, 3, 4: housing for, 73, 84–86, 137, 151–152; on welfare, 75, 83–84; care of in U.S. compared with that in Sweden, 83, 86, 137, 151–152; care of, 83–86. *See also* Basic Pension; Health insurance; Retirement benefits; Social Security program; Supplementary Pension
Agriculture, Department of, 100: employees of, 114
Aid to Families with Dependent Children (U.S.), 146, 153
Aid to the Blind (U.S.), 146, 153
Aid to the Disabled (U.S.), 146, 153
Akademiska Hospital, 57, 58
Alcoholics and alcoholism, 72, 87, 108, 125, 136, 155, 164, 165, 166: on welfare, 76, 77; rehabilitation for, 76, 166
Alexanderson, quoted, 123
Allmän tilläggspension, see Supplementary Pension
Allmänna Försäkringskassorna, see Regional public insurance funds
Allmänna Pensionsfonden, see National Pension Insurance Fund
American Medical Association, opposes general health insurance in U.S., 144, 145

American Psychological Association, 167
American-Swedish Monthly, 123
Andrén, Nils, quoted, 110, 115, 122
Ansokan om Allman Pension (Application for Public Pension), 21
Association against Polio, 89
Association against Rheumatism, 89
Association of Rural Areas, 74
ATP (*allmän tilläggspension*), *see* Supplementary Pension
Attorney General (U.S.), 118, 146
Austria, doctors in, 145

Bacteriological Laboratory, National, 55
Basic Pension, 5, 34, 35, 81, 83, 86, 90, 140, 141, 152: establishment of, 5, 10, 12–13; adjusted to cost-of-living index, 5, 21, 26, 27, 140, 142; number of recipients of, 13; coverage and eligibility of, 13–14, 16–17, 18–19, 20, 23, 138; financing of, 17–18, 22, 134, 163–164; administration of, 18–19, 20–21, 31; number assigned to every citizen, 20, 143; cut number on welfare, 76, 164; premium for, 131n, 132; compared with Social Security program (U.S.), 138–139; amount of, 141, 142. *See also* Children's allowance; Disability pension; Housing allowance; Retirement benefits; Widows' pension; Wives' supplement
Beckomberga Hospital, 59
Belgium, doctors in, 145
Bexelius, Alfred, quoted, 118, 121, 126
Bill of Rights (Swedish), 94
Bill of Rights (U.S.), 155

Biörck, Gunnar, quoted, 145
Birth control, 165: information about, 61, 62–63, 164; program of, 62–63
Blind: disability supplements for, 17; aid to in U.S., 146, 153. See also Disability pension
Block, Herbert, 170: quoted, 170
Boards, semi-independent, see Centrala Ambetsverk
Borgmästare (major judge), 105
Bromma home for aged, 84
Burial benefits, in U.S., 141
"But the Ombudsman Thought Otherwise" (Bolang), 123

Cabinet (Regeringen), 96: formation of, 97; members of, 100; decisions of, 100–102
California, pension payments in, 14
Camps, holiday: for housewives, 81; for children, 81, 83
Cancer, radiotherapeutic clinics for, 57
Cardozo, Benjamin Nathan, 169
Care homes, for chronically ill, 73
Carmichael v. Southern Coal and Coke Co., 169
Census registration (Mantalsskrilven), 20, 21: required for Basic Pension, 13–14, 20; required for health insurance program, 38; qualification for abortion, 66–67; necessary to vote, 98
Central Social Assistance Committee, 73. See also Social assistance committees
Central Statistical Bureau, 98
Centrala Ambetsverk (central administrative boards), 100, 110, 112, 113, 114, 117, 119, 120, 158: organization and responsibilities of, 103–104. See also individual boards
Cerebral palsy, classes for children with, 59
Chancery Building, 101
Child guidance clinic, 83: at Kungsholm, 60
Child welfare, 72, 74, 75, 76, 80–83, 109, 125: tasks of centers of, 59; local committees for, 73, 80, 82, 83, 98; provided by kommun, 106; in Sweden and in U.S. compared, 151
Child Welfare Act (1924), 10: provisions of, 80–83
Children: psychiatry for, 53, 59–60, 107; sex education of, 60–62, 63, 164; dental care of, 67–68, 83; camps for, 81, 83; care of preschool, 82, 83; illegitimate, 83; tax deductions for, 131; care of in Sweden and in U.S., 137; private services for, 154. See also Children's allowance
Children's allowance, general, 10, 15, 80, 83, 131, 141: eligibility for, 15, 16, 17, 80, 81; amount of, 17, 80, 83, 142; financing of, 80, 81, 134, 164
Children's Bureau (U.S.), 36, 137, 151
Children's Day organizations, 154n1
Cities, Federation of, 54, 55, 56
Civil defense, 55, 109: medical aspects of, 55
Civil liberties, protected in Sweden, 155–157
Civil service, 111–117: tenure in, 111, 112, 113, 116, 117; prestige of, 111, 115, 158; classifications in, 112, 113, 113–114; controls over, 117–128
Civil Service, Department of, 100, 102, 112, 113, 115: employees of, 113, 114
Civil Service Commission (U.S.), 113
Civil-ekonom (degree in business administration), 112
Colorado, pension payments in, 14
Columbia University, 167, 170
Commerce, Department of, 100: employees of, 114
Commons, House of (British), 127
Communications and Transportation, Department of, 100: employees of, 114
Congress (U.S.), 101, 126, 127, 128, 140, 142, 146, 169: compared with Riksdag, 96
Conservative party, 157
Constitution (Swedish), 94, 95n5, 99, 118: basic documents of, 94–95; Instrument of Government of, 94–95, 113, 118, 122, 155; Act of Succession of, 95; Riksdag Act of, 95; Freedom of the Press Act of, 95, 99, 155; on King, 96; provisions of for freedom of individual, 155
Constitution (U.S.), 94, 95, 155
Contraception: information about, 61–62, 62–63, 63; devices for, 62, 63
Cooperatives, in Sweden, 93, 93n1, 159, 160
Cost-of-living index: Basic Pension adjusted to, 5, 21, 26, 27, 140, 142; Supplementary Pension adjusted to, 5, 26–28, 140, 142; not consulted for children's allowances, 16; used by some state pension programs in U.S., 26; method of adjusting pensions to, 26–28

INDEX

Council of Responsible Authorities, 54
County Council Law (1862), 106
County councils, see Landsting
County Councils, Federation of, 54, 55, 56
Cripples, National Organization of, 89
Customs, National Board of, 129

Danderyd, Stockholm Län Hospital at, 59
Declaration of Independence (U.S.), 95
Defense, Department of, 100, 119: employees of, 114
Delinquency, juvenile, 72, 136
Denmark: health insurance plans in, 7; hospitals in, 58; ombudsman in, 121, 128; doctors in, 145; alcohol in, 166; suicide in, 167
Dental care: limited coverage of by health insurance, 11, 43, 45, 46, 68; in län, 67, 107; government program for, 67–68; free for children, 67–68, 83; covered by Medicaid, 147; covered by Medicare, 148
Dental Division, National Board of Health, 54, 67, 68
Dental Health Service, see Dental Division
Dentists: licensing of, 54, 67; in dental health program, 67, 68; association of (Tandvärnet), 68; schools for, 68; shortage of, 68
Depression, effect of on pensions, 5
Disability pension (förtidspension), 5, 8, 12, 15, 15n1, 15–16, 23, 24–25, 79, 86, 90, 137: eligibility for, 10, 15, 17, 19, 24–25, 45, 77; amount of, 15–16, 17, 19, 25, 27, 142, 143; administration of, 19; of Basic and Supplementary pension programs coordinated, 24–25; recipients of get free medical care, 47n6; funds for, 90. See also Rehabilitation; Vocational training
Disablement resettlement program, 87
District doctor, 31, 42, 43, 107: charges of, 39; duties of, 39, 54–55
Doctors, 54, 85, 145: fee schedule for, 38, 39, 39–40, 150; services of covered by health insurance program, 38–41, 46, 50, 51, 138, 141n, 147, 148, 149; shortage of, 40, 41, 91; distribution of in U.S. and Sweden, 40–41; licensing of, 52, 54; and civil defense, 55; education of for rehabilitation, 91; fees of covered by Social Security (U.S.), 138, 141n; block general health insurance in U.S.,

144, 145; complaints of in various countries, 145; fees of covered by Medicaid, 147; fees of covered by Medicare, 148. See also District doctor
Domsagor (judicial districts), 106
Douglas, William O., quoted, 156
Drugs, see Medicines and drugs

Economic Opportunity Act (U.S.), 150–151
Education, 110, 125: for crippled children, 59, 89; about sex, 60–62, 63, 164; of welfare recipients, 72, 136; result of lack of, 76; financing of, 81–82, 106; in län, 107, 108; in municipalblocks, 111; for civil service, 111–112; numbers of students receiving, 162. See also Vocational training
Education, National Board of, 60, 89
Education and Ecclesiastical Affairs, Department of, 100: employees of, 114
Ekelund, Wilhelm, quoted, 3
Elections: system of in Sweden, 96, 97–98; interest in in Sweden and in U.S., 98; social programs supported in, 157–158
Elmer Davis Memorial Lecture, 170
Emigration, from Sweden in 1930's, 80
Employers Federation, 163
Enskede, 85
Epidemiology, programs in, 53, 55
Epilepsy, 53: hospitals for, 55
Essays in the Public Philosophy (Lippmann), 169
Excise, National Board of (*Kontrollstyrelsen*), 129
Expeditionschef (legal secretary), 102

Family planning, see Birth control
Farber, Maurice L., quoted, 167
Federalist Papers, 169
Federation of Cities, 54, 55, 56
Federation of County Councils, 54, 55, 56
Federation of Swedish Industries, 160
Fee schedule: for doctors, 38, 39, 39–40, 150; amounts on, 39–40; for dental care, 43, 67
Finance, bureau of, of National Board of Health, 54
Finance, Department of, 100, 129: employees of, 114
Finance Bill (1967), 132
Finland: health insurance plans in, 7; ombudsman in, 121
First Fund, of National Pension Insurance

185

Fund: responsibility of, 32; amounts handled, 33
Fiscal Appeal, Court of (*kammarrätten*), 120, 130
Fleisher, Frederic, 36
Food and Drug Administration (U.S.), compared with National Pharmaceutical Laboratory, 56
Foreign Affairs, Department of, 66, 100: employees in, 114
Foreigners: covered by welfare laws, 9; some of covered by Basic Pension, 13; eligibility of for Supplementary Pension, 23, 25, 139; eligibility of for health insurance program, 38; eligibility of for abortions, 60, 66, 66–67; eligibility of for Social Security (U.S.), 139
Forensic Chemistry, National Laboratory for, 55
Forensic Medical Offices, National, 55
Försäkringanamnd (municipal insurance committee): duties and composition of, 31–32; salaries of, 32
Församlingar (parishes), 106
Förtidspension (advance pension), *see* Disability pension
France: medical profession in, 145; G.N.P. in, 161, 162; alcohol in, 166
Freedom of the Press Act (*1949*), 95, 99, 155
French Revolution, 95
Friedrich, Carl, quoted, 156
Froding, Gustaf, quoted, 12
De Fyras Bod (the Fours Shop), 154n1

Gävle, 105
Geijer, Erik Gustaf, quoted, 52, 154
General Accounting Office (U.S.), 126
General Salary Regulations of the State, 115
Generaltullstyrelsen (National Board of Customs), administration of taxes by, 129
Germany, West: ombudsman in, 121; doctors in, 145; G.N.P. in, 161, 162; alcohol in, 166
Göteborg, 58, 74, 89, 97, 105, 150: regional insurance fund in, 29, 30; medical treatment in, 39, 43; population of, 105
Grant-in-aid program: in U.S., 72, 106, 111, 137; in Sweden, 106, 108, 109, 110, 111, 158
Great Britain: citizens of eligible for Swedish social insurance, 13, 38; civil service in, 102, 118; ombudsman in, 121; medical profession in, 145; G.N.P. in, 161, 162; alcohol in, 166
Gross national product, growth of in Sweden and other countries, 161–162
Guilds, medieval trade, insurance programs of, 7
Gustafson, Lars, quoted, 165–166
Gustav VI Adolf, King, 96
Gynecology, on fee schedule, 39

Hälsingborg, 89, 105
Handicapped, mentally or physically: eligibility of for disability pension, 15; on welfare, 76; and aged, 85; vocational help for, 87; care for, 87, 89; number of, 88. *See also* Disability pension; Retarded, mentally
Härnösänd, 89
Harvard Medical School, 37
Health, Education, and Welfare, Department of (U.S.), 101
Health, National Board of, *see* National Board of Health
Health insurance, 4, 6, 6–8, 10, 11, 23, 37–51, 71, 144–150, 163: administration of, 11, 18, 19, 31, 52, 145; and dental work, 11, 43, 45, 46, 68; appeals of matters concerning, 34; premium for, 37, 47, 131n, 133, 134; coverage of and eligibility for, 38, 57; financing of, 46–48, 134, 149, 163, 164; lack of coordination of with rehabilitation program, 90; citizens approve, 92; blocked in U.S., 144, 145; compared with Medicare, 145–150; cut number on welfare, 152, 164; private, 163. *See also* Disability pension; Doctors
Health Insurance for the Aged program (U.S.), 145–150
Heckscher, Gunnar, quoted, 157
Heidenstam, Werner von, quoted, 69
Help for Self-Help, 72, 151, 152: administration of, 88
Helvering v. Davis, 169: decision quoted, 169
Hendin, Herbert, quoted, 167–168
Högdalen, 60
Hökaranger, 59
Home Affairs, Department of, *see* Interior, Department of
Home-help program, for aged and needy, 85
Hoover, Herbert, 169

INDEX

Hospital Administration, 93
Hospital Planning, Central Board of, 56
Hospitals, 56–58, 87, 125: publicly owned, 6, 56, 57–58, 92–93, 107, 134, 154; sickness allowance for patients in, 8, 44–45; provisions for expenses of children in, 10; patients in not eligible for disability supplements, 17; care in covered by health insurance, 38, 39, 41–42, 43, 45–46, 48, 50, 51, 147, 147–148, 149; maternity care in, 45–46, 51; bureau of, of National Board of Health, 53; equipped for national emergency, 55; number of, 56; construction of, 56–57, 109; for somatic disease, 57; teaching, 57, 58; care in for welfare recipients, 71, 74, 75; for chronically ill, 84; insurance for in U.S., 145, 146, 147, 148, 149; shortage of beds in, 150. *See also* Mental hospitals; Sickness
Housewives, 34: covered by health insurance, 38, 43, 48; eligible for additional cash sickness allowance, 46, 49; vacations for, 81
Housing, 109: for aged, 73, 84–86, 137; administration of, 101, 104, 105; for aged in Sweden and U.S. compared, 151–152
Housing, National Board of, 104
Housing allowance, municipal, 4, 5, 6, 15, 20–21, 28: subject to income test, 4, 15, 17, 19, 134, 141; amount of, 17, 19, 21; financing of, 17, 134; eligibility for, 17, 141; administration of, 19
"How Swedish Free Enterprise Co-Exists with Socialism," 160
Hungary, suicides in, 166
Hygiene, bureau of, of National Board of Health, 53

The Ideal Marriage (Van der Velde), 62
Illegitimacy, 83, 136, 155, 164–165: sex education about, 61
Immunization, 59: vaccines and serums for, 55; free for children, 83
Income tax, federal (U.S.), 81
Income test, 5, 6, 37: housing allowance subject to, 4, 15, 17, 19, 134, 141; for health insurance in Denmark and Norway, 7; not applied to Basic Pension, 12–13, 138; for wives' supplements, 15, 16; not applied to disability pension, 16; and children's allowances, 16, 80, 81, 82; administration of, 17, 31; for health insurance benefits, 37, 44, 47; for Social Security (U.S.), 138, 140; not applied to Supplementary Pension, 140
Industries, Federation of, 160
Infant mortality, 36: rates of in Sweden, The Netherlands, and U.S., 36–37
Institute for Social and Political Training, 74
Institutes for the Care of Cripples, 89
Instrument of Government (*1809*), 94–95, 113, 118, 122, 155
Insurance, *see* Basic Pension; Children's allowance; Disability pension; Housing allowance; Retirement benefits; Supplementary Pension; Survivors' benefits
Interior, Department of, 57, 100, 109: jurisdiction of, 53, 101, 102; boards of, 104; employees of, 114
Internal Revenue Service (U.S.), 129
Invalidpension, name changed, 15n1. *See also* Disability pension
Israel, ombudsman in, 121
Italy: eligibility of nationals of for Swedish social insurance, 13, 38; medical profession in, 145; alcohol in, 166

JK, *see Justitiekansler*
J.O., *see* Ombudsman for Civil Affairs
Johnson, Lyndon B., 150: quoted, 142–143
Judiciary, 125: in U.S. and Sweden, 95
Juris Kandidat (Bachelor of Law), 112
Justice, Department of, 100: employees in, 114
Justice Department (U.S.), 146
Justitiekansler (chancellor of justice), duties of, 118–119
Justitieombudsman, *see* Ombudsman for Civil Affairs
Juvenile delinquency, 72, 136

Kammarrätten (Court of Fiscal Appeal), 120: citizens' appeals to, 130
Karolinska Hospital, 57, 58, 87, 91, 145
Kennedy, John F., 150
King of Sweden, 97, 100, 101, 118: Oath of Coronation of, 94; role of, 96; presides over king-in-council, 101; ombudsman reports to, 124
King-in-council, 96, 104: National Board of Health reports to, 53; top executive agency, 101; appoints landshovding, 109; established duties of justitiekansler, 119; citizens' appeals to, 120
Kollegium Medicum, 52–53
Kommun (local unit of government), 98,

104: administration of public assistance in, 9–10, 10, 73, 88; income tax system of, 81, 130; care of aged in, 84, 85, 86; election of council of, 98; number of, 105; administration in, 105–106, 111; taxation in rural, 130
Kommunalborgmästare (chairman of kommun), 105
Kommunblock (cooperating kommuns), 106, 111
Kontrollstyrelsen (National Board of Excise), administration of taxes by, 129
Köpingar (boroughs), 106
Kunglig fullmakt (royal letters of appointment), 113
Kunglig Majestat (Royal Majesty), *see* Cabinet
Kungliga Medicinalstyrelsen, *see* National Board of Health
Kungsholm, 59, 60

Labor, National Board of, 87, 88
Labor Market Board, 104
Labor Protection Board, 104
Lagerkvist, Pär, quoted, 36
Län (counties), 106, 109: regional insurance funds in, 29; hospitals of, 57, 58–59, 84, 107; counseling in for women seeking abortions, 65; dental program in, 67, 68; welfare programs in, 70, 72, 80, 88; administration of, 72, 107–108, 109–110; taxation in, 129. *See also* Landsting
Landshovding (provincial governor), duties of, 109, 110. *See also Länsstyrelsen*
Landskommuner (rural kommuns), 105, 106: taxation in, 130
Landsorganisation (Swedish Federation of Trade Unions), 115
Landsting (county councils), 98, 104, 106–108, 109, 120: appoints two members of *pension delegation*, 31; agrees on doctors' fee schedules, 39; election of, 98; responsibilities of, 107–108; taxing authority of, 130
Landstingmän (county councilors), 107
Lanskap (provinces), 106
Länsstyrelsen (provincial governor's office; central government office in län), 98, 104, 108–111, 117, 120, 158: representation of on board of regional insurance fund, 30; district doctor in, 31, 39, 42, 43, 54–55, 107; welfare administration in, 72; and homes for aged, 84; compared with regional offices of federal departments in U.S., 108–109, 109n20, 110; administration of taxes by, 129
Law on Social Help (*1956*), 10, 11
Lawyers: on National Board of Health, 54; in civil service, 112
Legal and administrative affairs, bureau of, of National Board of Health, 54
Legislation, social, 3, 5–6, 7, 8, 13: early history of, 8–9, 10, 69–70; developed by ministries of executive branch, 95, 100; process of, 99; supported by voters, 157–158. *See also* National Insurance Act; Riksdag
Leopold, Carl Gustaf, quoted, 92
Liberal party, 158
Life expectancy at birth, 36: in Sweden, Norway, The Netherlands, and U.S., 37
Liljeholmen, 59
Linköpings Central Hospital, 58
Lippmann, Walter, 169
Lokalkontor (local social insurance offices), 18, 19, 45
Löneplans A and B (central government salary scales), 115
Long, Edward V., 127: quoted, 127
Los Angeles, 146
Lotteries, tax on winnings in, 132
Lower House of Riksdag, 96–97, 98
Lund, 58, 74, 112

Magna Carta, 95
Magnuson, Warren, 127
Maintenance homes, 73
Malmö, 58, 97, 105: regional insurance fund in, 29; medical travel reimbursement in, 43; population of, 105
Malpractice, review of complaints of, 54
Mantalsskrilven, *see* Census registration
Maternity benefits, 6, 38, 45–46, 48–49, 50, 51, 147, 149: dental care under, 43, 45, 46, 51; cash allowance (*moderskopspenningen*), 45, 46, 51, 149; supplementary allowance for working women, 46, 51; in län, 107; none in U.S., 149
Means test, *see* Income test
Medicaid (U.S.), 146–147
Medical bureau, of National Board of Health, 53
Medical care: in Sweden and U.S., 36–37, 145–150; free for disability pensioners, 47n6; free for children, 82–83; for aged, 85–86; for handicapped, 87; in län, 107. *See also* Doctors; Health insurance; Hospitals; Maternity benefits

188

INDEX

Medicare (U.S.): compared with Swedish health insurance program, 145–150; financing of, 149–150
Medicines and drugs: coverage of by health insurance, 41, 42, 43, 46, 48, 50, 51, 147, 148; investigation of, 56; injury of fetus by, 64, 66; free for children, 83; coverage of by Medicaid, 147; coverage of by Medicare, 148
Mental health, bureau of, of National Board of Health, 53
Mental health clinics, counselors in for women seeking abortions, 65
Mental hospitals, 56, 57, 87, 125: administration of, 54, 55; in län, 58–59; organization of, 58–59; financing of, 134
Michanek, Ernst, quoted, 113, 136, 157
Midwives, 52, 107: licensing of, 54; schools for, 55
Militieombudsman (Ombudsman for Military Affairs), 122
Minnesota, Medicaid in, 147, 147n
M.O., see *Militieombudsman*
Moderskopspenningen (maternity cash allowance), 45, 46, 51, 149
Montesquieu (Charles de Secondat), concept of check and balance of, 95
Mortality, infant, rates of, 36–37
Moscow, 171
Multiple Sclerosis Association, 89
Municipal housing allowance, see Housing allowance
Municipal insurance committee, see *Försäkringanamnd*
Municipal samhällen (limited towns), 106
Municipalblock (cooperating cities), 106, 111

National Bank, 32
National Board of Education, 60, 89
National Board of Health (*Kungliga Medicinalstyrelsen*), 30, 31, 53, 54, 57, 58: appoints district doctors, 31; organization of, 53–56; regulation of abortions by, 64–65, 66. See also *Centrala Ambetsverk*
National Housing Board, 104
National Institute of Public Health, 55
National Insurance Act (*1962*), 8, 16, 86: passing of, 4; quoted, 6; coordinated insurance programs, 15, 18, 24–25, 37, 49; costs of carrying out, 18; administration of, 93

National Insurance Court, 30: establishment and purpose of, 34
National Labor Board, responsible for vocational rehabilitation, 87, 88
National Mediation Board, 104
National Medical Board, see National Board of Health
National Organization of Cripples, 89
National Pension Act (*1913*), 5, 13: provisions of, 4–5
National Pension Act (*1946*), provisions of, 5
National Pension Board, 89: administered rehabilitation programs, 86–87
National Pension Insurance Fund, 32–34: financing of, 17–18, 22, 80, 81, 134, 163–164; three funds of, 32, 33; described, 133. See also Basic Pension; Health insurance; Supplementary Pension
National Popular Study Association, 162
National Social Insurance Board (*Riksförsäkringsverket*), 20, 23, 86, 88, 90, 103, 104: administers National Pension program, 18–19; supervises regional insurance funds, 30, 30–31, 32; costs of administration of, 33–34, 48; complaints division of, 34; supervises welfare program, 72; directives of on homes for aged, 84. See also *Centrala Ambetsverk*
National Tax Board (*riksskattenämnden*), 130
National Trade Education Board, 89
The Netherlands, life expectancy at birth in, 36, 37
Neurosurgery, 57
New York (state), Medicaid in, 147
New Zealand, ombudsman in, 121
Norrbacka Institute, 89
Norrköping, 105: regional insurance fund in, 29; medical travel reimbursement in, 43
Norway: health insurance plans in, 7; life expectancy at birth in, 37; ombudsman in, 121; doctors in, 145; suicide in, 167
Nurses: licensing of, 54; and civil defense, 55

Oath of Coronation, quoted, 94
Occupational therapy, 87, 108. See also Rehabilitation
Old Age Assistance (U.S.), 146, 152, 153
Old-age pensions, see Retirement benefits
Ombudsman for Civil Affairs (*Justitieombudsman*), 118, 119, 122, 158: duties

189

of, 120, 121, 121–123, 123–124, 125, 126; offices similar to in various countries, 121; superiors of, 122, 124; action of, 123, 124–126; interest in in U.S., 126–127, 128, 129
Ombudsman for Military Affairs (*Militieombudsman*), 122
Opthalmology, on fee schedule, 39
Örebro Central Hospital, 58
Överrevisorer (High Auditors), 119

Parliament, British, 94
Parliament, Swedish, *see* Riksdag
Parliamentary Commissioner: in New Zealand, 121; in Great Britain, 121, 127–128
Paymaster General, 119
Pell, Claiborne, 127
Pension fees, collected to finance National Pension, 17–18
Pension Fund, *see* National Pension Insurance Fund
Pension Law (*1959*), 6
Pension points, 21, 34, 35, 138: accumulation of, 23, 25, 27, 139; computation of benefits by, 25, 26, 27; derivation of, 27
Pensionähemen (apartment houses for the aged), 84–85
Pensions delegation (pension committee), 19, 98: composition of, 31; salaries of, 32
Pharmaceutical Laboratory, National, 56
Pharmacies and pharmacists, 42, 53, 54, 55, 145
Pharmacy, bureau of, of National Board of Health, 54
Philadelphia, 167
Physicians, *see* Doctors
Physiotherapists, licensing of, 54
Pinchot, Gifford, 170
Polio, Association against, 89
Politices magister (Master of Politics), 112
Poor laws, 10: in Sweden, 8–9, 70; in England, 69–70; in Ireland, 70
Poor Relief Act (*1918*), 9, 10: provisions of, 70, 73
Porter, Sylvia, quoted, 165
Post Office, employees of, 114, 117
Post Office Savings Bank, 32
Poverty program (U.S.), 76, 136, 150–151
Premiums for health insurance, 37, 47, 131n, 133, 134

Press Bureau, 79
Preventive health service, 52
Preventive Medicine, Department of, Harvard Medical School, 37
Product of Private Enterprise, 159
Providence societies, 7
Prövningsnämnd (Provincial Appeal Board), reviews tax assessments, 130
Psychiatry: on fee schedule, 39; for children, 53, 59–60, 107; role of in welfare program, 77. *See also* Mental hospitals
Psychiatry, bureau of social and forensic, of National Board of Health, 53–54
Public Accounting Office for Civil Administration, 119
Public Health, National Institute of, for research and training, 55
Public health programs, 37, 39, 52–53, 110. *See also* Health insurance; Hospitals; Maternity benefits; Medical care
Public Welfare, Department of, 74, 76, 78, 79: responsibilities of, 73; program of for aged, 84, 85
Public welfare committee, *see* Social assistance committee
Public Works and Economic Development Act (U.S.), 151

Radio-fluorography, center for, 55
Regeringen, *see* Cabinet
Regeringsrätten (Supreme Administrative Court), 120, 124, 130
Regional Action Planning Commissions (U.S.), 151
Regional public insurance funds (*Allmänna Försäkringskassorna*), 18, 19, 22, 29, 34, 50, 93, 145; boards of, 30, 31, 32; staff of, 30–31; administration of, 30–31, 39; reports of, 31
Regional Sickness Funds, *see* Regional public insurance funds
Rehabilitation, 59, 86–91, 108: of the disabled, 3, 4; of welfare recipients, 11, 76, 151, 152; of alcoholics, 76, 166; financing of, 88; administration of, 89–90; in län, 108; by private agencies, 154. *See also* Vocational training
Rental allowances, municipal, *see* Housing allowance
Reorganization Act (*1952*), 105
Responsible Authorities, Council of, 54
Retarded, mentally, 53: eligibility of for disability pension, 15; education of, 59, 107, 108; on welfare, 76
Retirement benefits, 4, 4–6, 8, 12, 13, 24,

INDEX

27–28, 137, 138, 140: financing of, 4; under National Insurance Act, 14–15; eligibility for, 14, 23, 24; compared with Social Security (U.S.), 14, 24; amount of, 23–24, 27, 27–28, 142, 143
Retroverse loans, 32, 33
Reuss, Henry, 127, 128: quoted, 127
RFSU (National Association for Sex Education), 63
Rheumatism, Association against, 89
Riksdag, 5, 6, 10, 71, 94, 95, 95n5, 96, 101, 102, 103, 104, 105: and compulsory health insurance, 8, 68, 93; process of legislation in, 13, 99; passes Supplementary Pension Act, 22; belief of that older workers useful to society, 24; legislation on public health, 54–55, 58; passes law on abortions, 63–64; passes welfare legislation, 70; passes law on homes for aged, 84; election of, 96, 97–98, 98; organization of, 96–97; and Cabinet, 101; employees of, 114, 117; and ombudsman, 122, 124
Riksdag Act (1866), 95
Riksförsäkringsverket, see National Social Insurance Board
Roosevelt, Franklin D., 170
Roosevelt, Theodore, 170
Rosenlund home for aged, 84
Royal Health Kollegium, 53
Royal Labor Board, 89
Royal Medical Board, 88–89, 89
Rudholm, Sten, quoted, 119
Rural kommuns (*landskommuner*), 105, 106: taxation in, 130
Rustow, Dankwart A., quoted, 99

Sabbatsborg home for aged, 84
Sahlgrenska Hospital, 58
St. Göran Hospital, 87
Sandburg, Carl, 172
Sanitation, programs in, 53, 55, 109
Scandinavia (excluding Sweden): health insurance compulsory in, 7; citizens of eligible for Swedish social insurance, 13, 38; ombudsman in, 121, 128; doctors in, 145. *See also* Denmark; Finland; Norway
Scandinavian Times, on health insurance, 7
School of Social Work at Göteborg, 74
School of Social Work at Lund, 74
School of Social Work at Umeå, 74
Schweinitz, Karl de, quoted, 171
Scientific Council, 54
Second Fund, of National Pension Insurance Fund: responsibility of, 32; amounts handled, 33
Self-employed, 138: eligible for basic daily allowance, 8; can accept or refuse Supplementary Pension, 8, 22–23, 44, 47, 139; pay own taxes and pension premiums, 27, 32, 130; eligibility of for sickness allowances, 43, 44, 47–48, 49; eligible for Social Security (U.S.), 139
Self-help program, 77, 78, 79, 86. *See also* Help for Self-Help
Semi-independent central administrative boards, *see Centrala Ambetsverk*
Serafimer Hospital, 57
Sex education, *see* Education
Sex Education, National Association for (RFSU), program of, 63
Sex Instruction in Swedish Schools, quoted, 60
Den sexuella samlevnaden (*The Sexual Relationship*), 62
Sickness: benefit societies for, 7–8; cash allowance, 43–44, 45, 46, 47, 48, 50, 147–148, 148–149; children's supplement to allowance for, 44, 45, 48, 50; reason for receiving welfare, 75; pay for civil servants during, 116; tax deduction for, 131–132; benefits in U.S. and in Sweden compared, 145–150. *See also* Disability pension; Health insurance
Sigtuna, community school at, 74
Social Affairs, Department of, 100, 136: responsibility of for public health and welfare, 53, 72, 101; organization of, 102–103; boards of, 104; employees of, 114
Social Assistance Act (1957): passing of, 70; provisions of, 70–72, 73, 84
Social assistance committee, 71, 72, 73, 77, 78, 79, 88, 98
Social Benefits in Sweden, 90–91
Social Democratic party, 5, 100, 158: supports retention of block pension, 13
Social Help, Law on, 10, 11
Social insurance programs, *see* Basic Pension; Children's allowance; Disability pension; Health insurance; Retirement benefits; Supplementary Pension; Survivors' benefits
Social Security Act (1935; U.S.), 14, 169: extension of, 137, 141n, 145, 146, 151
Social Security program (U.S.), 12, 14, 126, 134, 137: compared with Swedish pension program, 22, 24, 138–144;

191

penalizes older workers, 24; coverage of, 138, 139, 140; amount of, 140, 141–142, 143; payments for Medicare collected with, 150
Social Sweden, 136, 160
Social Welfare, Department of, *see* Public Welfare, Department of
Social Welfare, Royal Commission on, work of led to Social Assistance Act, 70
Social Welfare Board, 73, 104, 160
Social workers: relatively few employed, 73–74, 151; schools for, 74, 112, 151; in Sweden and in U.S., 74, 151
Soln, 105
Southern General Hospital, 59, 78
Spånga-Fristad home for aged, 84
Stad (six largest cities), 104: government in, 105, 106
Städer (towns), 106
Stadshagsgården home for aged, 84
State Forest Service, employees of, 114, 117
State Power Board, revenue from, 133
State Railways, 93: employees of, 114, 117
State Waterfalls and Power Administration, 93: employees of, 114, 117
Statens organisationsnamnd (office for organization and methods), 120
Statens Sakrevision (commission for efficiency audit and administrative supervision), 119
Statskontoret (Office of the Paymaster General), 119
Statsråd (Counselors of State), 96
Statssekreterare (secretary of state), 102, 103
Sterilization, 54, 77: sex education about, 61
Steward Sewing Machine Company case, 169
Stift (dioceses), 106
Stockholm, 33, 50, 76, 77, 78, 79, 89, 97, 105, 111, 112: regional insurance fund in, 29, 30; medical costs in, 39, 43; health insurance premiums in, 47; hospitals in, 57, 58, 59; län of, 59, 106, 107; welfare programs in, 70, 73–74, 74, 75; homes for aged in, 84–85, 85; rehabilitation in, 87, 88, 89; population of, 105
Stockholm Län Hospital at Danderyd, 59
Stockholm School of Social Work, 74: program of, 74
Stocksunds, 105

Strang, C. E., quoted, 136
Students, eligible for additional cash sickness allowance, 46
Study aid, 81–82, 83
Stureby home for aged, 84
Suffrage, universal in Sweden, 98
"Suicide and the Welfare State" (Farber), 167
Suicides, 155, 164, 165: care for attempted, 59; number of, 166; reasons for, 166, 167–168
Supplementary Pension: 5, 6, 11, 22–28, 34–35, 86, 90, 138: adjusted to cost-of-living index, 5, 26–28, 140, 142; eligibility for, 8, 15, 21, 22–23, 23, 44, 47, 138, 139, 140; administration of, 18, 31, 143–144; financing of, 22, 131n, 133, 134, 163; compared with Social Security program (U.S.), 22, 139–141; amount of, 27, 28, 139, 140, 141–142; appeals of matters concerning, 34; cut number on welfare, 75, 84, 152, 164. *See also* Children's allowance; Disability pension; Housing allowance; Retirement benefits; Survivors' benefits
Supplementary Pension Act (*1959*), 22
Supreme Administrative Court (*regeringsrätten*), 124: citizens' appeals to, 120, 130
Supreme Court (U.S.), 124, 146, 156: defines federal social responsibility, 169
Surgery, 39, 43, 50, 67–68
Survivors' benefits, 5, 8, 12, 15, 137, 138, 140, 154, 164: eligibility for, 16, 25, 27; under Supplementary Pension, 23, 25, 27, 140; under Basic Pension, 25; amount of, 25, 27, 142, 143. *See also* Children's allowance; Widows' pension
Svenska Vanforevardens Central kommittee (Swedish Central Committee for the Care of Cripples), 89
Sveriges Radio AB, 93
Swedish Broadcasting Corporation, 93: sex education programs of, 61
Swedish Central Committee for the Care of Cripples, 89
Swedish Employers Federation, 163
Switzerland: nationals of covered by Swedish Basic Pension, 13; alcohol in, 166

Tandvärnet (association of dentists in private practice), 68
Tanzania, ombudsman in, 121
Tax, National Board of (*riksskattenämnden*), 130

INDEX

Taxeringsnämnd (district assessment board), 129–130
Taxes and taxation, 163: pension fees part of, 17, 27, 32; income, 81, 130–132; in U.S., 81, 130, 134; Swedish system of, 128–134; sales, 130, 132; capital, 132; customs, 132; turnover, 132
Tegner, Esasis, quoted, 135
Telecommunications, Board of, 93: employees of, 114, 117; revenue from, 133
Temperance Committee, 73
Thalidomide, injury of fetus by, 64, 66
Third Fund, of National Pension Insurance Fund: responsibility of, 32; amounts handled, 33
Tjanstemannens centralorganisation, 115
Trade Unions, Federation of Swedish, 115, 163

Udall, Stewart L., quoted, 171
Umeå, 58, 74
Umeå Hospital, 58
Unemployment Committee, 73, 77
Unions: sickness benefits of, 7; can set up alternative to Supplementary Pension, 23; fear in U.S. of older workers, 24
Unions, Swedish Federation of Trade, 115, 163
United Nations, statistics for life expectancy compiled by, 37
United States, 74, 101, 105, 111, 122, 123, 126, 135, 136, 137, 144, 160, 169–172 *passim*: social programs in compared with those in Sweden, 3–4, 14, 16, 22, 24, 36, 37, 69, 76, 83, 86, 90, 145–150, 150–153, 168; Social Security program in, 12, 14, 22, 24, 126, 134, 137–144, 150; fear of older workers in, 24; use of cost-of-living index in, 26; life expectancy in, 36–37, 37; doctors in, 40–41, 144, 145; taxation in, 81, 130, 134; judiciary in, 95, 124, 146, 156, 169; elections in, 98, 158; political appointees in, 102; civil service of, 112, 113, 115–116, 117, 118; appeals systems in, 126; interest in ombudsman in, 126–127, 128, 129; no general health insurance in, 144, 145, 168; G.N.P. in, 161, 162; financing of social programs in, 163; attitudes in toward abortion, sex, illegitimacy, 164, 165; alcohol in, 166; suicides in, 166

United States v. Butler, 169
University Hospital, Lund-Malmö, 58
University Hospital at Uppsala, 107
Upper House of Riksdag, 96, 97
Uppsala, 57, 58, 112: cost of medical treatment in, 39; landsting of, 107

Vacations, provision of: for low-income families, 3; for housewives, 81; for children, 81, 83
Vällingby, 59
Van der Velde, Theodor Hendrik, 62
Venereal diseases, sex education about, 61
Vikariatsersättningar (Additional Payment for Higher Temporary Assignments), 116
Virus laboratories, 57
Vocational Schools and Orthopedic Clinic of Änggården, 89
Vocational training, retraining, 87, 88: for welfare recipients, 72, 77, 78, 150; schools for, 89, 162; in län, 108
Voters, number registered, 98

Washington, D.C., 170
Washington Post, 170
Welfare, 4, 8–10: obligations of local government, 8–9, 70, 71, 71–72, 106; for disabled, 10, 90; possible rehabilitation of recipients of, 11, 76, 151, 152; administration of, 72–74; vocational retraining of recipients of, 72, 77, 78, 150; amount of, 74–75, 76; number of recipients of, 74–76; aged recipients of, 75, 83–84; objections to, 76; in Sweden and in U.S. compared, 150–153. *See also* Child welfare
Welfare committee, *see* Social assistance committee
West German Federal Republic, *see* Germany, West
Widows' benefits, 15, 16, 81, 141, 164: eligibility for, 16; amount of, 142. *See also* Children's allowance; Wives' supplements
Wives' supplements, 6, 15, 140, 142, 143: subject to income test, 15; eligibility for and amount of, 16

X-rays: covered by health insurance, 39, 41, 43, 147, 148; injury of fetus by, 64; covered by Medicaid, 147